Letters from the Promised Land

Letters from the Promised Land

# Letters From
# The Promised Land

SWEDES IN AMERICA, 1840–1914

Edited by

## H. Arnold Barton

Published by the
University of Minnesota Press, Minneapolis
for the
Swedish Pioneer Historical Society

Third printing, 1990

*Library of Congress Catalog Card Number 74-22843*

*ISBN 0-8166-1009-6*

# Acknowledgments

In compiling this volume, I have incurred many debts. Special thanks go first of all to Professor Franklin D. Scott, chairman of the Swedish Pioneer Historical Society's Editorial Board, for first suggesting this project to me and for welcome help and counsel at every step along the way, and to the society itself for sponsoring the publication of this book.

The staffs of a number of libraries and societies provided valuable assistance: especially the Royal Library in Stockholm, where Dr. Ingrid Bergom-Larson in particular proved indispensable in repeatedly arranging for the prompt photocopying of needed documents; the Emigrant Institute in Växjö, where I received useful bibliographic leads; the Denkmann Library at Augustana College, Rock Island, Illinois; the University of Minnesota Library in Minneapolis, where Miss Mariann Tiblin rendered many services; the Minnesota Historical Society in St. Paul; and the Morris Library at Southern Illinois University, Carbondale, where Mr. Charles Holliday gamely contended with undecipherable and unpronounceable Swedish names and titles on my constant requests for interlibrary loans. Mr. Michael Brook, now of the University of Nottingham library in England, gave expert advice on materials dealing with Swedish immigrant radicals.

Numerous individuals (in Sweden) and publishers (in the United States) kindly permitted me to make use of copyrighted materials. Several persons provided—often on their own initiative—or allowed use of previously unpublished documents. Others supplied pictorial material. All these persons, societies, and publishing houses are gratefully and individually acknowledged in the list of Sources and Credits, and in the captions to the illustrations. All were unfailingly courteous and cooperative; several touchingly kind and helpful.

In addition to Professor Scott, Dr. Wesley Westerberg, director of the American Swedish Institute in Minneapolis, and Dr. Nils William Olsson, director of the Swedish Council of America, read my manuscript and made valuable suggestions.

To my Swedish-born wife, Aina, go heartfelt thanks for her patience and encouragement, as well as for more insights into the subject of this work, gathered over the years, than she, or even I, are ever likely to realize.

Finally, this book is dedicated to the memory of my father, Sven Hildor Barton, to whom I owe both my love of history and pride in my pioneer heritage.

H. A. B.

Carbondale, Illinois
March 1974

The publication of this paperback edition has made possible the correction of a few minor errors in the original edition, as well as an updating of the Select Bibliography.

# Contents

         Sections of illustrations follow pages 56, 152, and 248
         A map of the Swedish provinces and districts
            appears on page 312

# Letters from the Promised Land

# Introduction

W<br>
e are, as President John F. Kennedy and others have reminded us, a nation of immigrants.[1] In 1800 the United States had a population of only 5.3 million, approximately the same as that of Sweden a century later. During the next century and a half more than 35 million immigrants came to these shores. Of these, some 1.2 million were Swedes, the overwhelming majority of whom arrived between 1840 and 1914, the period covered by this book. In absolute numbers Sweden ranks seventh among the countries of origin for immigrants to the United States and first among the Scandinavian lands. Relative to total population, only Ireland and Norway have experienced heavier emigration. The American census of 1930 showed the record number of 1,562,703 persons born in Sweden or in the United States of Swedish-born parents, out of a total population of 122,775,046.[2] If the Swedish element forms only a small part of the total American population, it has nevertheless played a proud and distinctive part in the history of the nation. Emigration has meanwhile had a profound impact upon Sweden: by 1910, it was estimated, one out of every five Swedes was in America. It is a rare family in Sweden that does not have relatives across the Atlantic. Innumerable grass-roots contacts have tied the two countries together.

Some Swedes came to America before 1840 and some after 1914. It is not unlikely that some took part in the Norse expeditions to North America around 1000 A.D. In 1638 the Swedish crown itself established a colony at the mouth of the Delaware River. New Sweden, as it was called, fell in 1655 to the Dutch, who lost it to the English in 1663, but descendants of the original colonists long maintained their Swedish identity and language with the help of pastors sent out to them by the Swedish state church, the last of whom died as late as 1831. During the War of American Independence a considerable number of Swedes fought in the French and some in the Continental forces, though it is not known whether any of them later remained in America. By the early nineteenth century the Delaware Swedes had become thoroughly assimilated, but occasional Swedes continued to turn up in the United States before 1840. World War I drastically reduced Swedish immigration after 1914. Although there was a brief upswing in the early 1920s, improving economic and social conditions in Sweden effectively brought the transatlantic movement to a close.

The great Swedish migration to America thus took place between 1840 and 1914. During this three-quarters of a century there were considerable variations in the numbers of emigrants from year to year, their reasons for emigrating, their home regions in Sweden and destinations in America, the balance between occupational groups, the age, sex, and marital status of the emigrants, and the rates of remigration. Broadly, I see three main phases within the great migration on the basis of these variables: from 1840 to about 1865, from 1865 to around 1890, and from 1890 to 1914. In the commentaries to the corresponding sections in this book I examine the changing picture of Swedish migration to America.

The purpose of this work is to let the Swedish immigrants tell their own story, mainly through the "America letters" they wrote back to their homeland. Since an anthology requires selection, it may well be asked how representative the letters given here are of the immigrant letters as a whole. They are in fact not altogether so, nor can they be. Of the millions of letters written by Swedes in America only a few thousand have survived, by chance or design; of these a smaller number have been cataloged or printed. Those given here have, moreover, been selected with an eye to variety, interest, and appeal to the reader. Many have been chosen for colorful and exciting episodes, keen observation, sensitive feeling, the writer's attractive personality. Most immigrant letters have in fact little of interest to relate. They are often filled with clichés, concerned with mundane matters and local news from the old home parish. Many consist largely of religious platitudes, hearsay information, accounts culled from newspapers, comments on the weather, reports on wages and the prices of commodities, news of family affairs, and greetings to long lists of relatives and friends at home. I have sought to include enough "typical" immigrant letters in their entirety to give their characteristic flavor; otherwise I have not hesitated to make deletions or where necessary to reparagraph, punctuate, or even slightly modify wording in the interests of clarity.[3] My aim has been to produce good readable texts that are as faithful as possible to the originals. In some cases documents are reproduced here as given by previous editors and translators, and are so indicated. Otherwise all translations are my own. The sources for the original materials are in each case provided for the interested reader.

Regretfully, the translator must admit that no translation can do justice to the full flavor and rough, unvarnished quality of most of these letters in their original Swedish, with their often outlandish spelling, quirky capitalization and lack of punctuation, their rich admixture of archaic local dialect, solemn biblical turns of phrase, anglicisms and English words and expressions, often in quaintly phonetic guise. Though I have sought within acceptable limits to substitute colloquial English for colloquial Swedish, the letters in translation cannot but frequently appear more polished and well groomed than the originals. The Swedish-American jargon in which many of these letters were written must often have been the despair of their recipients, but it can be a rare delight to those capable of appreciating it.[4]

In selecting materials for this collection, I have given first place to personal letters written by actual immigrants in America and a lower priority to such things as diaries, memoirs, reminiscences, letters from Sweden, public documents, and travel accounts by Swedish visitors to America. As for subject matter, I have sought above all to include the actual experiences of the immigrants themselves, as well as their reactions to them and to the American environment in general, particularly in ways characteristic of their ethnic and social origins, and the times in which they lived. I have for the most part excluded hearsay information, impersonal descriptions of places or events, and purely family matters such as Aunt Ernestina's rheumatism or Uncle Olof's will, except where they may provide some insight or atmosphere. I have tried to retain from these documents the essence of the immigrants' experience in coming to and making their home in a new land. Theirs is often a story of hardship, loneliness, disillusionment, despair, and sometimes tragedy. But it is even more one of courage, cheerful optimism, a sense of adventure, good humor, sturdy common sense, hard work, neighborliness, and well-earned pride in both the new country and the old.

The writers of these letters came from all parts of Sweden and from all social levels. Some, such as Baron Axel Adelswärd and Rosalie Roos, were highly cultivated and articulate. C. J. L. Almquist was one of the leading figures of Swedish literature.[5] The great majority of the letter writers, as of the immigrants as a whole, were nevertheless persons of humble origins and little schooling, though some surprise us with their self-acquired learning. The fact in itself that such large numbers of common people wrote so many letters is meanwhile of epoch-making significance. Since the dawn of civilization literacy was the preserve of small upper-class elites, which produced virtually all the written documentation upon which the historian must rely to reconstruct the past. It was only during the nineteenth century that considerable numbers of people from the broader masses started to become literate, beginning in northern Europe and North America. Among the most advanced countries from this standpoint was Sweden.[6] The America letters sometimes show that help was needed to write and occasionally even to read them. Yet the letters of Swedish emigrants give striking testimonial to the early and broad diffusion of literacy in their homeland. Even though literate, however, common people would ordinarily have left behind them little if anything in writing. It took the great migration beyond the sea and separation from home and family to cause such people to take up the pen in large numbers, with hands—as they themselves often complained—more accustomed to the plow, ax, or washtub. The letters thus provide not only a deeply moving picture of one stream in the great migration that peopled this land, but also reveal how, for the first time in human history, the common man began to speak directly to posterity.

PART ONE: The Pioneers, 1840–1864

# Background

In the sixth century A.D. the Gothic-Roman historian Jordanes called the Scandinavian North the "workshop or womb of nations." By his time the pressures of population growth had already driven forth a great wave of Nordic migrants in search of land elsewhere in Europe. The same phenomenon recurred some centuries later during the Viking age, when large colonies of Scandinavians settled in the East Baltic region, England, Ireland, and France, while others, via Iceland and Greenland, explored as far as North America.

To understand the great Swedish migration to the New World in the nineteenth and early twentieth centuries, one must again look first of all at the growth of population. In Sweden as elsewhere in Europe, it had been steadily on the rise since the early eighteenth century. The establishment there of the first regular census in 1749—some forty years before the United States and fifty years before Britain or France—gives a unique insight into this development. At the end of the eighteenth century there was already growing concern over the loss of several thousand Swedish subjects who settled in other European countries, especially in Denmark and Russia.[1]

After 1800 the rate of population increase climbed rapidly as the result, said the poet Esaias Tegnér, of "peace, vaccine, and potatoes." Sweden indeed did not go to war after Napoleon's defeat in 1814; vaccination brought smallpox, the most deadly epidemic disease, under control; and the potato, introduced into Sweden in the later eighteenth century, provided a cheap and plentiful new source of nutrition. Yet the potato was only one of the more striking changes that affected the Swedish countryside around 1800; more basic still was the enclosure movement which in the early years of the century began to break up the old, tightly integrated village communities in most parts of the country and to regroup scattered peasant holdings into farms that could be more rationally cultivated. In 1815 Sweden's population was close to 2.5 million; by 1910 it had more than doubled to around 5.5 million, and this notwithstanding the net loss of over a million emigrants, to say nothing of their foreign-born descendants.

No less significant is the fact that as late as 1870 the agricultural part of the population still made up nearly three-quarters of the total, a proportion almost as large as it had been a century earlier. Industrial expansion from the 1850s onward at first absorbed only a relatively small part of the population increase. The result was heavy pressure upon the land. Much new ground was brought under the plow, but here too there were limits, for though Sweden is a large country by European standards, only about one-tenth of its area can be considered good arable land. By mid-century many were forced to scratch a living out of patches of poor, stony ground. While the number of substantial *bönder* or independent farmers increased slowly, the poorer classes of the countryside grew far more rapidly: small *bönder* with properties not large enough to support them, *torpare* or small tenant farmers, and farm laborers without freeholds or leases of their own, often the younger sons and daughters of small *bönder* or *torpare*.[2] For such people life was hard under the best of circumstances; in years of poor harvest they might be reduced to eking out their bread by mixing rye with ground-up birch bark and moss, and their ranks were thinned by malnutrition and disease. Low prices for agricultural commodities likewise caused widespread distress.

From the middle of the nineteenth century onward, these pressures led to a flight from the countryside which is still continuing in part today. Although emigration was the most notable aspect at first, it was only a part of this great movement of population. Internal migration was ultimately much greater: to other parishes, to the developing north of Sweden, to towns, cities, and industries. A single example may show something about population growth and movement, both internal and external, by the third quarter of the century. In 1867, when 5,893 Swedes left for the United States, Djursdala parish in Kalmar *län* (Småland) had a population of 1,178, representing a net gain of 18 over the year before. During 1867 there were twice as many births (34) as deaths (17). Forty-five persons moved into the parish as against 49 who left; of the latter, 28 went to "North America," according to the pastor's report, including my great-grandparents and those eight of their eleven children who were not already in the United States.[3] Historians and sociologists are submitting such developments to detailed statistical studies. Swedish literature meanwhile gives valuable insights into the effects they had upon individual human lives: the novels of Vilhelm Moberg for emigrants to America, those of Eyvind Johnson for life on Sweden's own northern frontier, those of Per Anders Fogelström for Stockholm's proletariat after about 1870.[4]

Thus economic factors more than anything led to the Swedish emigration. The "push" of circumstances in the homeland is clear. Yet the "pull" of hopes for something better across the ocean, based upon belief in America's boundless resources, is fully as important, in some ways more so. The early emigrants were indeed for the most part not poor. The expenses of the journey and of getting settled in the New World were at first quite considerable; the emigrant leader Peter Cassel advised from Iowa in 1846 that a family of four should not attempt to come over with less than 1,000 *riksdaler riksgälds*, a sum relatively few could afford.[5] On the whole the wealthy and socially prominent stayed home, and reports from America repeatedly reminded them that they had much to lose and little to gain by emigrating. So, generally, did the very poor, who lacked the necessary means. Emigration was largest from the elements in between and was evidently inspired very largely by insecurity and fear of impoverishment and the social degradation that went with it, rather than by poverty itself. To keep family farms in one piece, the land often went intact to one of the sons; the other sons and daughters, if unable to acquire land of their own at home, often preferred to seek it in America rather than go to work for others, move to the cities, or become industrial workers. The heirs to small farms were often heavily burdened with supporting their aging parents, compensating their brothers and sisters for their share of the inheritance, and paying off long-term mortgages. Poor crop years or falling agricultural prices often drove them to sell out for the best terms they could get and to seek a fresh start across the ocean.

Other factors likewise played a part, of which religion was of particular importance. Protected by law, the Lutheran state church held a virtual monopoly over religious practice in Sweden and laymen could be fined, imprisoned, or exiled for conducting unauthorized services or seceding from the established church. From the 1830s forward there nevertheless took place a powerful wave of lay revivalism, largely in reaction to the dry formalism and rationalism of the state church. In part this "Awakening," as it was called, consisted of a kind of Puritanism which sought to reform the church from within, to return it to a purer evangelical piety, and to combat public immorality in such matters as the flagrant misuse of alcohol; it is thus reminiscent of the Puritanism of seventeenth-century England, which played so great a part in the settlement of New England. Some people went further and, risking official persecution, disavowed the state church to join various sects with their own exclusive messages of salvation. Most important at first were the followers of the self-styled prophet, Erik Jansson, mainly in Hälsingland. When Jansson was brought to trial for heresy in 1845, he escaped and made his way to America. He was joined there the following year by some 1,200 of his followers who founded the Christian-communal colony of Bishop Hill in northwestern Illinois. The janssonists, who sent back glowing reports from their new home, gave a great stimulus to further Swedish emigration. They were joined over the next several years by continual new arrivals at the same time that disaffected members of the group spread out into neighboring communities to form the beginnings of new Swedish settlements. Thus Bishop Hill became the focal point for early Swedish immigration into northern Illinois, the basic "mother-colony" of Swedish America.

The Janssonists meanwhile gave a powerful impetus to sectarianism in Sweden, where Baptists, Methodists, and Mormons—denominations of American inspiration—rapidly gained ground, to be joined by the purely Swedish Mission Friends by the 1870s. The Free Church movement itself swelled the ranks of emigrants, for the sectarians saw America as a new Land of Canaan, free from religious oppression and flowing with milk and honey. Although the laws against religious dissenters were repealed by 1860 and the sects sought thereafter to build their strength at home, religion continued to affect emigration for some time to come.

Religious revivalism was in part a reaction to social and political discontents. These derived partly from the breakdown of immemorial ways of life through the enclosures and the growing agrarian crisis. But in large part too they resulted from an antiquated social order. Down to 1866 Sweden was governed by a parliament, the *Riksdag*, composed of the four traditional estates of the nobility, clergy, burghers, and peasantry, directly representing only a small part of the population. This system gave rise to much jealousy: of the unenfranchised toward the enfranchised; of wealthy commoners toward the nobility; of tenant farmers and landless farm laborers toward the landowning *bönder*, who alone were represented in the peasant estate. Such jealousy tended to alienate the poorer classes from the state "establishment," which they naturally regarded as an upper-class preserve, and accounted largely for the rather lukewarm patriotism noted among Swedish immigrants in America as compared with those from oppressed nationalities such as the Irish, the Poles, or even to some degree the Norwegians. Even after the establishment of a bicameral *Riksdag* in 1866 the vote was limited by high property qualifications to a minority of the population until early in the present century.

Aside from the political sphere life was pervaded by social distinctions. A person's station in life could be immediately identified by his occupation, manner of speech, customary form of dress, and exact degree of deference or condescension with which he was treated by others in the social scale. The Swedish-American journalist Ernst Skarstedt, home on a visit in 1886, was reminded that there were at least four proper ways to address married women, according to their social rank, and four more for unmarried women, at which point he longed for America where all women were simply "Mrs." or "Miss." America offered an escape from this class-bound society, and the emigrants' letters constantly extolled a land where free republican institutions formed the character of its citizens, where one man was as good as another, where honest labor was respected and determined one's place in life. "Here we have rich men, here we have learned men, here we have smart men," a Swede who had emigrated in 1868 later wrote, "here we have bosses who sometimes work us like dogs,—but masters we have none."[6] That the upper classes soon took alarm at the emigration and sought to impede it hardly served to discourage those in the classes below from departing.

Though sheer lust for adventure often played its part, the decision to emigrate was not at first one to be made lightly. For the early emigrants it usually meant a clean break with the old home, for only by selling out completely could the necessary funds be raised. Hardships began during travel overland by cart or canal boat to the port of departure, where the far greater ordeal of the ocean crossing awaited. The first emigrants shipped on small Swedish sailing vessels, usually as additional cargo on top of a load of pig iron, in which a lively export to the United States continued up to mid-century. Soon larger numbers were carried by American ships sailing from Swedish and other northern European ports. In either case the crossing under sail was long, normally lasting between eight and ten weeks, sometimes longer. The emigrants were packed into cramped quarters below deck. The air was foul, especially in heavy weather when the hatches had to be battened down. Provisions became moldy and wormy, the water putrid and sometimes scarce. The passengers were racked by seasickness and many succumbed to shipboard fevers, especially children, the weak, and the old. Some were lost in disasters at sea. The experience was such that most could hardly contemplate repeating it.

Further trials awaited in America, where the journey into the interior could take another two to six weeks. Most, arriving in New York, traveled by river and lake steamer and horse-drawn canal boat, sometimes with short connections by railroad, up the Hudson River to Albany, through the Erie Canal to Buffalo, on the Great Lakes to Chicago, thence by canal to Peru, Illinois, or later to the Mississippi. Others made their way from Boston or Quebec to the Great Lakes, from middle Atlantic ports overland to the Ohio River, or up the Mississippi from New Orleans. Ignorance of the language caused constant difficulties, and the immigrants had to be on their guard against "runners" and swindlers who tried to fleece them at every turn. Weakened by the long journey, many fell victim to cholera or the ague. On the last lap the emigrants trudged across the open prairie or into virgin forest, beside wagons piled with their belongings, to their final destinations in Illinois, Iowa, or Minnesota.

The first year after arrival was usually particularly hard. A dwelling had to be found or more frequently built, often a primitive dugout, sod hut, or log cabin, to be replaced with something more permanent as soon as circumstances allowed. Small plots were cleared and broken, but it was usually the following year before the first crop could be harvested. Funds brought from Sweden soon gave out and the men often had to seek temporary work on farms, with railroad construction gangs, or in logging camps, leaving wives and young children to fend for themselves until they could return, carrying a sack of flour and if possible leading a cow.

The character of the early immigrants was determined by these circumstances. They included at first a number of upper-class persons who came to America either for idealistic reasons, like Gustaf Unonius in 1841, or because of personal failure or scandal at home, like the writer C. J. L. Almquist in 1851. Some of them, particularly Unonius, played an important part in arousing public interest in emigration to America. More commonly, however, immigrants were moderately prosperous *bönder* who brought with them their entire families and sometimes a hired man or hired girl who contracted to work off the cost of the journey in America.[7] Such persons made up the group of seventeen emigrants from Östergötland who in 1845 accompanied Peter Cassel to southeastern Iowa, where they founded New Sweden, the first lasting Swedish settlement in the Midwest. Such too were most of the Janssonists who the following year established Bishop Hill, though by pooling their resources they managed to bring a number of their needier brethren with them. In both these cases, and in a number of others besides, the early Swedish immigrants traveled in groups of relatives and neighbors under chosen leaders and settled in colonies in the new land, to cooperate in facing their common problems. After the expenses and hardships of the journey and of making new homes in the wilderness, few expected ever to see their native land again.

One may wonder what sources of information the early immigrants had about the great land to the west upon which to base their decisions. Among the educated classes there had long been much interest in America, stimulated by the travel accounts of such Swedes as Baron Axel Klinckowström (1824), C. U. von Hauswolff (1835), and C. D. Arfwedson (1835), or of foreign observers like Morris Birkbeck (1818), Frances Trollope (1832), Charles Dickens (1842), and above all Alexis de Tocqueville (1835–1840).[8] During the early emigration period as well, a number of Swedish travelers visited America and published their accounts in books and newspapers, the best-known being Fredrika Bremer, whose *Homes of the New World* (1853–1854), promptly translated into English, caused a sensation on both sides of the Atlantic. The California gold rush, beginning in 1848, naturally created much excitement. Among the broader masses, newspaper accounts of America, rapidly increasing in scope and in number from about 1840, had considerable impact. Even before the school law of 1842 required elementary schools in each parish, literacy in Sweden was high by European standards and the early nineteenth century saw the rapid development of the newspaper press, not least in the provinces. In 1840 liberal elements in Stockholm, concerned about the prospect of overpopulation and progressive pauperization, founded a controversial and short-lived Emigration Society, which publicized opportunities in the New World. There appeared thereafter a long series of emigrant guides, some of them translations of works by Germans or Norwegians, whose countrymen had commenced emigrating at earlier dates, giving descriptions of America and advice to prospective settlers. One of the most influential was Johan Bolin's vivid *Description of North America's United States* (1853), which belied the fact that the author had never been across the Atlantic.[9]

Even the earliest immigrants after 1840 frequently encountered Swedes already established in America, or were referred to them from home. Both Unonius in 1841—who called himself the "first emigrant," since he was the first to leave under a new law which allowed emigration without the king's special permission—and Peter Cassel in 1845 received valuable assistance from countrymen in America, to say nothing of those who came after. Many of these forerunners were former seamen who had stayed on in the New World, such as the Methodist missionary, Olof Hedström, with his Bethel Ship moored in New York harbor, who between 1845 and 1875 gave aid and comfort to thousands of his arriving countrymen, and whose brother, Jonas, in Victoria, Illinois, welcomed many of them to the prairie west.

By far the most important source of information about America, however, were the letters the emigrants themselves wrote home, for accounts from relatives and friends overcame peasant skepticism in a way that books or newspapers never could. These "America-letters" tended to paint a bright picture of the new land, for the emigrants, having committed themselves to a new life there, were naturally anxious to justify themselves. Surely, too, the "Royal Swedish Jealousy"—what Anders Larsson in 1876 called the "hereditary sin"—played its part, for no Swede would willingly admit to being less successful than his neighbors. "There are certainly many who write home," a man who had emigrated from Stockholm in 1891 later commented, "but they do not speak about their hardships so as not to worry their people back home, rather they talk about everything to America's advantage. And so there are many who are blinded by that and in that way many have been lured on their way. I speak from my own experience."[10]

What is striking about many of the earlier immigrant letters is how long and, despite often uncertain spelling and grammar, how carefully composed they were. These characteristics were due to the slowness of the mails—six to eight weeks from the Midwest to Sweden by steam packet across the Atlantic—remoteness from post offices, and above all the high cost of postage, payable either by sender or receiver. Gustaf Unonius related how in the 1840s he once walked twenty-seven miles from the little settlement at Pine Lake, Wisconsin, to Milwaukee when he heard that an unfranked letter from Sweden was being held for him at the post office there. The postage evidently cost him about a dollar—a very good day's wages for a working man at the time—which he had to borrow from a Dane. When to his infinite disgust he found that the letter was simply an inquiry about American conditions from a total stranger, he walked all the way home again the same day![11] Thus the early immigrants could not often write home; when they did, they composed carefully, wrote small, and filled up the paper. Such letters were eagerly received, read aloud at every opportunity, passed from hand to hand, copied and recopied, and not infrequently printed in local newspapers. Sometimes, as in the case of Peter Cassel's particularly influential letters, they were published in book form.[12]

A final source of information about America was provided by some emigrants who went back to Sweden at an early date. Such returned "Americans" caused a great stir in their old neighborhoods, as people came from far and wide to inquire firsthand about America. Those who went back to America often took with them groups of new immigrants. In the mid-1850s the Illinois Central Railroad began the first organized recruitment of emigrants by sending the Swedish-American, Oscar Malmborg, as its agent to Sweden and Norway. By this time there was already talk of a regular "America fever" raging in those parts of Sweden from which the earliest emigration had come. In 1854 nearly four thousand Swedes departed, but the number declined thereafter because of generally favorable conditions in agriculture at home, the American depression of 1857–1859, and the outbreak of the Civil War in 1861.

The Swedes in America enthusiastically supported the Union and President Lincoln. More than three thousand served in the Union army during the war, most of them volunteers, while only some twenty-five have been identified on the rolls of the Confederate forces. As had been the case in the American War of Independence, a number of Swedish officers took part, including three brigadier generals and twelve colonels in the Union army. American entrepreneurs recruited Swedish contract laborers for the Northern states and American diplomats made thinly veiled attempts to find volunteers for the Union forces. After the Homestead Act of 1862 there was an increase in the emigration of young Swedes who promptly enlisted in hopes of gaining bonuses, quick citizenship, and free land. Not all, however, joined up of their own free will, for some innocent souls were shanghaied by unscrupulous persons who made off with their enlistment bonuses, as recounted, for instance, by Måns Hultin.

The pioneering period saw the founding of the first Swedish-American cultural institutions. Here religion naturally played a central role, for its significance in the lives of the early immigrants can scarcely be overestimated. Their attitudes, as revealed in their letters, show the tension between traditional and newer ways of thinking characteristic of their times. The emigration itself strikingly reveals how far the new secular ideal of material progress had replaced the traditional Christian acceptance of one's earthly lot and of this world as a vale of tears. Yet at the same time most of the early emigrants could hardly have faced the hardships they did and their permanent separation from family and friends without an abiding faith in a better world to come, where loved ones would be eternally reunited.

Most significant was the development of the Swedish Lutheran church in America, beginning in 1849 with the immigration of Pastor Lars Paul Esbjörn to Andover, Illinois, largely with the aim of keeping newly arrived immigrants out of the snares of the Janssonists at Bishop Hill or the Methodist preacher, Jonas Hedström, in Victoria. Others soon followed, including that guiding light of Swedish Lutheranism in America, Pastor Tufve Nilsson Hasselquist, in 1852. These pioneer clergymen were strong proponents of the great revival movement in Sweden and from the start imparted to Swedish-American Lutheranism a strongly evangelical, low-church character, in contrast to the state church at home. By 1860 thirty-six Swedish Lutheran congregations joined their Norwegian brethren to form the Augustana Synod, though the Norwegians seceded in 1870. In 1858, meanwhile, Esbjörn undertook to train the first Scandinavian candidates for the ministry. Two years later the Augustana College and Seminary were founded in Chicago, moving in 1863 under Hasselquist's leadership to Paxton, Illinois. In the same period smaller groups of Swedish Methodists and Baptists began to organize. The early Swedish congregations often provided the first schools in their districts, and when public schools were established many of them long continued to give their own instruction in religion and the Swedish language.

In 1851–1853 a Swede published in New York the newspaper *Skandinaven*, intended for immigrants from Norway, Denmark, and Sweden. The first purely Swedish paper was, however, the Lutheran *Hemlandet, det Gamla och det Nya,* founded in 1855 in Galesburg, Illinois, by the versatile Pastor Hasselquist "to free our people from immoral and unchurchly papers." It fulfilled an invaluable service by regularly providing the early immigrants with reading matter in their own language. After a few years *Hemlandet* moved to Chicago, where it was published until 1914. During the later 1850s and early 1860s Swedish-language newspapers appeared in Galva and Galesburg, Illinois, and in Red Wing, Minnesota. As early as 1836, meanwhile, New York's Swedish Society was organized. Two decades later, in 1857, the Svea Society of Chicago was founded.

These were, to be sure, modest beginnings, but they laid the groundwork for Swedish-American religious and cultural life in the era of mass immigration which followed.

What did the immigrants make of their meeting with America? The physical environment impressed them above all by its sheer size and the immensity of its resources. To new arrivals journeying into the interior, the continent must have seemed endless. Their letters again and again express incredulous delight at the lush grass and deep, stone-free loam of the prairie, the giant trees of the undisturbed forest, the lakes covered with wild fowl and swimming with fish, all there for the taking. Yet if the sea of grass on the virgin prairie, the windswept plains to the west, and the primeval forests to the north held the beauty of promise to the practiced eye of a land-hungry farmer, they could be frightening or depressing in their vast emptiness after the old, settled landscapes at home. The elements were extreme, often violent. Most of the immigrants were ill prepared either for the burning summer sun or the icy blasts of winter in the great interior. There were blizzards, tornadoes, prairie fires, floods, droughts, plagues of locusts. Yet they took these things in stride and laid the wilderness under ax and plow.

The human environment was no less impressive. To raw immigrants fresh from the Swedish countryside the great city of New York could produce an overwhelming introduction to America and its many marvels. Railroads, river steamers, farms and factories, other cities farther west, but above all the people and their ways in the new land aroused interest and wonder. Almost all were exhilarated by the new freedom they found: freedom from meddlesome bureaucrats, army officers, and pastors of the state church; freedom for all citizens to take part in public affairs; freedom too from the deadening constraints of social convention. They welcomed the cheerful informality of American life. Yet they often found manners crude and Americans indifferent to comfort, relaxation, taste, and cherished traditions. They were frequently shocked by the evident lawlessness of much in American life: false advertising and blatant swindles in business affairs, corruption in politics and justice, the high incidence of murder and arson in the cities, vigilante law, Indian massacres and savage reprisals against them. It is, incidentally, remarkable how similar the observations of Swedish commentators today are to those made by Swedish immigrants and visitors over a hundred years ago.

No feature of the American scene impressed the immigrants more than the mixture of nationalities; the new land must have appeared to them as a veritable Tower of Babel. Their reactions to the different inhabitants varied. The native Yankees they admired for their practical ingenuity, frontier skills, ambition, drive, and lack of social pretentiousness. They were bemused by their frank materialism, their love of the Almighty Dollar, and often repelled by their penchant for braggadocio and sharp business practices. Yet on the whole the Swedes got on well with the Yankees and sought to emulate them, sometimes to excess. The most numerous of the other "nations" they encountered were the Germans and the Irish. The Germans they generally appreciated for their orderliness, sobriety, and industry, especially if they were

Protestants. Toward the Irish, however, the Swedes often felt a strong aversion, considering them slovenly, unreliable, ill-tempered and, perhaps worst of all, papist in religion. The folklore of Swedish America contains its share of stories in which Irish claim jumpers are thrown off the land or disputatious sons of Erin are hurled bodily through barroom windows by Swedes, slow to anger but once aroused wrathful in the extreme. Yet how many miles of track they laid and how many city blocks they built together! An old Irishman once told me with pride that "the Irish and the Swedes built America."

Settlement on the frontier meanwhile often brought the Swedes into close contact with the original inhabitants of the land, the Indians, at whose hands they suffered some violence, particularly in the 1862 Sioux Uprising in Minnesota. Yet though they sometimes feared the red man, there is little evidence that they hated or despised him. On the whole relations were peaceable and the Swedes tended both to respect the Indian and to sympathize with his lot. Settling, as they did, overwhelmingly in the North, the Swedes had far fewer contacts with Negroes. They were in principle strongly opposed to slavery, although those who witnessed it in practice in the South sometimes claimed that black slaves there were on the whole better treated than poor tenant farmers and landless hired hands at home in Sweden. Their emotional response to the Union cause in the Civil War has been noted. Yet toward the Negroes as people the Swedish immigrants tended to share more or less uncritically the attitudes of their Yankee neighbors.

When immigration from southern and eastern Europe greatly increased in the later nineteenth century, the Swedes generally came to regard themselves as more "American" than the later arrivals because of their earlier settlement, rising prosperity and social status, and the more kindred nature of their native society. Increasingly they identified themselves with the old Americans rather than the new immigrants.

Finally, those with whom the Swedes had closest and most cordial relations were their fellow Scandinavians from Norway, Denmark, and Finland. Despite old rivalries from home which now and then flared up in the new land, the history of the Scandinavian immigrants is above all one of neighborliness, cooperation, and intermarriage. The role of the Norwegians as forerunners—their immigration had begun in the 1820s—was great indeed, and again and again we see arriving Swedish families taken in hand by hospitable Norwegian pioneers who gave them invaluable help in making new homes in the New World.

# Letters and Documents

*It seems fitting to begin this anthology with a letter from four lads who had settled near Salem, Wisconsin, in 1838. Here the eldest, Carl Johan Friman, not yet twenty, writes to their father and ailing younger brother, who had returned to Sweden.*

Salem, January 18, 1841

Our Dear Father:

Your welcome and long awaited letter of July 26 was received today, and I will not delay a minute to answer it. God be praised, we are all well. Adolf has not had a single minute of indisposition since he arrived in the free world; Otto has grown perceptibly; Janne is almost as heavy as I am, and in language he and I are regular Yankees; Adolf and Otto have not yet reached that stage. I give lessons in English reading and writing to my three brothers as often as I have time. That is not often, because we are so busy splitting rails in the winter and breaking land in the summer. We have eighty acres inclosed, but it is exceedingly hard work to split oak rails—the only timber available.

Only people capable of heavy work or possessed of wealth are equal to the life of a pioneer in America. But if the vigorous and efficient Swedes would ever arouse themselves and come here, they would find the best land for pioneers; *but they ought to come soon*, because the land is rapidly being settled, largely by Norwegians. Last summer about one thousand Norwegians came to this territory. I met them and was told that only one Swede came over from Gothenburg to New York. There is room enough here for all the Swedes who can come. . . .

Last year and this year we had pretty good crops and the prices of grain are quite low. Wheat is fifty cents a bushel, corn thirty-six cents, oats eighteen cents, and potatoes twelve cents. A yoke of oxen which sold for one hundred dollars when we came is now sixty dollars and a good cow only twenty dollars. Times are hard for farmers but the best for new settlers. If the Swedes are coming, they ought to come soon or next summer; if they wait longer everything will be more expensive and the best land will be bought up. . . .

The whites and reds cooperate in killing off deer. The price is low: a deer that weighs about two hundred pounds brings two dollars. The skins are excellent and are worth two dollars each. The meat is delicious, excelling everything. I wish you had a portion. Janne has shot six and has divided the proceeds. We have purchased a Yankee rifle that shoots a deer at a distance of five hundred ells[1] on the run, because we cannot get any closer to them. . . .

George M. Stephenson, trans. and ed., *Letters Relating to Gustaf Unonius and the Early Swedish Settlers in Wisconsin*, Augustana Historical Society Publications, vol. 7 (Rock Island, 1937), 55–57.

*In 1841 Gustaf Unonius, a government clerk from Uppsala, together with his young wife, maid, and two university students, emigrated to America. They settled at Pine Lake, Wisconsin, near Milwaukee, where they idealistically hoped to live a life of pastoral simplicity and republican virtue. Their departure and Unonius's letters from America, which were printed in the newspapers, aroused widespread interest in Sweden. A number of other Swedes joined the Pine Lake settlement, which nonetheless broke up after a few years, largely because of the practical inexperience of the settlers, most of whom, like Unonius himself, came from educated, upper-class backgrounds. Here Unonius describes his impressions of the new land.*

Milwaukee, Wisconsin, 13 October 1841

The soil here is the most fertile and wonderful that can be found and usually consists of rich black mold. Hunting and fishing will provide some food in the beginning, but they must be pursued sparingly, otherwise time which could more profitably be spent in cultivating the soil is wasted. I beg the emigrant to consider all these factors carefully and closely calculate his assets before he starts out. In spite of this, he will have to suffer much in the beginning, limit himself considerably, and sacrifice much of what he was accustomed to in Europe. Without work, often with work that is hard and painful, he cannot hope to achieve success. I caution against all exaggerated hopes and golden air castles; cold reality will otherwise lame your arm and crush your courage; both must be fresh and active.

As far as we are concerned, we do not regret our undertaking. We are living a free and independent life in one of the most beautiful valleys the world can offer; and from the experiences of others we see that in a few years we can have a better livelihood and enjoy comforts that we must now deny ourselves. If we should be overcome by a longing for the fatherland (and this seems unlikely), we could sell our farm which in eight years will certainly bring ten or twelve dollars per acre, perhaps more if the canal is finished by that time. But I believe that I will be satisfied in America.

I am partial to a republican form of government, and I have realized my youthful dream of social equality. Others may say what they will, but there are many attractive things about it. It is no disgrace to work here. Both the gentleman and the day laborer work. No epithets of degradation are applied to men of humble toil; only those whose conduct merits it are looked down upon. In the future, with more experience and facts at my disposal, I shall probably discourse more fully on these subjects. Liberty is still stronger in my affections than the bright silver dollar that bears her image. I do not agree with Hauswolff that in order to appreciate the blessings of a monarchy, one must live in a democracy.

*Ibid.*, 50–51.

Pine Lake, Wisconsin, 25 January 1842

. . . I admit that I am no friend of the big city of New York. The shopkeeper's spirit is too prevalent, but to judge the American national character from that is incorrect. I have found the Americans entirely different. We live in an industrial era and it is true that the American is a better representative of that than any other nationality. Despite this fact, there is something kindly in his speculation for profit and wealth, and I find more to admire in his manner than in that of the European leaders. The merchant here is withal patriotic; in calculating his own gain he usually includes a share for his country. We need only to remember that the universities and other educational institutions, homes for the poor, and other institutions of value to society are dependent on and supported by the American merchants. Canals, railroads, etc., are all financed by companies composed of a few individuals whose collective fortunes serve the public for its common benefit and profit. One must, therefore, overlook an avariciousness which sometimes goes to extremes.

It is true that the American is a braggart; his love for his country is a predilection; the experience he has had with European culture and institutions often leads him to censure them and in considering the advantages of his own country to pass over the good things which the Old World still retains. We find him to be a proud egotist, a quarrelsome patriot, and, if I may say so, an intolerable fellow citizen. Instead of the jealousy that prevails among other nationalities, he has these faults, if faults they be. During the struggles which rend and agitate the countries of the Old World he sees in the progress of his peaceful fatherland the results of liberty and equality which he considers impossible to obtain under any other conditions. Even though I do not wish to blame him for this, yet I do not deny that his resulting self-satisfaction expresses itself in a highly ridiculous fashion in trivial matters. . . .

I find myself joyful and happy in my work; so far, praise God, my family and myself have been in good health. Many a refined European would perhaps feel sorry for us when he entered our log house and saw the single room with its bare walls and its simple furnishings and our sacrifice of many of the necessities to which we were accustomed at home. After spending twenty-four hours with us, he would see our joy and our contentment; he would see us arise happily in the morning to take up our tasks; he would either accompany us to the magnificent oak forest and hear how merrily the American ax resounds from the mighty trunks, or on a merry hunt for the wild animals so abundant in the forest where he could admire the beautiful and luxuriant prodigality of nature, or he could go with us to visit the neighbors where, among simple and wholesome customs, many of which he might consider peculiar, he would better be able to study the national characteristics of America than in New York boardinghouses and in Broadway's great stores.

After such a day an hour or two in the evening would be spent in our simple home pleasantly discussing liberty and independence; he would hear our plans for a future without unnecessary troubles and imaginary dangers; he would see refined elegance, imaginary needs, and all actual poverty exiled from the house; perhaps he would even see us shed tears at the memory of friends and relatives in the distant fatherland; but he would also experience how with pious hearts we thank God for the position we now enjoy and how trustingly we commit our future into His hands. From this and from the heartfelt "goodnight" which we wish one another he would recognize four contented persons.

Such has been my experience in America, such has been my mood. Committing myself to the care of the All Highest, I see no reason for a change in either. Many might expect a more poetic description of my life here, happy as it is by love and friendship and by daily tasks, but reality has seized me, though not with iron clutches. Nay, on the contrary, it has become poetical since my writing ceased to be so; my spirit is more poetical than formerly, thanks to that reality in which I live and work. . . .

Somewhere in my letter I have referred to the Americans as the most enlightened of people.[2] If by that is meant the greatest number of scholars, authors, and artists, I am in error. America has few of them, and I admit that neither the states nor the nation show much inclination to encourage science and the arts. . . . If one understands "the most enlightened people" as referring to those among whom one finds the least ignorance, then my contention is correct. Visit any American log cabin you please, even in the outlying western districts, and you will find the man who wields the ax and guides the plow civilized and able to express his ideas on a variety of subjects in grammatical language and with intelligence and insight. If you try to find out how well he understands the creed of the church to which he belongs, you will learn that it was not by chance, birth, or custom that he became a member, but, with the ease of expression which is characteristic of this free people, he will give his reasons and defend the teachings and precepts of his faith. If the conversation drifts to the history of his country, you will scarcely find a native-born citizen of the United States who is ignorant of it; almost everybody is well grounded in it and shows a knowledge of the political situation and the governmental organization that will astonish you. You will find him no less informed on many other topics. It may be that in many cases his knowledge is superficial and based on the newspapers, but in any case it is greater than it is among the lower classes of any European country. Public education among other things in America merits the highest praise. In every township one section (640 acres) is set aside for school purposes. Every day the children are instructed in the fundamentals, principally in Christianity, by a resident teacher. In addition missionaries are sent to the distant west, by the various sects, it is true, but all have a common purpose: to give the people a Christian education. I feel that Tocqueville is right in seeing in this not only Christian zeal but also political considerations.[3]

In a few words I have described the culture and customs I found in America. Perhaps you expect me to express myself on the American system of government. There has been a great deal of discussion and writing about it and more capable writers than I have dealt with this subject, so that my comments would be superfluous. I merely wish to say that I have found realized one of the boldest and sweetest of my youthful dreams of liberty, independence, and equality. It seems to me, as Tegnér somewhere says: "Here the European at last must send his household gods." Wise men may quarrel about the superiority of this or that form of government; but if the results of a form of government are to be the guide for our judgment, then, at least for the present, conditions in the American free states justify my homage to the principles upon which the Constitution rests. Even though I assume that there is a sort of equality in other countries, yet in reality what is the relation of the upper to the "lower classes" (an expression that should never be used)? Is not the bullying attitude of the officials and the "better folk" everywhere in evidence? . . . Everyone knows that these conditions do not prevail in America. Mr. von Hauswolff correctly adds in the appendix to the "Sketches": "Every person, no matter who he is, is respected here, not only with reference to his rights as a citizen but also with reference to his individual worth."[4] This complete equality exerts a no less beneficial influence on the public than it does on the individual. As yet there has been no perfect government and no body politic without sores and blemishes, and the American free states furnish no exception. I willingly admit that there are deplorable shortcomings and much room for improvement; nevertheless I am convinced that America more closely than any other country in the world approaches the ideal which nature seems to have intended. for the happiness and comfort of humanity.

*Ibid.,* 68–76.

*Largely through letters from one of the Pine Lake settlers to his father near Kisa, Östergötland, Peter Cassel, a prosperous local farmer and miller, became interested in America. In 1845 he led a group of twenty-one relatives and neighbors who established the New Sweden settlement in southeastern Iowa. Cassel's letters were printed in newspapers and published in book form. Coming from an experienced farmer, they aroused great interest among the Swedish peasantry. Cassel wrote:*

Post Office, Jefferson County, Iowa Territory,
United States of America, February 9, 1846

Friends and Countrymen:

In accordance with our promise on our departure from Sweden we are sending you a few lines to tell you how and where we are situated at present. After a fortunate voyage of eight weeks between Gothenburg and New York we arrived at this place the 16th of last August. We are under heavy obligations to Captain Nissen for the promptitude with which he satisfied our desires and the attentiveness with which he always ministered to our welfare and needs. We also had the pleasure of hearing him expound the Word of God in rich measure, not only at the regular morning worship every Sunday but also with a reverent prayer every morning.

From a complete map showing all the land that was offered for sale, which we obtained in New York, we learned that the best land in Wisconsin had already been taken, and accordingly we decided to settle in Iowa. This territory borders on Missouri to the south and on Illinois to the east and is reputed to be the best of the hitherto unsold lands. It has an abundance of water power, contains metals, marble, and several other natural resources, and only a very small part of this extensive territory is settled.

After a sojourn of eight days in New York we embarked on our journey with Burlington, the capital of Iowa, located about thirty-three Swedish miles[5] from St. Louis on the Mississippi River, our first destination. At New York we met many Swedes who reside there; and these countrymen showed us many favors and much kindness. The long journey from New York to Burlington, which is made by steam power over land as well as by water, cost us twelve dollars per person. It should be noted that children under three ride free. In each case provisions are not included. Among the larger cities we passed were Philadelphia, Pittsburgh, Cincinnati, and St. Louis. The first named is the most beautiful city in America and probably one of the most beautiful in the whole world. On the journey we could eat as much fruit as we desired, including grapes, which grow wild in great abundance.

We had made a sort of agreement with a Mr. B. of Stockholm, who was in our company on the journey to Iowa and was in better financial circumstances than we, that he was to purchase land for all of us. We promised to reimburse him as soon as we were able. Accordingly he bought four hundred *tunnland* situated about six and one-half Swedish miles from Burlington from a man in this city for two dollars per *tunnland*[6] on credit and with interest. We immediately went to view the land. After a short time, when it became evident that we could not possibly make a deal with Mr. B., we decided to leave him. We had no difficulty in securing employment and lodging in the neighborhood.

For the present we are in Iowa Territory, Jefferson County, near Skunk River, a Swedish mile and a half from Mount Pleasant, about 42° north latitude. We have everything we need and feel secure for the future. Our plan is to found a Swedish colony about twenty-three and a half Swedish miles west of here, where the government has recently acquired land from the Indians. Each family can take a claim of three hundred and twenty *tunnland*, and when the time for payment comes, which is usually four years later, as much thereof as desired can be purchased at $1.25 per *tunnland*, the remainder reverting to the government. Two educated countrymen from Västergötland, whose longer residence in the country has made them thoroughly familiar with conditions and in whom we have the highest confidence, have associated themselves with us and we have taken a common claim to one thousand *tunnland* of the aforementioned land, whose fertility and excellent location on the navigable Des Moines River is not excelled by any tract in the entire state of Iowa. Next month some of us will go there, the others remaining here another year, since we are getting along reasonably well and have most excellent neighbors.[7]

The ease of making a living here and the increasing prosperity of the farmers, year by year and day by day, exceeds anything we anticipated. If only half of the work expended on the soil in the fatherland were utilized here, the yield would reach the wildest imagination; but the American farmer, content with enough to give him a living and comfort, confines himself to plowing, planting, and harvesting. Timbered land is broken with a yoke of oxen, the expense being $1.50 per *tunnland*. The hard prairie requires four yoke of oxen at $3.50 per *tunnland*. There is not a single stone on the surface but small hills almost in every case contain at a depth of four or five feet limestone and sandstone, so there is never a lack of stone for building purposes. Coal is found nearly everywhere along rivers and creeks. A yoke of oxen is worth from twenty-five to thirty-five dollars and a cow ten to twelve dollars.

Barns and cattle sheds are seldom, if ever, seen in this vicinity; livestock is allowed to roam the year around, and since pasturage is common property, extending from one end of the land to the other, a person can own as much livestock as he desires or can take care of, without the least trouble or expense. Every morning or evening the cattle are fed corn or oats, in order that they may become attached to the place. Hogs thrive and increase very fast. One of our neighbors, who has farmed only four years, has one hundred head of hogs, raised on his farm. Their food consists largely of acorns, a product that is so abundant that as late as February the ground is covered in places. This winter pork is worth four *rdr banko* per *lispund*.[8] All crops thrive and grow to an astonishing degree. Cornfields are more like woods than grain fields. Ordinarily corn grows to a height of from ten to twelve feet, and a special kind of ax is used to cut it. A bushel of seed corn yields as high as seven hundred bushels, and the ears are so large that a single one makes about a *kvarter*.[9] We have counted from one thousand to fourteen hundred grains in an ear. Since corn must be planted thin, various things are planted between the hills—cucumbers, beans, melons, and pumpkins. The last named grow so large that a single one makes a meal. There are several varieties and they are quite good. From them can be made ale, syrup, and several other products. I have seen hemp, but I do not know what it is used for, because it is so coarse. I measured a hemp fiber which was thirteen and a half inches long and at the root two inches in diameter.

Game of many kinds—geese, turkeys, pheasants, etc., etc.—is abundant. All domestic animals in Sweden are in use here, and in general they are large, especially sheep. Cows yield milk generously and on the average milk from a single cow makes at least five *skålpund*[10] of butter per week. A day's wages is equivalent to two bushels of cornmeal (about one Swedish *halftunna*).[11] Last October for fourteen days' work I received twenty-two Swedish *lispund* of finely ground wheat flour. We have raised and threshed buckwheat on half shares, including food. It is to be noted that nobody furnishes his own food when he works for others. The Americans have unusually good food. Skilled laborers are well paid. A tanner gets half of the leather he prepares. In this vicinity a tanner ought to do well, but I do not think leather is tanned by the method used in Sweden. A carpenter is paid eight dollars for making a bed—four days' work. A farm wagon costs from one hundred to one hundred and thirty dollars. This is a heavy wagon with large wheels. The necessary iron costs only sixteen dollars, so you can judge how good wages are. I do not think it would be profitable for an artisan who confines himself to carpentry to come here, because the Americans probably excel all other people at this trade, and there is an abundance of carpenters in all parts of the country.[12]

Emigrants ought not to bring implements with them, because this country has perhaps the best implements in the world. They are made of cast steel and are not very expensive, but of excellent quality. Moreover, it does not pay to transport from New York to the remote western states more effects than is absolutely necessary. Each passenger on a steamboat is allowed five *lispund* of baggage free of charge, but on canal boats and on railways only two and a half *lispund*. Excess charges are so high that they eat up the value of the article.

If any of you decide to join us, we will be at your service, as far as we are able, until you reach your destination. We will plant our own little Sweden. If you will notify us in advance with reference to your departure from Sweden and the approximate time of your arrival at New York, one of us will meet you in that city and guide you the entire way out here. A *bonde* with a wife and two children ought not to emigrate unless he has at least one thousand *riksdaler riksgälds*,[13] because after paying all the expenses of the journey he will have scarcely enough money left to purchase necessary livestock and a few household necessities; but with this sum and good ability to work he can undertake the journey with confidence and with the assurance that a hopeful future awaits him and his children.

Freedom and equality are the fundamental principles of the Constitution of the United States. There is no such thing as class distinction here, no counts, barons, lords, or lordly estates. The one is as good as another, and everyone lives in the unrestricted enjoyment of personal liberty. A Swedish *bonde*, raised under oppression and accustomed to poverty and want, here finds himself elevated to a new world, as it were, where all his former hazy ideas of a society conforming more closely to nature's laws are suddenly made real and he enjoys a satisfaction in life that he has never before experienced. There are no beggars here and there never can be so long as the people are ruled by the spirit that prevails now. I have yet to see a lock on a door in this neighborhood. When people leave their houses everything is left unlocked, even though they expect to be away several days, yes, even months. Their houses can be entered by anybody, but I have never heard of theft.

As regards the language, we are getting along quite well. Our children attend school. The population of Iowa is composed for the most part of Americans and some Germans. The Americans are extremely good and friendly, but the Germans are more industrious. The Americans compete with one another in helping the needy. If a person does not make his wants known, they come of their own accord to those they think are in need of assistance and inquire if they can be of service; but everybody in good health who is able and willing to work gets along by his own efforts.

At this time of the year the sap of the sugar maple is running and we have made much sugar and syrup; we are still engaged in this. Here grain is stored in a building roofed and lined with straw to prevent the grain from leaking through. In December we had fairly cold weather; I guessed the temperature was from twelve to sixteen degrees.[14] From

Christmas on, however, the weather has been pleasant, and now in February everybody has the doors open all day.

Space forbids me to write any more, although I have much more to tell you. We hope we will soon receive a few lines in reply to this long letter. May God be with you and may He grant you good fortune and success in all honorable and useful undertakings is the wish of your honorable and upright friends across the ocean.

Peter Cassel

George M. Stephenson, trans. and ed., "Documents Relating to Peter Cassel and the Settlement at New Sweden," *Swedish American Historical Bulletin* 2, no. 1 (1929):55–62.

~~~~~~~~~~~~~~~~~~~~~~~~~~~~~~~~~~~~~~~~~~~~~~~~~~~~~~~~

*Some fantastic stories soon spread through the Swedish countryside, as shown by a report printed in a Småland newspaper in 1846.*

The desire to emigrate to America continues to increase in the Kisa area and has evidently spread to neighboring regions. A beggar girl from Kisa, who went up to the plain region to carry on her activity, is said to have described America in much more attractive colors than Joshua's returning spies described the Promised Land for the children of Israel. "In America," she is supposed to have said, "the pigs go and eat themselves full on raisins and almonds, which everywhere grow wild, and when the pigs are thirsty, they drink from the ditches, where nothing but wine flows." Naturally, the simple peasantry must draw the conclusion that it is far better to be a pig in America than a human being in Sweden. The desire to emigrate overwhelms them and the governor's officials get no sleep at night from preparing emigrant passes. More than a hundred of these are supposed to have been issued.

*Jönköpingsbladet*, 26 May 1846.

~~~~~~~~~~~~~~~~~~~~~~~~~~~~~~~~~~~~~~~~~~~~~~~~~~~~~~~~

*Such tales call to mind the numerous "America ballads" that soon
began to circulate. The following, of uncertain origin, was recalled by
an old sailor in 1900 and is a particularly exuberant example.*

Brothers, we have far to go,
Across the salty water,
And then there is America,
Upon the other shore.
Surely it's not possible?
Oh yes, it's so delightful!
Pity that America,
Pity that America
Must lie so far away.

The trees that grow there in the land,
Sweet they are, as sugar,
The country there is filled with girls,
Lovely little dolls.

And if you would like one of them,
You right away have four or five,
Out there in the fields
There grows English money.

Ducks and chickens come raining down,
Roasted geese, and others yet
Fly onto the table,
With knife and fork stuck in 'em.

The sun, it never does go down,
Or go out for each of us,
Here is gaiety and song,
Cellars filled with fine champagne.
Surely it's not possible?
Oh yes, it's so delightful!
Pity that America,
Pity that America
Must lie so far away.

[August Bondesson], *August Bondessons visbok*, 2 vols. (Stockholm, 1903), 2:231–32.

*When the self-proclaimed prophet Erik Jansson fled persecution in
Sweden for his sectarian activity in 1845, he and his followers sought a
haven in America, where the following year they founded their Bishop
Hill community in northwestern Illinois. Among the first arrivals was
E. Myrén from Västmanland, who here describes the marvels of New
York—"Nefyark," he calls it—where he left the group.*

New York, North America, 28 September 1846

Since I have now reached the long-awaited shore and together with
my fellow travelers have set foot on American soil, I feel obliged to
report in a few lines how our journey passed. We went on board the
brig *Charlotta* as is known on 3 June and landed here in New York the
15th of September the same year; but during this voyage more happened to our pietists than I can describe. Most of them were dissatisfied
with it, as the letter addressed to my wife says; you alone may read it,
and read it to her only. Since the piece of paper I wrote the letter to her
on did not leave me room to describe New York's life and ways, I will
therefore describe here what little there is room for.

When we came to the American coast after not having seen anything
but sky and water for nearly two months, on the 15th of September we
saw before our eyes a bit of land which we soon came up to. It rose into
the sky like the Swedish ridges, but much higher. Upon it the most
unfamiliar trees were swaying in the warm breeze. Scattered about,
here and there on the slopes, we could see fields already harvested.
There were also countless small white houses built of clay, like our
Swedish camping places of canvas, where the farmers live with their
small patches of land around them, which they can cultivate with the
least effort and in the greatest prosperity provide for themselves
throughout the year without any state demanding their harvests as
in Sweden.[15] This was the first sight of America.

Soon we saw through a narrow passage of the sea the long-awaited
New York, which was not built all together like other ordinary towns
but quite different from what I could see. When we had passed through

this narrows we were once again in quite a large bay of the Atlantic Ocean which we could not see until there, suddenly, unexpectedly, we had New York around us on all sides, for right around the sound where we were, the most important parts of the city were built on the shores and inland on all sides.

We anchored a couple of stones' throw from the city because there was no place there yet such as the captain wanted. We lay there for five days before we could winch ourselves into a mooring, which took place on 20 September. But while we lay out there we could see what I could almost call the liveliest place in the world. There were hundreds of ships, larger and smaller, all together in New York's bay, with its beautiful surroundings, while in the harbor lay millions of the same, from all the nations and kingdoms of the world. Different flags waved colorfully from the mastheads along miles of waterfront, so crowded that there was hardly room for them all. The number and magnificence of the many steamboats was such that at any minute of the day or night I could not count less than ten or twelve leaving the harbor and the same number arriving. If one were to describe their splendor, it would take a whole book to do it, but the length of the largest is supposed to be 360 feet, upon which is built three stories without any outer walls, the most beautiful iron fences around each story, and great salons and rooms in the middle. For the rest there are the promenade decks, extending fourteen or sixteen yards inside the fence, so you can easily walk until you are tired without having to go around so many times.

I must not keep describing this but turn to the city, which is also beyond my understanding with its mechanical marvels. First of all, the strange passages for water caught my attention. On almost every house in the city there is an iron contraption beside the steps which looks like a cannon with a screw-like spigot on top. If somebody needs water, all he has to do is have his cup in his hand, sit down, and turn the spigot, and the freshest water you ever could wish for comes out without any pumping. In many places I have even seen the spigot left open and the water running out steadily. There are even two places in the city where they have the same contraption, only on a larger scale, so that just by turning a little screw I can open a vein in the earth and water shoots right up into the air twenty to twenty-four feet high. These waterfalls are open every afternoon.

In the second place, it is no less remarkable that many of the houses in the city never need to use candles in any room, because in each chamber or room there is a spigot to turn and there then comes the brightest light you ever saw. But I have found out that there is a certain house in the city where the light comes from, through pipes, and these pipes are laid right under the streets. Then in every room in this house I talked about, where this comes from, there are supposed to be big contraptions for burning gas for this purpose.

The third strange thing I will describe does not surprise me at all, that there are fires almost all the time in many places and the bells in the city's towers ring the whole night through just because of that. You would not believe the carelessness with which fire is handled here if I described it. One evening at eight o'clock, I was going to the Swedish church for evening prayers.[16] But no sooner had I set foot in the entrance than I turned back, for I could not help noticing that there was a fire in the neighborhood, since thick smoke was coming down over the roofs of the nearby houses. Surprised, I turned immediately to find where it was coming from. I went up a back alley and there, a short distance away, I saw that about two hundred small boys had come with three tar barrels which they had put in a row along the street and set fire to. They all had sticks in their hands which they stuck into the burning tar and hit against house walls and steps so that the sparks flew. Meanwhile a crowd of older people looked on and laughed, clapped their hands, and cheered. I soon went and laughed with them. It is the same when a house is on fire; everyone laughs, even the house-owner, for everyone in the city is insured.

Now all the pietists[17] have traveled inland so that we are only three from Hälsingland and two of us from Västmanland still in New York. You know those who are left here; they are Jöns, the boy from the sexton's place, and I. We left their sect completely, for they were a devilishly selfish crowd and also we did not want to follow them out there into the wilderness, twenty-five miles from any passable road, where they said they were going. I do not know anything more.

You can imagine the sort of upright life Jon Olsson lived when he came here to New York. To start with, he said he would not pay out more than he wished and that no one he did not want could go along with him out to the country, and when someone said give me back my money, he answered, I have never gotten any money from you. But this did not last long for Johan Olsson, for the Swedish consul read him the law and told him, if you have brought people here with you, you must either take them with you out into the country or else pay for them to return home. At this, Jonas had to give way and let as many go with him as wanted to.[18]

For us, the consul has been and is a father who does not fail us. He has now recommended me for a place three days' sail south of New York on a manor farm for a wage of five hundred Swedish *riksdaler*[19] until the 1st of April, 1847. Since I can in the meantime learn something of the language, I will be able to earn a much larger salary or day wage. I forgot to say that I will also get board, bedclothes, and room. The three men from Hälsingland will also go to the same farm, but we will have different work, for I will be inside doing handicrafts and carpentry, and they will be out in the woods cutting timber. But the master will pay our way down and also back again in April if we do not want to stay. Since Monday, we have gotten our day wages and pay, as well as our food here in the city from our employer, who is staying here until the ship is ready to sail, which should be tomorrow.

I beg you to be so kind as to help my wife write back to me. If she should be in great need of a few *styver*[20] just now, give her the fourteen *riksdaler* I have coming to me on account with AAS in Thorstunaby.

Respectfully
E. Myrén

Albin Widén, *När Svensk-Amerika grundades* (Borås, 1961), 56–59.

*A Janssonist named A. Andersson writes home to the district police superintendent in Torstuna, Västmanland:*

North America, Illinois State, Henry County, and
Bishop Hill, November 30, 1847

I now take pen in hand, moved by the spirit of the Lord, when I consider how God has blessed us here on this new soil by a hundredfold in both spiritual and worldly goods over what we possessed in our

fatherland, so that I may say like David: I cannot tell of all Thy goodness, which Thou doest with the sons of man who fear Thee. For: 1. We
have bought lands that could not be exchanged for a quarter of all
Sweden. You ask how this could be? Indeed, if we should take all the
plain which lies around them, forest, sawmills and flour mills, and
other useful places, we could, besides the produce of our own land, harvest all that was needed for several hundred thousand people. 2. We
have on our own land found a lime pit so that we can build houses of
brick, which we can do ourselves, as many as we need for building the
whole town. And we cannot use ourselves all the lime we burn, but
have enough to sell for several thousand dollars each year. 3. We do not
need much seed grain, for when we plant a *tunna* of corn, it can yield
from five to nine hundred *tunnor*, according to how the soil is cultivated and looked after, etc.; wheat yields from fifteen to forty *tunnor*,
Swedish corn[21] from thirty to fifty *tunnor*, oats about the same; innumerable other fruits that do not grow in Sweden can produce a thou-
sandfold. Swedish rye grows here unusually well but since our friends
were not here last fall to sow any, I cannot say for sure how much we
can get from a *tunna* of seed. But according to what people say, we can
get at least forty *tunnor* from one. 4. The word of the Scripture has
been fulfilled for us, that hundreds of cattle may graze upon a pasture
so great that all Sweden's cattle could have enough fodder there for
both winter and summer. 5. We can sow our plowlands every year without manuring or ditching, and if we plow in the spring, we can plant
as much corn and buckwheat as we need the same year, as well as oats
and flax and potatoes. And many other kinds of useful fruits, as well as
turnips for the cattle, grow on newly plowed soil without our having
to do anything more than put them down in the ground. 6. We never
have to buy sugar or syrup here because we can get it from the woods[22]
in the spring and from cornstalks in the fall, as much as we need for
ourselves and even some to sell. 7. I need hardly tell how this land is
flowing with milk and honey, for here we can take wild bees and honey
right from the wilderness itself and also grapes and wild plums and
apples and many kinds of berries and herbs, and so on. 8. We can also
get as much coal as we need from the ground; a man in a blacksmith
shop can earn from five to ten dollars a day, for here blacksmith's coal
can be had for nothing more than it costs to haul it from the special
places where such mines are found in the ground. 9. There are great

earnings here of many kinds. We have harvested flax and given only the seed to the owner and gotten all the flax for the work, and this even though we have hardly seen such good, clean flax in the fatherland. We also sent out nine of the young men, who are going to the English school, to cut wheat; when they had laid it in windrows they got a third of it for their work, so their gain was seventy-five *tunnor* of good wheat in about a month, during which they also threshed and winnowed it, etc. This autumn we harvested fall and spring wheat together, at least eight thousand bushels, amounting to about sixteen hundred *tunnor*, Swedish weight, as well as barley, oats, corn, potatoes, cucumbers, melons, beans, cabbage, all in such unusual amounts that they cannot be reckoned, and we also have an herb garden with many kinds of English herbs, the names of which I cannot tell you. 10. We now have thirty horses, forty oxen, two hundred cows, six hundred sheep, and at least three hundred pigs. We have built barns and stables for our livestock, so that the people of this land are greatly amazed. And, 11. We have built houses of brick and the brick we made ourselves, and about five *mil* from here we have the Mississippi River, where we caught fifty-three *tunnor* of good fish this summer. Here there is hunting, a great abundance of buffalo, elk, and deer, and many other animals and birds in great plenty which we both trap and shoot. . . .

I would point out above all that there is here, as you know yourself, freedom to serve God according to His sacred word. And from this it follows that the light God has brought forth through Erik Jansson cannot be dimmed through either prison or madhouse. They have, to be sure, already tried through slander to have him arrested, but thus far they have gotten no farther than the jailhouse before those who have lied have been brought to shame. . . . There is much more to write about, how we have the opportunity here to edify each other in the most sacred faith, but it need hardly be said that we may listen undisturbed to Erik Jansson, who explains the Bible in its true meaning. And since the Spirit tells me that you cannot believe he is the only one in the whole world who now, in these times, shall in Christ's place reconcile all men with God, I will write no more about it; for you along with many others will not believe a foolish preacher. But why? Indeed, just because you are among those whom Isaiah, 65th chapter, verses 2 to 6, speaks of. But I say unto you, once and for all, that if you do not give up your own thoughts—namely, that you think you already belong to

Christ because you have sought to do good to all men—on judgment day I will see you descend alive into the eternal torments of Hell. But if you can now repent from the snares of the Devil, fly without delay, in accordance with Zachariah, chapter 2, verse 7, from the Land of the North and you will find here the New Jerusalem preserved, according to the above-mentioned chapter, verses 4 to 5. Yes, if you believed, here you would see God's glory. If you hear that even here in this land of freedom, they wish to persecute us, be not surprised but remember what Jesus says to his disciples, namely: Ye shall be hated by all men for My sake; and we must all pass through much tribulation into God's kingdom.

Still, you know that this country's laws are different from those of our fatherland. We are protected here by both the secular law and the secular power, and thus have the rights of citizenship which a true Christian could not enjoy in our fatherland; everyone has the right to serve God according to his conscience. See now how Jesus' word has been fulfilled in us, namely that we who have forsaken all have already been repaid a hundredfold, and according to His promise our final reward is to be life everlasting. And so I do not ask too much of you when I urge you to forsake everything and come here to us. For you know there must be a sheepfold and a shepherd, and if we do as God commands us, namely forsake everything, only then shall our reward be eternal life. I would have much to tell you, how the Scripture is fulfilled in us, but it would be, as I say, too much to write, the one thing with the other. I should also remind you why I address you in the familiar manner. It is the custom of the land in America and especially when we wish to edify one another; God Himself takes no account of persons, for we are all the work of His hands. . . .

J. E. Ekbloms arkiv, Uppsala landsarkiv. (See also Widén, *När Svensk-Amerika grundades*, 21–24.)

*A woman who had left the Janssonists wrote:*

City of Chicago in the State of Illinois of North America, 4 March 1848

Dear Brother,

I must now tell you about my present circumstances, and I must thank God for the priceless gift of health, which is the greatest treasure one can wish for in a foreign, faraway land. I and my children are living very well here and have, praise be to God, not suffered any want as far as the needs of this earthly life go, though it looked dark when we first came and was harder still when my husband died on 7 February a year ago. But praise be to Providence which has granted me and mine health up to the present. I long greatly to hear how you and your family and my children in Sweden are. I have sent greetings to them all but have not heard a word from any of my relatives. I beg of you, Brother, that you tell my children the contents of this letter and tell them all that we live better here than they can imagine, for whoever has health need fear no want. I have sent word several times to my girls, that if someone intends to come over here they should come along, for they would be much better off here than in Sweden. Until they learned the language they could not get more than four dollars a week plus food and gifts, but as soon as they got more used to things they could surely get more; women do not have to do any other work here but wash clothes and cups and keep the house tidied up and at some places also cook food. And here people live well, there is nothing but wheat bread. There is no need to tell about conditions, for word has surely spread through various letters that have been sent from here. If you cannot see my children, you know in any case where they are, so send this letter to them or tell them to send some word about their situation. It is up to Providence whether we shall ever meet again in this earthly life, but let us then meet in a better world. . . . If anyone should possibly want to come over and they could get some help with money for the journey, they could quickly repay it here. Oh! How happy I would be if I had with me my boys and girls who stayed behind in Sweden; I could dance with joy to my grave and be sure that they would soon earn enough here to assure themselves of a carefree old age. Many greetings to you all. God be with you. So wishes your loving sister,

Christina Källström

*Ibid.* (See also Widén, *När Svensk-Amerika grundades,* 90–91.)

*In a letter from Bishop Hill was enclosed the following note:*

June 26, 1848

The old soldier, Jonas Blixt, sends greetings to his old woman and wants to know if she is living or dead. I wrote a letter a year ago which I have not gotten any answer to, and I wrote that letter so that she could come over to me if she wanted to. If you are getting along well, stay where you are; but if you have made up your mind to come here you will be welcome. I have thought about going to Sweden but I don't know what I ought to do until I get some answer. This is a very good land here, but I don't want to get too attached to any piece of land until I find out how it is, whether you are married or not. So I wanted to write and let you know about how things are with me nowadays. The Lord has helped me and been close to me to this day and I have by the Lord's great grace and mercy always enjoyed good health. . . .

former soldier Blixt

Albin Widén, *Amerikaemigrationen i dokument* (Stockholm, 1966), 18.

*The pain of separation could be heartrending. From Alfta, Hälsingland, the old Swedish center of Janssonism, a woman wrote to her daughter in Bishop Hill:*

Alfta kyrkby, April 3, 1848

Dearly beloved but greatly missed Daughter and Son-in-Law,

I will herewith without delay send you a few lines; whether these lines will reach you is in the hands of the Lord. But my heart grieves and my eyes flow with tears when I think of your emigrating, and the sorrow and longing you left me with. You can well imagine the sorrow with which you burdened my weak shoulders, and the other pains, when you forsook the earthly good God allotted you, first and foremost your late father and me. Then when through God's merciful help and support, I wished to leave all this to you, dear children, you did not regard it as a gift from God but rather as a poison that repelled you. This was the reward you gave me for all the unstinting efforts I made for your earthly future. You surely think you have behaved toward your parents as befits obedient children. But dear children, I would turn from your offense and gladly forgive you everything if only you would return from your erring footsteps and pray to God for His grace to forsake them and be obedient to Him and to me. For you see, this is what God will have of both parents and children. Consider, dear children, how first of all you were the means of the early death of your little son, which your letter from Gräsö described, over which many a tear of pain and sorrow has run down my cheeks, sunken with grief. But I can still comfort myself that your little son has a better Father than any on earth. But this is a reminder the Lord has given you to return to your fathers' land.

You think you have no means to make a living, but there is surely some way out. For you are only a father in the flesh here; He has revealed Himself to me, and I can tell you this. For think, dear daughter, how you used to lie at my breast and in your innocent years would trample on my knees; now you trample upon my heart, so that I shall go with sorrow down into an early grave. I must often say, Maria, my daughter, and son-in-law, how could you do this to me? Grieving, I search for you day and night, and I wish and pray fervently to God that

I may someday cry out with the Patriarch, it is enough for me that my daughter and son-in-law live and will go to visit their mother before she dies. Signed, your mother, with tears of pain and longing. . . .

Kare Jons Dotter

*Ibid.*, 14–15.

*The Bishop Hill colony had its critics, including various disgruntled former Janssonists. A letter from 1848 reported:*

They have acquired a lot of land. They carry on all kinds of crafts and sell and save up money. They even make liquor. I want to ask if these are God's folk, but they say that what they do is to God's glory. Morning and afternoon they have prayers and on Sundays divine services, but even so they sell liquor on the Sabbath.[23] The people get food and clothes, but not coffee or sugar, which are kept only for the Apostles.[24] Their food is of the Swedish type. They have three dining halls and four long tables in each dining hall. No one can prepare his own food. The people are like serfs, who must work according to the bell. At six in the morning it rings when they are to get out of bed, at half past six it rings for prayer, which lasts until eight or nine, and then it rings for breakfast. When they have eaten, it rings for work, and it goes on like this morning and evening. After the evening meal, it rings after it gets dark for prayer, which lasts as long as in the morning.

*Ibid.*, 24.

*In 1849 the first Swedish Lutheran pastor to come to the Midwest, Lars Paul Esbjörn, sailed with his family for America and established himself in Andover, Illinois. Here he describes their voyage across the Atlantic.*

Diary of a journey from Gefle to New York with the ship *Cobden*, in the summer of 1849. According to contract, this ship was to be ready to sail on Midsummer's Day, but as many things on the ship were unfinished . . . one had to wait, which, both before and after embarking, caused a deplorable strife between the shipowner and the captain on one side and a part of the emigrants on the other. . . . Truth and justice also demand the admission that the shipowner had not kept to what he had promised them, that he had a part of the water taken in the bay where it was somewhat salty, etc.

On the 25th and 26th of June we moved our things to the ship where there was great crowding and confusion in arranging and packing one's belongings.

June 27 we moved out to the ship in the name of the Lord and took in possession the lower cabin, our future home for several weeks, and under wholly new and strange conditions. In the cabin it was crowded and very unfinished; there was not a chair to sit on, and a trunk was moved in, to serve as a table during the whole journey. We sat on the floor. The two little twins were placed in a hammock which was stretched across the whole room. Yet we were happy and cheerful. . . .

Friday, June 29. After two days' arranging of our things, we sailed today. . . . The office clerk of the shipowner, a sea captain, and some store clerks boarded the vessel and inaugurated our journey by drinking and worldly singing. This, together with the wrangling with the captain on account of the closing of the big hatch, which made the big room entirely dark, aroused a nauseous and sad feeling among the God-fearing. . . .

Sunday, July 1. 9 A.M. I conducted service, and in the evening the captain led evening devotions.

Monday, July 2. We traveled over the Åland Sea. Storm arose and made many seasick, among them all of mine. . . . My dear wife remained sick and could not leave her bed, where she felt somewhat at ease, as long as the sea was rough. . . .

Monday, July 9. This day Bornholm appeared. It bore the stamp of the wealth of the more southern nature, which especially gladdened our eyes, used to the poverty of the north. Seals appeared here and there around the ship.

Tuesday, July 10. An unexpected and affecting event happened to us today. Our little twin son, Emanuel, unexpectedly suffered from a heart attack, and after a few minutes he died a blessed death in my arms. Universal sympathy was shown among the people, and the occurrence made a deep—God give, also a lasting—impression.

Wednesday, July 11. This day we saw Zealand and received aboard a Danish pilot who brought news of a victory which his countrymen had recently won over the Germans.[25] His boat was greeted by the singing of "Up Friends," etc.

Thursday, July 12, we anchored at Helsingör[26] at 7 P.M. Now off to the commissioner of our vessel, where we were well received, and I secured one of the sons of the household as a guide. He followed me very willingly to the police, the Swedish consul, and the customs guard, all of whom were to sign my pass, and to the doctor of the quarantine who gave me a certificate about the dead child. Everywhere I was shown the greatest of friendship and accommodation. After the pass had been inspected in Helsingborg, off to call on Dr. Wieselgren, who was greatly surprised. After conversing a while with these Christian friends, who carefully and with especial interest listened to the conditions and occasions leading to my mission journey, we went to Mlle. Fryxell's pension. Later we went back to Dr. Wieselgren's and afterward we all, including the whole group of lovely girls, accompanied each other to the beautiful cemetery of the rural congregation, where the remains of our Emanuel were buried, Dr. Wieselgren conducting the service.

Friday, July 13, our feet stepped on Swedish soil for the last time, for at 6 P.M. the inexorable steamer departed for Helsingör. After the return to Helsingör, the pass must again be exhibited and visaed in the police and customs offices, so that it became a long document. Then a lot of supplies were bought, money exchanged for me and others, etc. On reaching the ship, we found Dr. Wieselgren with wife and two children, Provost P. G. Ahnfelt, and others, before us. On request, Dr. Wieselgren delivered a farewell speech in which he expressed that he did not approve the removals, but, seeing that they had come to pass, he wished them accompanied by God's blessing, and urged the emigrants to emulate the Swedes who journeyed to New Sweden in the time of Queen Christina. He admonished us all not to dishonor the Swedish name.

Sunday, July 15, we bade good-bye to Sweden, when, at four o'clock in the morning, the last place in the fatherland, namely, Marstrand, disappeared. In the evening Swedish fishermen visited us, lying here at a distance of thirty miles from home, and offering cod, ale, bread, and brandy[27] for sale.

Monday, July 16, Paul and John fished a lot of mackerel by hook and line. Many began and continued this fishing all day and got more or less, but quarreled deplorably about places.

Tuesday, the 17, twelve or thirteen dolphins appeared just as on Sunday the 15th. When the mate, the last-named day, wanted to lance them with the harpoon, they all fled. The weather was usually fine the whole week, except on Wednesday when there was much wind. As usual, the wind was against us.

Friday, July 20, at 11 P.M., a girl was born to Anders Ersson's wife. As a certified midwife was on board ship, it turned out well. The mother soon became strong.

Saturday, July 21, just before the evening prayer, we were visited by a boat of English fishermen from London. They had been out for seven weeks. They seemed just as poor as the Swedish fishermen and wanted only brandy in exchange for their peculiar red-finned skin-fishes. My advice not to drink brandy they refused to consider right. Abstinence, they maintained, would not do for fishermen and sailors. While we sang a stanza at the evening prayer they departed.

Sunday, July 22. Service was held at nine o'clock. In the afternoon Anders Ersson's child, Brita, was baptized, and many were regaled in the captain's cabin. . . . The wind was quite severe so that the captain himself had to serve the coffee.

Tuesday, July 24. The storm continued. In the forenoon, after much cruising, we came to the narrowest passage between Dover and Calais, but could not get any further because of the strong head wind, the sea, the storm, and the tide.

Wednesday, July 25. The storm grew, and the waves rolled and rushed in upon us majestically. Many were sick, but many were driven to humility and prayer. The carnal temper of many was, however, unfortunately unchanged and unbroken. At noon the air thickened so that we, who had cruised back and forth the whole day between Dover and Calais, without being able to get further, had to withdraw a little. We soon turned, however, because it soon became clear. In the afternoon a big steamer with two smokestacks, black coal smoke, and rapid speed passed us.

Thursday, July 26. Because the storm and the seas did not abate, the captain again turned back toward the North Sea during the night, and it happened with great speed. Early in the morning a turnabout was again made, and all day we cruised up towards the Channel again. Because we had not been able to continue our song practices for several days on account of the wind, the opportunity which better weather offered was used in the afternoon; but we had not continued long before an attack of storm and rain put an end to it all. Swedish slothfulness shows itself here also in indifference in regard to singing and the school instruction of the children. Food and drink seem to be the chief end for many.

Friday, July 27. During the night favorable weather has prevailed so that in the morning we again have come close to Dover. But a father has with sorrow found a former store clerk with his daughter and given them a well merited chastisement. At noon letters home were sent with English pilots. In the afternoon I conversed with above-named wanton girl, who now cried and confessed. The same warning was given to two other women. From Dover proceeds a railroad which soon enters into the big, steep mountain by the coast, and further ahead again comes forth. In the evening we found much pleasure in witnessing how the steam wagons rushed on and later again came into view further in the west, after their subterranean journey.

Saturday, July 28. After the evening prayer we were sadly constrained to listen to the songs of the carnally minded, sung from the bow. The emigrants suffer great harm from the two young cabin passengers whom the ship owner or the captain has admitted.

Sunday, July 29. During the divine service it rained, and the wind was, besides, strong enough, so that the sermon had to be short and the service soon thereafter discontinued.

Monday, July 30. On account of rain and storm the morning prayer was conducted in the Big Room. . . . Today, as usual, I conversed with several on spiritual matters.

Tuesday, July 31. The sea has been very rough during the night, and my dear wife and others have been very sick. She has been very weak for several days. At noon we are only two Swedish miles further west than yesterday noon. In the evening I had to go up and admonish some young folks who were noisy and swore and played on the deck after the evening prayer. . . .

Thursday, August 2. . . . After I had taken the boys away from the worldly songs of the two youths in the afternoon, the two and one more were heard singing worldly songs in thé bow after the evening prayer. . . . We found a whole lot of young people and seamen who thus with play and hilarity drove away the spirit of God and of prayer. . . . One especially became angry and spoke vehemently. . . . After conversing for a while we separated. . . .

Friday, August 3. On awakening, the vessel was found to be in a fog, and the terrifying sound of the warning horn was heard incessantly all morning. . . . The afternoon turned into the most beautiful and warm day we have had during the journey. . . .

Saturday, August 4. After having cruised outside of Falmouth all night and been unable to secure a pilot, in spite of all the usual signals, with the wind, besides, turning southeast, and quite vigorous, we had to put to sea in the morning, without being able to fulfill our desire to enter Falmouth, in order to secure more water and wood . . . and traveled with a speed of nine knots, and with a good wind—for the first time during the whole journey hitherto. Lord, guide us now as we set out upon the great ocean. . . .

Sunday, August 5. . . . We did not get far this day, on account of poor or no wind. . . .

Monday, August 6. At 5 P.M. I conducted a mission prayer when $3.23 were collected for the Lapp mission. Later we met a Danish ship and exchanged greetings. After the prayer a lot of women bathed in the darkness in a specially arranged vessel. Here a lot of youths gathered, among them probably also seamen. When the misbehavior became worse the captain had to send a couple of emigrants with a rope's end, to keep order there, which method, of course, was of little avail.

Wednesday, August 8. During the night has occurred the worst rolling we have had so far. Now as before the children stand it the best.

Thursday, August 9. In the morning I stayed in bed long because I had slept little during the night, and consequently sent word to the captain that he must conduct prayer. After the prayer it was announced that we were only to get three-fourths pottle[28] of water per person, or just half as much as the contract contains. This, besides the constant quarreling and snubbing of the officers toward the emigrants, which had taken place in regard to the consumption of water, led us to . . . ask the captain to go to the Azores Islands and secure more water, if the amount on hand did not allow one pottle per person. . . . To this we received an abusive answer, and especially I was covered with abuse. On measuring and reckoning, it was found that there is still water for one pottle and one and a half for the seamen daily for fifty-four days. . . .

Sunday, August 12. . . . In the afternoon we sang in parts. . . .

Monday, August 13. Mild weather today also, but the speed, which ever since we left Cape Lizard on August 4, has averaged twenty-three Swedish miles per day, was now only a little over eleven since yesterday noon, and that strongly southward. . . . In the afternoon I distributed a lot of Christian and temperance tracts among the seamen and the emigrants. They thereupon all began to read eagerly. The evening was unusually beautiful and bright. We sang and praised God in the darkness.

Tuesday, August 14. . . . and sang in parts hymnal nos. 124 and 102 and in unison 498.

Wednesday, August 15. The calm continued all day, and we made little headway. The sky was clear, the sun warm. Everybody had their bedclothes up to be aired.

Thursday, August 16. On awakening we rejoiced at a good and speeding east wind which continued all day. . . . I spoke to a sick youth who had been ailing from consumption, and prayed with him, as I had done before. He died in the evening. . . . My dear wife became so well that she could prepare food herself.

Friday, August 17. In the evening it was intended to bury the dead youth in the sea; but the weather became so bad and rainy in the afternoon that it was impossible. The storm continued until midnight, when it was worst. . . .

Saturday, August 18. . . . Soon after the morning prayer I conducted the funeral service over the dead youth who after the service was inconspicuously sunk into the sea, sewn into sheets with weights. . . .

Monday, August 20. . . . From noon until Tuesday noon was calm and fine weather so that the sick could recuperate. . . .

Tuesday, August 21. . . . In the evening we found two English ships, one of which went to Europe and showed longitude 42° 36′. The other one went the same way as we and was overtaken by us, and showed exactly the same longitude as we, namely 45°, which also later was found to be correct; although the captain, convinced that the current had carried us eastward, showed only 43°. . . . In the cabin had been made a transparency with the name Josephine, with a royal crown above it and crossed laurel branches underneath, etc. This was unveiled at the evening prayer. The captain besides caused illumination with three lanterns under a canvas roof in the stern and saluted with two shots. . . . A couple of sick women became very ill because of all this, especially as the oft-named youths roared . . . so that the emigrants were not allowed to end this name day of the Swedish queen in stillness and peace. . . . In the evening I and A. Björklund saw two big whales a short distance from the ship. . . .

Wednesday, August 22. . . . In the afternoon the wind became cold, the sea rippled, while a lot of porpoises panted on the surface of the water and countless seabirds were in view. One began to suspect that we had already, against expectations, reached the Newfoundland bank. On sounding, at six o'clock, a depth of thirty-five fathoms was found, and a new sounding at eight o'clock showed thirty fathoms. God had thus not, as is usual, allowed the current to hinder us; on the contrary, we were a little more than one degree longitude ahead of the reckoning. . . . The following night we traveled fast, eight to nine knots.

Thursday, August 23. . . . The whole forenoon, after the weather had improved, we tried to fish for cod at a depth of forty-five to fifty fathoms. My household got nothing, but others did, so that the whole amounted to seven fish. . . . During the night the feebleminded girl was wild again, and the parents gave her a taste of a rope's end which the mother had brought along. Ye fathers, provoke not your children to wrath. . . .

Saturday, August 25. . . .

Conrad Peterson, trans. and ed., "Letters from Pioneer Days," *Yearbook of the Swedish Historical Society of America*, vol. 9 (1923–24), 54–62.

*D. A. Peterson went to America with his family from Östergötland in 1849, settling in Iowa. In 1880 he reminisced (in his own English) for the* Fort Dodge Messenger.

In the winter between 1848–49, my father resolved to emigrate to America. One family from our parish had three years ago preceded us, and their flattering account of their new home was a powerful aid in forming that resolution. As soon as it became a fixed fact that the old home should be left, hundreds of things came up to be thought about and to be seen to; clothes to be made; chests procured to carry clothing and provisions in; money to be collected and paid out; personal property to be disposed of (happily most of emigrants are not encumbered with real estate) and the Rector's certificate of good character and the King's passport to be procured. The first was obtained by weaving the cloth at home, and then calling in the parish tailor, who with his apprentices, worked away two or three weeks to make each of us, both male and female, two suits apiece, while the men folks have an extra suit, consisting of sheepskin coat and pants of reindeer skin. Boots and shoes were made by the parish shoemaker. I should here state that the tailors and shoemakers went from place to place and did the work: not in shops of their own as the case in this country. The chests were made by carpenters versed in the art, and ironbound by my father who was a blacksmith, and then a painter was called in to put the finishing touches on the work, and when done the chests looked large and strong enough to cross the Atlantic in. The property was disposed of by public sale, much the same as in this country, with the exception that the auctioneer, at the close of the sale, would pay to the seller the amount the sale brought, with the exception of a certain per cent, which the auctioneer retained for his trouble of conducting the same and collecting the proceeds.

Meantime we were harassed daily by our neighbors who came to see the preparations for our leave-taking, and who were always proffering advice, and many of them sadly bewailing the fate in store for us, such as falling into the hands of the Turks (the terror of them have not yet died out in the lower classes in Europe), shipwrecks, famine, all these painted in most vivid colors. Many, though, wished themselves ready to start on the journey; with most of them means to carry out the wish was lacking.

The next move was to get a certificate of good character from the parish Rector, which was of the utmost importance, as without one a person could not get a passport, and consequently could not leave the Kingdom, but it was an undertaking that anyone would shrink from as the Rector was known to be a bitter opponent to immigration. But done it must be, at all hazards, so one day my father presented himself at the parsonage and made his business known. He was met by something like the following, which in his (the Rector's) mind seemed unanswerable.

"Well, Mr. Peterson, I am both shocked and grieved at the resolution you have taken. You certainly know that you are committing a wrong against your country of birth and a sin against God to thus throw yourself and family into dangers that you have no conceptions of. The danger attendant to crossing the great ocean between here and America is something that I shudder to think of. And if you should get there— which by the blessing of God I hope you will if you are determined to go—you will find a people without religion or morality of any kind whatever, churches and schoolhouses there are none, laws there may be but none have any respect for them and your life will be at the mercy of anyone who is disposed to take it, whom I assure you are not few, and if as you say you are going to the western part of the United States you will find it to consist of an impenetrable forest in which it will take an immense amount of labor to make a home and where your only neighbors will be ferocious wild beasts and bloodthirsty Indians and the lives of yourself and family will be in daily peril from both. And if a war should break out between these lawless Americans and some strong foreign nation the result can easily be told, the country would be overrun and you would find yourself a fugitive in a strange land."

Here my father meekly suggested that the United States seemed fully able to take care of itself in its late war with Mexico. The Rector somewhat nonplussed continued:

"Well, I know that, but the ways of an overruling Providence are not always clear to [us] poor blind mortals. Certainly it appeared to us that Mexico was the richest and best qualified of the two to gain success, but then most likely the United States was a chosen instrument in the hands of God to punish the Mexicans for some great national sin, most likely to be its obstinate adherence to the wild beast popery, but what do you suppose would have been the result if our noble army or even a portion of it led by our gracious Sovereign had come in conflict with these contemptible Americans? Why they would have been swept from the face of the earth as well they deserve to be. By this step that you contemplate I am afraid that you do yourself an irreparable injury both for this world and the next. I pray you to not disregard the advice and warning that I have now given you, and when disaster and misfortune overtake you there will be no occasion for you to say that a true friend did not warn you in time."

Nothing would do however but the Rector must issue the certificate which set forth the following points: "That the within named person having decided to remove from the parish it is hereby certified that he was born (here insert date and year) that he was baptized according to the rites of the Evangelical Lutheran church. That he has been vaccinated and that he can read and write, that he has been confirmed in the church and has served his term in the militia, has been a good and law-abiding person heretofore, and has good and sufficient knowledge of the Christian religion according to the ritual of the Evangelical Lutheran church of this realm."

And then [were] added to the above the names of wife and children with dates of birth, baptism, and confirmation. This document being procured, and receiving the Rector's final blessing, the next move was to present the above to the Bailiff of the district, and get the following endorsement from him: "That the above-named person being to me personally known, this is to certify that he has paid his taxes for the previous year; has no law suits pending in any of the courts in the kingdom, leaves no unpaid debts behind, and is a person of eminent and exalted respectability."

And then this most weighty document had to be presented to the Governor of the province in order to receive a passport from that august personage and to do this was a serious affair as a person heard nothing but jeers and insults from the time one entered the anteroom and gave his name and business to the liveried flunky, until one had safely got outside again of the executive mansion. After having presented the credentials from Rector and Bailiff, the Governor with all the eloquence at his command tried to dissuade one from so foolish and fatal a step (as in the Governor's belief) one is about to take. About the same arguments were used as the Rector thought would bring my father to his senses but nothing would avail. The Governor finding all his efforts fruitless, with bad grace ordered his secretary to make out the following piece of pompous nonsense.

"*To all whom it may concern*, be it known, that we, being duly authorized and empowered by our most gracious Sovereign and King of Sweden, Norway, Goths and Vandals, to carry out his Royal wish and will. Therefore with the power in us thus vested do we grant and permit the within named person, with his family and goods to him belonging, without let or hindrance to peacefully depart the Kingdom, of which he has this day made application."

Attached to the above document was a stunning seal, gotten up, I am confident, for the express purpose of striking awe into the breasts of barbarous Americans when we should exhibit it to them. Also a signature, alongside of which the autograph of General Spinner would be voted a failure.

Having received authority from everyone concerned to migrate, it was our next duty to get away as soon as possible. Accordingly our chests were packed with clothing, provisions, and a few such articles as we did not wish to sell, or thought would be necessary on our arrival in this country. Teams were hired to convey us to the nearest station on the canal running between Stockholm and Gothenburg. And now the old home is left forever, a home rough and rugged to be sure, but still a house where our cradles have stood, and where our pleasantest days of childhood have been passed, a place which to us children seemed a very paradise, but in our parents' eyes a place of misery and want to us after their efforts to secure a meager subsistence for their offspring should cease. But how many tender associations of our childhood we had to depart from. Often yet in my dreams am I carried back to that place. . . . The wagons are at the door, load up and hurry, the teamsters are impatient, neighbors are there to take leave, tears and lamentations are seen and heard on all sides. "Write us a line and let us know how you like it" is the last exclamation by everyone left behind, and of course everyone was promised the desired missive; promises made to be kept to few and broken to many. Now we are away, up hill and down at a rattling pace. Here and there along the road an acquaintance steps out from his domicile and waves us a final adieu.

D. A. Peterson, "From Östergötland to Iowa," *Swedish Pioneer Historical Quarterly*, 22 (1971):138–42.

1.  An Emigrant Couple. (From Knut Brodin, *Emigrant visor och andra visor*, Stockholm, Åhlén & Åkerlund, 1938. Courtesy of the publisher.)

2. Gustaf Unonius and his companions at Pine Lake, Wisconsin.
(Engraving from Gustaf Unonius, *Minnen från en sjuttonårig vistelse i
Nordvästra Amerika*, Uppsala, 1861–1862. Courtesy of
Carolina Rediviva Library, Uppsala, University.)

3. The emigrant's farewell. (Anonymous peasant painting
from Värmland. Nordiska muséet, Stockholm.)

4. Emigrants on their way to Gothenburg. (From Sjöfartsmuséet, Gothenburg. Courtesy of the museum.)

5. A family of Erik-Janssonists at home in Bishop Hill around 1860. (Courtesy of the Bishop Hill Heritage Association, Bishop Hill, Illinois.)

6. Andrew Peterson outside his log cabin in Laketown, Minnesota, built in 1855. (Minnesota Historical Society, St. Paul.)

7. Emigrant ships moored alongside South Street, New York. (Statens sjöhistoriska museum, Stockholm. Courtesy of the museum.)

8. The Bishop Hill volunteer company musters at the beginning of the Civil War. (Courtesy of the Bishop Hill Heritage Association.)

*The experience of emigrant parties traveling overland to their Mid-western destinations could be bitter, as witnessed by this letter written in 1850 by Lars Magnus Rapp in Andover, Illinois, to a brother-in-law in Östergötland:*

. . . In Chicago we met many Swedes we knew, who have written glowing letters to Sweden but who now can hardly be said to be earn-ing their own bread. So one ought not believe all the favorable letters. A good many people, who perhaps were not used to earning their living in Sweden, when they first come over think that things are remarkably fine, for here they can eat wheat bread. And some people find this so marvellous that they cannot praise their situation highly enough. When I was in Sweden I saw many letters from America where it said that the food was as good here as on the finest banquet tables in Sweden. . . .

We learned that cholera had broken out in Chicago before we got there and it was not completely gone when we passed through the city. But we were not affected by it while we were there; not before the third, fourth, and fifth days' journey thereafter, when we were traveling by canal boat from Chicago to Peru. Then my mother-in-law came down with cholera and after that Magnus's whole household. The old-est of their daughters died on the evening of the same day she took sick; the youngest girl died the next day. The first was buried without a coffin by the canal bank but the little one was taken dead to Peru. When we went ashore in Peru things looked bad, for by then we had six sick people who could not move a muscle. We had to carry them out of the boat and lay them on the shore, the dead child too. We were now in sore need of help, for all in our company were afraid of the sick. But many are aided by God's wondrous Providence, and we were too, this time. I saw no act of charity by anyone during the journey before then. Three gentlemen of the town's inhabitants came and looked at the sick and discovered the dead child. They quickly provided a coffin for the child and went with us a way along the canal bank and dug a grave under an aspen tree and helped us both to bury the body and to hold a service over it. After that was done they arranged for a horse and wagon to take the sick to a house where no one was living. There we were able to stay and tend our sick as best we could. A doctor called on us twice a day and gave out medicine. But we could talk to no one and no one could talk to us; rather, we had to make signs to each other like deaf-mutes to show what we meant. Some of the townspeople brought food so that we did not have to buy so much. We stayed there for four days. Mother-in-law died the second day we were there, the seventh of September, Greta from Govik on the eighth. Coffins and transportation and a burial place were provided by the town's inhabitants without payment. Both the deceased are buried in consecrated ground. Finally the doctor got hold of a Swedish girl who had been in town for a year. She could speak the English language but she was so shy that she could hardly pass on our ideas. We asked her to request that her master arrange for wagons to take us to Andover. But now we came up against those who knew nothing of charity. They could not be persuaded to drive ten Swedish miles for less than thirty dollars a wagonload, and as we ourselves could not bargain with them we had to give in to their demands, for we were sick and tired of staying on where we could not talk to anyone. On the second day's journey out of Peru Magnus died. He could not be taken along because the sickness stank so badly and he had to be buried on a broad plain by the side of the road. Now we had three sick, orphaned children. Our boy was sick too. We arrived here in Andover on 12 September. The three orphaned children were taken in hand. The oldest of Magnus's boys died eight days later and a lad called Carl Oscar was taken in by an American and a girl was taken in by Swedes from Tjärstad parish. I have a place to stay with a widow from Boda in Hägerstad. . . .

Now we are all feeling somewhat better, though God knows whether we can ever completely regain our health, for this is a rather sickly tract for nearly all its inhabitants. Brother-in-law Carl has been kind enough to lend me money to buy leather and for a stove to cook food on. If he had not helped me I do not know where I would have turned. I have now begun with my shoemaking so I can earn something, though my health is still not restored. Now we would like to tell of the goodness of the land, and that nobody can deny, for out here in the western states the soil is uncommonly fine, consisting of black loam. . . .

We would not want to advise anyone to come over here, for one must consider carefully all the grievous hardships that can arise. You and others can see here what we have had to go through. We will never be

able to forget the journey, even if we should find ourselves in the most
fortunate circumstances in the world. . . .

*Norra Kinda-Boken* (Linköping, 1973), 302–303.

*In 1851 Lars Johan Berglund of Dalarna sailed with a Norwegian ship
from Christiania (now Oslo) to San Francisco around Cape Horn, an
unusual direct voyage in those days. In February 1852 he wrote to
his mother:*

In San Francisco in May there was a great fire. When we arrived in
San Francisco, the city was already built up again, for they build houses
quickly here, but then they consist only of the frame with boards nailed
on; they are not made as tightly as in Sweden and therefore when it
rains hard, water gets into the rooms. Many stone houses have been
built since the fire, as well as houses all made of iron, where the bankers
have their offices and valuable goods. The city is built on a number of
hills so that the streets are steep and in marshy places thick planks are
laid crosswise over the whole street. In places there are mires of deep
sand. The harbor is large and excellent, protected from the winds.
There lie a great many ships, tightly packed together, all over the harbor, their masts like a great forest. Their number is almost unnatural;
I believe almost as many ships lie here as in London. The reason there
are so many ships here is that as soon as a ship docks in the harbor, all
the sailors immediately desert, and therefore they must be unloaded by
day laborers who demand around twenty *riksdaler riksgälds*, five dollars, a day in wages; and then there is no return cargo to be had so if a
ship sails from here it must take on ballast, which also requires day
laborers. This ballast therefore becomes altogether too expensive. Then
the captain must try to find new sailors, whom he cannot get for less
than sixty to seventy, even one hundred dollars' wages per month.
Most of them have therefore considered it more advantageous to sell
their ships to the city people, who have turned them into warehouses.
Many ships lie unsold. During the last year there has been such an

enormous inflow of goods of every possible kind that prices have been forced down below European prices. Clothes have been unusually cheap. The sailors on the *America Packet,* the same one we sailed on, also deserted as soon as we came into port, all except a cook and the officers.

. . . When the passengers on the *America Packet,* my traveling companions, left the ship in San Francisco harbor, most of them left together for the southern mines (except for a few persons who stayed in San Francisco); they stopped at the first place where gold was being washed, Jamestown, but later spread out around Stockton, however not too far from each other. After two months some of them left this place for Sidney, Australia, believing they would have better luck there than here. Up to now the others have stayed in the area around here, so that we are presently a large number of Swedes and Norwegians, including those who were here before and have come after us; we meet together in friendship and harmony, and help each other with digging and washing gold. But none have yet gained any great wealth or made a lucky find. We live here in tents or log cabins with canvas roofs and stone fireplaces. In the beginning, before a fireplace can be made from fieldstone, food is cooked under the bare sky over log fires, for there is plenty of firewood. In these houses there usually live four persons, who sleep on canvas cots and prepare their own food, for which the ingredients and necessities are to be had in the small towns around here, usually Jamestown, Camp Seco, and Sonoma, the last being the largest of them. The food consists mainly of fried pork, brown beans, fresh beef and stew, rice and apple soup, pancakes, potatoes, cheese, coffee, tea, chocolate, and so on. A kettle and frying pan are necessary items, glass and porcelain are not to be found in our tents, but rather tin cups and plates to eat and drink out of.

Björn Hallerdt, ed., "Emigrantminnen," in *Dalarnas hembygdsbok 1966* (Falun, 1968), 64–65, 70–71.

*Hans Mattson, who emigrated to the United States from Skåne in 1851
at the age of nineteen, was one of the leading figures of the earlier
Swedish immigration. He was among the first Swedes to settle in Minnesota, arriving there in 1853. He was later a colonel in the Union
army during the Civil War, secretary of state for Minnesota, and the
principal promoter of Swedish settlement in that state, working for the
state and the Northern Pacific Railway. His memoirs remain an important source for the period. The following selection describes the early
days at the Vasa settlement in Minnesota.*

Looking back to those days I see the little cabin, often with a sod
roof, a single room used for domestic purposes, sometimes crowded
almost to suffocation by hospitable entertainments to newcomers; or
the poor immigrant on the levee at Red Wing, just landed from a
steamer, in his short jacket and other outlandish costume, perhaps
seated on a wooden box, with his wife and a large group of children
around him, and wondering how he will be able to raise enough means
to get himself ten or twenty miles into the country, or to redeem the
bedding and other household goods which he has perchance left in
Milwaukee as a pledge for his railroad and steamboat ticket. And I see
him trudging along over the trackless prairie, searching for a piece of
land containing if possible prairie, water, and a little timber, on which
to build a home. Poor, bewildered, ignorant, and odd-looking, he had
been an object of pity and derision all the way from Gothenburg or
Christiania to the little cabin of some countryman of his, where he
found peace and shelter until he could build one of his own.

Those who have not experienced frontier life will naturally wonder
how it was possible for people so poor as a majority of the old settlers
were, to procure the necessaries of life, but they should remember that
our necessaries were few, and our luxuries a great deal less. The bounti-
ful earth soon yielded bread and vegetables; the woods and streams supplied game and fish; and as to shoes and clothing, I and many others
have used shoes made of untanned skins, and even of gunnysacks and
old rags. Furthermore, the small merchants at the river or other points
were always willing to supply the Scandinavian emigrants with necessary goods on credit, until better times should come. Our people in this
country did certainly earn a name for integrity and honesty among

their American neighbors, which has been a greater help to them than money.

Some of the men would go off in search of work, and in due time return with means enough to help the balance of the family.

Frontier settlers are always accommodating and generous. If one had more than he needed, he would invariably share the surplus with his neighbors. The neighbors would all turn out to help a newcomer—haul his logs, build his house, and do other little services for him.

The isolated condition and mutual aims and aspirations of the settlers brought them nearer together than in older communities. On Sunday afternoons all would meet at some centrally located place, and spend the day together. A cup of coffee with a couple of slices of bread and butter would furnish a royal entertainment, and when we got so far along that we could afford some pie or cake for dessert, the good housewives were in a perfect ecstasy. The joys and sorrows of one were shared by the others, and nowhere in the wide world, except in a military camp, have I witnessed so much genuine cordial friendship and brotherhood as among the frontier settlers in the west.

One fine Sunday morning that summer, all the settlers met under two oak trees on the prairie, near where the present church stands, for the first religious service in the settlement. It had been agreed that some of the men should take turns to read one of Luther's sermons at each of these gatherings, and I was selected as reader the first day. Some prayers were said and Swedish hymns sung, and seldom did a temple contain more devout worshipers than did that little congregation on the prairie.

Hans Mattson, *Reminiscences: The Story of an Emigrant* [trans. Axel Lundeberg] (St. Paul, 1891), 48–50.

*Following the disappointment of a broken engagement, Rosalie Roos, a young woman of good family, spent four years in America, from 1851 to 1855, principally in South Carolina, where she taught at a girls' school and served the Peronneaus, a wealthy planter's family, as a governess-tutor. Her letters give an almost unique Swedish view of the*

*antebellum South and hint at her later career as a leader in the Swedish feminist movement.*

Limestone, 26 February 1852

I am still in Limestone, as you see, Papa, from the above, but with the difference that I have now moved over to the school, where I have been engaged for a year as a teacher of French and music at a salary of three hundred dollars. This arrangement came about rather quickly, for eight days ago I had no idea of it. Last Monday Frantz[29] came and said Dr. Curtis wished to speak with me. I went to him and we agreed on terms, and the next day I began giving lessons. It was not without some trepidation that I took the position, for it is not so easy to teach one foreign language through another. I must therefore work very hard myself outside of classes. . . . They are not as concerned with foreign languages here as they are in Sweden; only French is studied and among the seventy pupils who have now arrived (they do not all come at the same time), there are only nine who study this language. The music students are more numerous, but interest and inclination for this, as for the fine arts in general, is very slight. They will not learn properly but only for the sake of appearances, so that exercises and études are quickly put aside and replaced by a few pieces, which are generally forgotten as soon as they finish school. I have five music students and am expecting more this afternoon. May I succeed in what I have taken upon myself! . . .

Rosalie Roos, *Resa till Amerika 1851–55*, ed. Sigrid Laurell (Stockholm, 1969), 75.

Limestone, 30 July 1852

. . . I cannot quite get used to the American gentlemen's ways: they sit and rock on their chairs, put their feet up on chairs, tables, benches, indeed even on window sills, chew tobacco constantly and spit. On Monday afternoon, a Dr. Sloan from Dallas, a little town three years old and with three hundred inhabitants, was at Hammarskiölds'[30] and stayed the whole afternoon. He sat down on the sofa beside Mrs. Hammarskiöld and said: "I must sit here beside you so I can spit out the window." What do you think of that? And he was one of the most distinguished gentlemen of that place! . . .

*Ibid.,* 88.

Dungannon [South Carolina], 4 May 1853

I have now finally managed to obtain *Uncle Tom's Cabin*[31] and have just begun reading it. In Charleston this book cannot be bought. No bookseller has it for sale there. We have been able to borrow it from Mrs. Peronneau's sister, and Eliza read it through in a day and has halfway become an abolitionist from it. She is the only Carolinian whom I have heard disapprove of slavery and who considers it unjust. Otherwise, the slaveowners and others, indeed even countrymen of ours, believe that it is ordained by God and will exist for eternity. Eliza and I got into a dispute just the other day with a Dr. Matthews on this subject. He sought in every way to discredit Mrs. Stowe and said that he had written something to ridicule her book, which he wanted to send us. Eliza began the argument and I kept quiet as usual, for I think with Papa that when I cannot do any good by speaking it is better not to speak; but when he became unreasonable, this became impossible for me and I said to Mr. Matthews right out that I was fully convinced that God had bestowed the same spiritual qualities on the blacks as on the whites, and that in a better life he should not expect to find the same caste and color distinctions as here.

I very much like what I have read of *Uncle Tom's Cabin*; the Negroes' and also the plantation owners' ways and speech are faithfully described. It seems to me the book ought to be very difficult to translate, for the Negroes speak very badly and their speech is impossible to understand for those who have not been together with them. Any such owners as a couple of those who are described there, I have not seen, thank God, nor have I seen the slightest mistreatment; on the contrary, they are treated more kindly and are freer in their speech than white servants at home. . . .

*Ibid.,* 110–11.

8 May 1853

[To Hedda Hammarskiöld in North Carolina]

. . . My conviction remains the same as it has always been: that God has not created races of men to be the domestic animals of others, that such a condition is unnatural and repugnant, and that sooner or later it will be ended, though not without a hard struggle. If the masters are good and noble persons, the lot of the slaves is perhaps preferable to that of the majority of white servants—but everything depends upon this *if*.

*Ibid.*, 112.

24 October 1853, Bentwood [South Carolina]

. . . black servants are considered more suitable here than white. No agreements with white servants are binding, for they simply go their way without their masters being able to force them to return. As soon as they have been in America for a little while, they pick up distorted ideas of freedom and equality, and come to regard all heavy labor as beneath their dignity, which foolish arrogance continues until necessity convinces them of their mistake. The Hammarskiölds in North Carolina are in complete despair over white workers, so much have they suffered from those they brought out with them; they caused endless difficulties and finally disappeared, except for a couple of them. The blacks are usually less skilled than the whites, however, and in Mr. Peronneau's opinion one can reckon that two blacks equal one white.

*Ibid.*, 126.

20 November 1853, Dungannon, South Carolina

. . . One evening we were invited to a concert, quite good for the Philharmonic Society in Charleston. They also had a full house, but only a few who understood and appreciated good music, for which reason one or another was seen napping; most yawned and wished that it would soon be over. In fact, if I were a performer, I would not want to give a concert in Charleston, for Negro minstrels are the only thing that is a success with the public.

*Ibid.,* 133.

## 12 January 1854, Dungannon, South Carolina

. . . It is strange to see how these words are borne out everywhere: "one only wishes for what one does not have, and what one has cannot please." Thus, for instance, Papa considers the form of government in the United States to be the best and wishes to enjoy its advantages, while Mr. Peronneau and many others with him disapprove of it and maintain that it cannot last another century. He says the only possible basis for a republic's existence is slavery, for otherwise power will fall into the hands of the raw, uneducated masses. He calls me a republican. General suffrage, which is so greatly desired at home, gives rise here to many intrigues and much baseness, for it is not the most deserving who are elected, but rather whoever can buy the most votes. Mr. Hammarskiöld therefore says that if he was a liberal before, he will now be the most conservative man who ever returned to Sweden.

*Ibid.,* 140.

## 21 January 1854, Dungannon, South Carolina

[To brother Gustaf]
You know of old with what special fondness Papa has always regarded America and how eagerly he has wished that one of his sons would come to enjoy the advantages which, in his eyes, this country has over the Old World. Whether all these advantages are as great as he imagines them, I will leave unsaid, for I do not trust myself to pass judgment on them. Certainly, however, those objects we regard through imagination's telescope take on a rosy hue, a kind of nimbus, which disappears when reality brings us close to them; but much of

value can meanwhile remain even after the nimbus pales. So it is with America too; we from the Old World find much here that does not meet our expectations, does not agree with our ideas, and offends our prejudices, but also much that is good and useful, perhaps better than what we left behind. I do not doubt that a steady, industrious, and determined young man with good principles can make his way more quickly here than at home in our country; the resources are greater, the rewards greater. But if he lacks these qualities, he can also go to his ruin faster and fall deeper than elsewhere. America is a land of contrasts; refinement and crudity, luxury and misery, high virtue and profound immorality are found closer to each other here than in Europe. . . .

*Ibid.,* 141.

13 August 1854, Bentwood, South Carolina

No commandment is so much violated at home as that which has to do with keeping the Sabbath, and none is more strictly observed here. Many go so far as to consider taking a walk in God's glorious creation a sin; they will not pick a flower or fruit on Sunday, and even to cook any food or read anything but a Sunday book is considered highly improper. But they do not find it offensive to sleep a good part of that day which is dedicated to the glory of the Lord, not even to take a nap in church, nor to talk in a vain and superficial manner, nor to complain that the day is long and dull. The use of the Sabbath, properly and in a manner befitting its purpose, is a subject to which we give very little attention at home. . . .

*Ibid.,* 151.

18 September 1854, Bentwood, South Carolina

. . . I believe I have sufficiently refuted any accusation of lack of courage. I have already shown that when I have once made up my

mind, I do not let myself be frightened by others' representations. . . .
Meanwhile, Mr. Peronneau and his friends have begun to point out
to me the unpleasantness and risk for a woman undertaking a tour
such as I have arranged for, without a protector. Such statements are
disagreeable to me, for I see I cannot make my journey without thereby
offending the prejudices of a family which I love and respect, yet they
do not persuade me to abandon the path I have set for myself. Here is
one of the many instances of the power of prejudice in this, freedom's
promised land, and I could recount many more. Mrs. Peronneau became very upset with me when I, following my old custom of walking
alone when I cannot find company, took little walks on my own in the
Pineland, where hardly anyone was to be seen except the inhabitants.
She affected to fear that someone could offend me, but I am afraid that
the real reason was that it is not considered proper for women to go
out alone. Neither convention nor fear of insult would thus have
restrained my wishes at home; there I could stroll around freely at any
hour of the day.

*Ibid.*, 166.

*Pastor Tufve Nilsson Hasselquist, who emigrated from Skåne in 1852,
was the central figure in early Swedish-American Lutheranism, especially after Esbjörn's return to Sweden in 1864. Here he broaches to his
colleague, Pastor Erland Carlsson of Chicago, the idea of founding the
first Swedish newspaper in the United States,* Hemlandet, det Gamla
och det Nya,[32] *which first appeared in 1855.*

15 November 1853, Galesburg, Illinois

. . . Have you given any thought to the proposed Swedish newspaper? I hear many people express a longing for one, especially for
complete news from the home country. You must not put the matter
out of your mind, for we must seek to free our people from immoral
and unchurchly papers. The Lord lend you courage! For his sake we

will do all; He deserves what we can do for Him. May our faith be greatly increased and may we be consumed by love for our brethren! May God bless us! . . .

S. W. Olson, trans. and ed., "Early Letters to Erland Carlsson," *Augustana Historical Society Publications*, vol. 5 (Rock Island, Ill., 1935), 111.

*By the mid-1850s various districts in Sweden had been seized with the "America Fever," as shown by the following letter to Pastor Carlsson in Chicago from a Swedish colleague.*

1 March 1854, Berga, Sweden

Dearly Beloved Brother:

For a long time I have intended to write you, but I fear you are so overwhelmed with letters and inquiries, besides many official duties, that you will hardly find time to reply. You are stationed at a point where the harvest is plenteous but the laborers few; may God give you grace to garner a great harvest for His kingdom!

I have read a brief extract from a letter of yours to Rector Andersson, which describes the spiritual condition there as being deplorable; but I have also read several letters from other persons in America, in which temporal conditions in particular are described as most glorious and excellent, so that according to indications emigration from Sweden this year will increase considerably. From Långaryd we are told that sixty to seventy families want to go; there they are studying English eagerly, and in our neighborhood there is a clergyman who is teaching English. Last year two families left this parish, one a deaf man who tinkered with clocks, the other a crofter[33] from Toftaholm by the name of Jonas with six children; but now for some time we have had auction sales here every week, and eight or nine households, not counting hired men and working girls, are outward bound. A man reputed to be somewhat of a Christian and known as Lars in Hörsset, with two small children and wife, intend to go there. They have not much more than one thousand *riksdaler riksgälds* to start out on. People are attacked as if by some epidemic, and to try to dissuade them is useless. They shy away and will not let any minister or public official talk to them about the matter. They are afraid they might be swerved from their decision and get mad if one refers to the subject. The other Sunday, in a funeral address, I spoke of the true fatherland, stating that man ought to seek that land above any other; also pointing out what a precious gift an earthly fatherland is, including house and home, etc., and that without a call from God or being in peril of one's soul no one ought to desert his native country, and that those who carelessly or thoughtlessly can exchange all these advantages for something uncertain are ungrateful and act foolishly. This caused bitterness in some, so that on their way home they said, "Now the preachers are getting worked up; they are getting anxious about their privileges, and fear a shortage of servants," etc.

Now I should like to know how things are in America. What shall we say about this emigration?

Do you intend to remain? Would you favor freedom of worship here? Do you expect that the emigration from here will increase? Could it be on an even larger scale? In that case, would it hurt this country? Might it not result in a shortage of working people, or in a rise in wages? Or does the population grow as fast as they are emigrating? How about Ireland? Isn't there a lack of people? Ought people to do as I do, bring up their children in such a way that they may go over there—teach them to read and write, and to read English and work? For here, as you know, the professional career is a rather slippery road. An Englishman, Chamber,[34] says he would advise the working men to go out there—could not communications soon be improved to the extent that one might go across in about three weeks?[35]

I wonder whether a great deal of imperfection does not adhere to our native land after all—the laboring classes are driven to their wits' end to keep alive—I know very well that if whiskey[36] distilling were abolished, conditions would be entirely changed—America must surely enjoy great advantages, especially material ones, and those are, sad to say, the things that people mostly strive for in our day.

How about the high wages for labor? the fertility of the soil? the low price of land? How can the grass stand upright when it grows six to nine feet tall? How about free pasture and hay lands? Most of the emigrants also write that you have a better brand of Christianity over there than we have here, that there is no swearing, no drinking, etc. How is it possible to control and hold together such a motley mass of people in the long run? You speak of the snares of the Baptists and the Methodists—I beg your pardon, I am not familiar with their errors, but tell me, was not Scott[37] a true Christian, a good deal better one than many a Lutheran—we ought indeed to thank God for the pure evangelical doctrine; but I wonder if most Christian sects do not think they have understood the Bible correctly—and yet, is there not strife on this point—and without a fight no victory is won? Is there any real strife here; are we not rather sleeping? Everything that is preached is accepted without question, like the coin of the realm, whether it is true or not. What do we accomplish by all our preaching after all? Most people remember nothing at the close of the sermon—possibly the fault is ours.

Now as to the letters—a hired girl from Hjortsberga writes that she hears you preach once a month, and a friend of Hofven who does likewise and conducts Bible exegesis the other three Sundays, says: Here I get twenty *riksdaler* per month in wages and don't have to work outside. She could not wish for anything better, does not miss Sweden, will never regret her going, and only wishes she could get her spinning wheel sent over. This, she says, is something different from Sweden, where one worked for twelve *riksdaler*, ate oatmeal bread, and had to sleep in a bunk with a few rags on it. She wishes with all her heart that her relatives were with her over there. The cows are in pasture, where one must ride horseback to hunt them up.

Bengt Månsson, a hired man now in Illinois (Knoxville, Oct. 2, 1853) writes (starting with grace and peace) that he could wish nothing better than to have all his relatives and acquaintances with him in this glorious land. He came to Knoxville Aug. 3, meeting acquaintances from Åkarp parish—got work at forty *riksdaler* a month—is offered 528 *riksdaler* a year—cannot wish anything better in life—No count in Sweden fares better—oats and corn the horses eat. Here one needn't cut straw for them after sundown—His master owns fifty head of cattle, forty hogs, five horses, and milks the cows himself—Oh, such a comfortable existence for men and animals, different from being downtrodden farm laborers back home—all those who advise against the trip do so either from envy or ignorance; therefore don't listen to their advice—don't even talk to them—works about a mile and a half from the town of Galesburg, where there is a Lutheran church—Wheat costs twelve *riksdaler*, corn four and oats three—corn yields one hundred bushels—calls Sweden oppressed—Too bad that my old friends must slave in Sweden—Americans gladly adopt Swedish children, and if they may keep them to the age of eighteen, they give them a horse, a bed and bedclothes, and forty acres of land—I am not lying, for of that there is enough in Sweden—There are many who want to dissuade; because it gives them a pain to think that anyone should crawl out from under their yoke; but the day of reckoning is drawing nearer, soon the time will come when the tears and sweat of the laboring class will be demanded out of the hands of the bloodsuckers; for he who stands at the helm, the Lord of all lords, when he says, so far, etc.—Mentions Hedström[38] in New York—Thanks Trued Kjerstensson who helped with money— Thus reads the extract from Romans . . .

Another letter, from Anders Jönsson, living near the parsonage in which Pastor Esbjörn lives[39]—tells of the hardships of the voyage—passed through cities where the cholera was raging, lost his wife in the epidemic, yet he never regrets the day he came—left Gothenburg July 5, 1852—heard Pastor Hedström in New York, but he was a Methodist—came to Andover the 8th—of all he had talked with only one had regretted going—If one becomes a pauper the government provides aid—If servants in Sweden only knew of conditions in America and were able to leave, Sweden would soon be without servants, he writes—Finely sifted wheat flour is used for bread—If any one sends his children they will gain more than if they were given two thousand *riksdaler banko* in Sweden—Lives ⅜ Sw. mile from Andover church.—One boy is being prepared for confirmation—The other children are reading English in school—The state is defraying the cost of education—Good protective laws, four times as decent conduct as in Sweden—all equal, the farmer, the minister, and the judge, all are addressed the same way—One does not have to go hat in hand and bow and scrape before another—Lordly titles have been discarded there, etc. Here endeth that farmer's letter. Such and other similar letters are being circulated here, and they make bad blood—Servants are already beginning to speak up, saying that nobody can stay here and keep on slaving till one spits blood—to answer all this is well-nigh impossible.

But be so kind as to reply to some of these things, so that, if possible we might dissuade some or give them correct information—A true description of America I should like to read—Why don't you Swedish ministers get together and put down the actual facts and a full account of conditions and send it here—It is a peculiar fact that all who go there want to get their relatives over there, too. See to it that those who regret having left write home about it and advise against others going there. Certainly there are many who shed tears of regret—Why don't these write?—Look them up, beg them to write—

Now please do not let my numerous questions tire you—Your letter gave me reason to ask for further information—It is very well for those who go there that they are feeling well in body; but if their souls should be damaged, that would be worth more than tears—God help us in these troublous times lest lukewarmness or coldness get the upper hand in the things that are most precious and important to us mortals. Write soon, begs, while wishing you God's mercy and peace, your humble friend and brother

S. Stenvall<br>Assistant Pastor in Berga

Olson, "Early Letters to Erland Carlsson," 113–17.

*In a celebrated case still much debated in Sweden, the prominent poet and novelist Carl Jonas Love Almquist was tried for the alleged poisoning of a creditor and fled to America in 1851. Although this effectively ended his literary career, his letters to his wife and daughter give a vivid picture of America in the fifties. He died in 1866 in Bremen after vainly seeking permission to return to Sweden.*

Philadelphia, 8 July 1854

This *excitement* or condition of exhilaration of which I have spoken extends to all social classes here and is truly a distinguishing characteristic of the United States. *Freedom to think and act* gives rise to unbelievable activity in the souls of all; and the Europeans are mistaken if they believe that this concerns only material and outward things. On the contrary, there is speculation about everything here; the most spiritual, indeed one could say the most curious things in the world are subject to the Americans' speculations, often along with mechanical and mercantile matters, and many times before them.

To speak only of religion, there are at present nearly 300 churches in Philadelphia (240 according to an earlier source); and these are in use both on Sundays and sometimes on weekdays, both mornings and afternoons. To be sure, these churches are not all as large as our Swedish churches in Stockholm; many of them consist simply of large salons (such as Lacroix's salon), where they preach and sing; but quite a few are also sizable buildings with one or two massive towers and, especially the Catholic ones, are very handsome. There are besides an unbelievable number of public halls, so-called academies, and meeting-houses, where lectures and disquisitions are held on every subject in the world, and which are frequented as much by women as by men. But the lecturers are always on their own, that is, they are not employed by the government; but rather when any person finds he has something of interest to make known, he announces the day and place, a modest admission fee is charged, and the lecture is held. One describes some new discovery in chemistry, mechanics, or agriculture, wine cultivation, livestock breeding (a la Nathorst)[40] and so forth; another lectures on mysticism, on spirits, dreams, clairvoyance, etc.; a third gives a political speech, on relations between Europe and America, on Cuba, Mexico, Japan, China, Russia—nothing is too remote, nothing barred.

The Americans are from childhood, and through their very upbringing, practiced speakers; they express themselves very well, energetically, and often with that practical clarity that belongs to the English character. That a great deal of humbug, charlatanry, and unfounded nonsense is mixed in, is doubtless true; but this is discovered and revealed very quickly here, for everyone has the right and most also the desire to criticize and point out whatever foolishness and stupidity he has found in anyone else. It is not like European humbug, charlatanry, and unfounded nonsense, which are often so deeply rooted that one is not aware of them, and held so sacred by the laws themselves that they cannot be touched. The Catholics here also complain bitterly, not only over all the souls that are already lost and condemned (that is, all men besides themselves), but even that many of the Catholics themselves no longer wish to submit so unconditionally to the Pope or to let the bishops here treat the parishes as they will. There will soon be, the way it looks, a life-and-death struggle between the Jesuits and the Republicans.[41]

That all of this must appear as indescribable confusion to those who see things only on the surface or to whom they are too unfamiliar and new, is natural. In New York recently there was a great riot over a man who preached a new religion on the street corners and who was called "The Angel Gabriel" (I do not know if he called himself this or was so called only by his followers). Fighting broke out between opposing parties. The same kind of thing has also recently taken place in Boston. One great reason for such disorders is the great number of Irishmen who arrive here each year, who are characteristically very superstitious, very hot-tempered, very poor, and very inclined to idleness. They are Catholics; at the slightest cause they pull knives: in the name of the Pope and the Virgin Mary, blood must flow. . . . This riotous disposition is general in the United States and constitutes one of their worst traits, although it is meanwhile not by far as dangerous as one might believe. It exists not only among the lowest classes (especially between the Germans and the Irish, or within these two elements separately), but sometimes even as high up as in the legislative assemblies. A representative who cannot silence his opponent with arguments gets up from his bench and seizes the other member by the collar. Recently there took place an imbroglio of this kind in the Senate in Washington itself, between two senators, in which one drew a pistol. The senators were separated by the Senate's sergeant-at-arms and peace was restored. Such things are also generally regarded as a "scandal," the newspapers censure the persons involved, and they lose their positions.

Such disorders *can* thus happen here, and *do* indeed sometimes occur, but without any apparent consequences except for the rioters themselves. A European can hardly imagine how easily and quickly the seemingly most serious disturbances can be put down here. The reason is that disorders here constitute—if I may make a comparison—only a mass of boiling, seething bubbles, under which the river, for the most part deep, quiet, and sure, flows toward its goal. These bubbles burst like nothing at all. The law and its guardians (the officials) in this country have the greatest power one could hope to find; for there is no law here that has not been instituted in the public's best interest by the public itself, which likewise has elected and established its highest administrators (judges, sheriffs, mayors, etc.)—consequently every violation of the law (disturbance, riot) is only something *partial,* which the public itself has the greatest interest in quelling; for which reason, every wise and just magistrate, policeman, or peace officer immediately has the broader public *on his side*, and often its actual physical assistance, as soon as disorder arises. This intervention by the public itself to maintain justice and order, when the police do not arrive in time or hesitate to show themselves, sometimes goes so far that one can say it goes too far. . . .

I shall now say a few words about the *celebration of the Fourth of July*, which has taken place within the last few days and is the most notable holiday in the whole Union as the commemoration of 4 July 1776 when the *Declaration of Independence* was made. This celebration was all the more remarkable here in Philadelphia, for it was right *here* (in one of the rooms in the city hall) that this bold document, influential for all human civilization, was promulgated. I may also add that the very manner in which the celebration took place gave further witness, in its remarkable extremes, to what I have just now recounted about American *order and disorder at the same time*. . . .

Further, to give some idea of the humbug here, I send (a) an advertisement by a Mr. and Mrs. Van Horn, among the many who claim with full assurance to be able to *tell people's fortunes*. They begin their announcement by *warning* against all other astrologers; only *they* are qualified! Further, (b), a little example of the hundreds of *medical charlatans* with which America swarms, who claim to have invented medicines that cure everything, and to which they give all sorts of curious names (*Tonic, Syrup, Cordial, Invigoratine*, etc.). *Every* doctor's medicine is *the best in the whole world*, and *never* fails in its good effects. This boastfulness in advertisement moreover extends to everything and is highly ridiculous, especially since no one can be fooled by it. Here in Philadelphia there are surely a couple of thousand shops for *ready-made clothing*: all quite cheap, but all just *the same*. Still every person advertises *his* shop, claims it is *the best*, not in Philadelphia, whatever that may mean—not in Pennsylvania—not in the United States—no!—but in the *whole world*. See a little example of this in enclosure (c). When a cobbler wants to make himself known, he calls his little shop an *Emporium*, which actually means a *depot for international commerce*; he puts his business (in jest) under the protection of a saint (for instance *St. Crispin*), prints an advertising flyer, and hires some boys to throw copies of it into every doorway in the city to inform the public. See also (f), an example from the cobbler (Mr. *Pritchett*), whose handbill I found one day in the doorway here. . . .

R. G. Berg, *C. J. L. Almquist i landsflykten 1851–1866* (Stockholm: Bonniers, 1928), 504–8, 514–15.

*After the first number of* Hemlandet *finally appeared, Pastor Hassel-quist wrote to Pastor Carlsson in Chicago about the problems facing the new venture.*

2 February 1855, Galesburg, Illinois

Dear Brother:

Long have I been expecting a few lines from you, especially after the first number of *Hemlandet* reached you. You have not sent me any news from Sweden, nor any other article for the paper. I can not possibly single-handedly write all that is required for the paper, although it is not large; you too must contribute, furnishing historical information about your congregations, articles on practical matters, etc.; Swedish letters would also be good material. Now, however, the publication of the paper is interrupted temporarily, possibly for quite a while. The type has not arrived, and I don't know when it will come; the first issue was printed in Knoxville under difficulties and at a cost almost twice what it ought to be if the enterprise is to carry itself. Nevertheless I decided to print one issue per month, despite the expense, until the type arrives; I had everything in readiness last Monday, but the printer answered me that he could not possibly let me use his type; the case was the same here in Galesburg. So here I stand helpless, not knowing what to do. You must exert yourself to the utmost to get an issue printed in Chicago; I have plenty of manuscripts on hand. The whole newspaper enterprise is jeopardized, and a failure would mean an equally great loss to each one of us. The paper will no doubt be a success, just so long as it can be issued regularly. The number of subscriptions, paid and unpaid, is not far below five hundred. . . .

Olson, "Early Letters to Erland Carlsson," 127–28.

*In 1850 Erik Jansson was shot to death by a disgruntled former follower. Under his successor, Jonas Olsson, there was increasing dissatisfaction in the Bishop Hill colony and many left it, as described here.*

Victoria, Knox County, Illinois, North America, August 1855

. . . As far as Bishop Hill is concerned, I can say briefly that they still continue in their misled doctrine, which is rapidly going from bad to worse, not better, but otherwise they are prosperous. Still some of the members are constantly leaving them. Especially this summer a crowd of persons have left them, especially from among the oldest in the place. Even Erik Jansson's widow has now left them and gone away, as well as a lot of others from both the later arrivals and the earlier people. Anders Persson's children from Domta have also gone away. And now they have recently rejected Jansson's teachings, which has contributed considerably to several people's falling away and to old Jon. Olsson's holding the power at present and considering himself God or something more, trying to mislead people into believing that the world and everything else will be destroyed. But the prophets there claim Bishop Hill to be Noah's Ark, which will be preserved, and in this way seek to hold on to at least simple-minded persons on such false grounds. There is much more that cannot now be described about their foolishness, which in a word changes by the day and by the hour. . . .

Petter Andersson

Widén, *När Svensk-Amerika grundades*, 38.

*A young Swedish engineer, Baron Axel Adelswärd, was sent by his gov-
ernment in 1855–1856 to study the railroads in America. His letters
provide a fresh and enthusiastic picture of his extensive travels between
the Atlantic and the Mississippi. Here he gives a rare impartial account
of the controversial Bishop Hill colony at the height of its activity,
before its economy was ruined by the crash of 1857 and its properties
were divided up among its remaining members in 1860.*

8 May 1856, Clifton Hotel, Niagara Falls, Canada

My Dear Mother,

. . . I made a couple of days' excursion (from Chicago) to the
interior of the state of Illinois to visit the Erik-Janssonists' colony at
Bishop Hill. . . . Their settlement lies about three English miles from
the station where I got off. Around the station there is already a little
town, although it is not yet two years old. The Janssonists have a large
brick warehouse here, in which I saw I don't remember how many
thousand hams, salted and piled up. What is more, they have a large
general store and divers other buildings. Here I met a Mr. Cronsiöe, a
Skåning;[42] he was in the midst of setting up a printshop with the
Janssonists' help and will publish a newspaper in Swedish.[43] He was
the biggest talker I have ever run into in my life. He talked the first
evening so that I, who am by no means nervous, nonetheless felt ill and
got a headache. Aside from the endless stream of words, he happened
to be hoarse and that caused his vocal organ to be most painful to the
auditory nerves. Still, since he had known Erik Jansson he was an excellent guide and we went together on foot over the prairie to Bishop
Hill, where we arrived a little before dark. It has the appearance of a
large manor at home; the great, white-plastered schoolhouse, which was
originally intended as a hotel, with its columns and its cupola on the
roof, looks like the *corps de logis*.[44] Round about are large, solid brick
buildings, unplastered on the outside as is the custom in America.

They also have a small hotel for travelers and we went there. Since
it soon became dark we did not go around to look at the place but only
talked with some of the Janssonists. To my great surprise I found that
the man in charge of the inn was from Södermanland, had been with
*Perioden* in Nyköping for twenty-five years, and had finally been in
charge of the paper mill. When that burned down he had gone up to

Norrland and been in charge of another mill, and while he was there he had heard Erik Jansson preach "and thought he ought to join the Janssonists," as he put it, and is now in his tenth year in America. The next day I made the acquaintance of his wife, a good-natured old woman, now toothless and over sixty. She had served at Stora Sundby manor in her youth and was glad to talk of home and times gone by. Both were so overjoyed to meet a Sörmlänning,[45] the only one, they said, they had met on this side of the ocean. I had a simple but good supper and for the first time in nearly two years broke and ate Swedish *knäckebröd*,[46] which I had often longed for. When I left them I was not allowed to pay for my food and lodging but they bade me consider myself as having been their guest.

The Erik-Janssonists are communists, have everything in common; no one owns anything as an individual, but the society taken together is already remarkably wealthy and will become more so if it can preserve itself. They came here under Erik Jansson ten years ago. They brought a fair amount of money with them from Sweden but a large part of it went for the journey, and when they had bought oxen, horses, and several thousand acres of land, which then sold at a good price, they had almost nothing left. When Erik Jansson, who was possibly a great prophet but certainly no economist, was shot six years ago, the society's affairs were in such poor shape that even their bedding was confiscated and the society was on the point of breaking up. Since then a couple of smart fellows have placed themselves at their head and within these six years they have so improved their situation that they are now worth at least four or five million *riksdaler riksgälds*. They have, for instance, ten thousand acres of land, every acre worth at least one hundred *riksdaler riksgälds*, fine, large buildings, forest, which is worth much there, easily accessible coal, several hundred horses and mules, oxen and cows by the thousands, pigs, chickens, geese, etc., by the tens of thousands. I have never seen so many pigs in one place as I have here. Moreover, they have a steam-powered sawmill and flour mill, which earns them a great deal, water mill, general store, etc.; they manufacture a kind of broom and from that article alone they have earned 150,000 *riksdaler riksgälds* in the past year. It sounds unbelievable in Swedish ears, but is true and not much to be surprised at in America.

The day after my arrival I went around and looked at the colony, saw the school where thirty or forty children were gathered, learning to read in English, naturally. Erik Jansson's daughter, an unpleasant-looking girl of fourteen years, was one of the schoolmistresses. Their infirmary is a good little facility where there was nonetheless no patient to be found, even though there are eight hundred colonists. I saw their agricultural implements, harvesting machines, and so forth, stables, chicken coops, pigsties, steam saw, brewery, where I drank near beer, bakery, where the *knäckebröd* hung on its poles from the ceiling, their kitchen, where they happened to be cooking enormous quantities of porridge, their dining halls where they ate their meals together, and finally departed Bishop Hill highly satisfied, riding with the endlessly babbling Cronsiöe in a so-called "buggy," belonging to the society.

They seem to live contented and happy. I do not know much about their religious ideas. Their fantasies have abated considerably, but they have recently begun to introduce a new dogma into their teachings, which, if they hold to it, will soon put an end to the society. They have, namely, begun to forbid marriage and are hereafter to live entirely as brothers and sisters; this has caused a number of young people to leave them and to bring suit against them, the consequences of which are hard to foretell. Except for this last dogma, I have nothing against them. They are capable and hard-working, and to join together, as they have done, is a sure way to amass wealth here in America, although it seems to me they can have precious little joy from their riches. They are meanwhile very good to other poor Swedes who come to them. If they wish they may join them, but if not they may stay with them for some time and are fed and housed free.

Cronsiöe eats at their common table in the station town, Galva, where a group of them are located, and when we returned there, I was also invited to have my dinner there. The others had already finished so we were alone. The dinner was better than any workingman at home gets and although the dishes were not many they were very good. Spareribs and mashed potatoes, something similar to marrow pudding, milk of the finest quality, and plenty of *knäckebröd* and white bread. In the afternoon, I left Galva and by evening was back in Chicago.

Unpublished letters of Baron Axel Adelswärd, 1855–1856.

*An undated letter, apparently written by a Janssonist in the 1850s, provides advice to a prospective emigrant in Sweden:*


. . . We are not surprised that you raised some questions in your letter concerning your departure, for we have all tried to get advice at such times and it is also our duty to tell you about what we ourselves have been through. First, you wished I could come to meet you. I would not fail to if I thought it was necessary, but since I know that when it comes to business and contracts of that kind you have a better understanding of how to manage your affairs than I did when I came over, I am sure you will have no trouble with this. And as for going on an American ship, I don't think there would be any advantage to this because it probably is more expensive and it's also hard with the language. And as for clothes and bedding, you shouldn't take with you more than you need to be comfortable on the trip in both cold and hot weather. It doesn't pay to bring things over for the future because it is expensive to haul them out here from New York, and also a lot of trouble to keep everything together when you have a lot of stuff. The prices are the same here as in Sweden. Also with household things, you should take along enough to manage with the food on the trip, tin and copper utensils and so on. But you should not take along any kind of tools for your work, because there are such good tools of all kinds here that the Swedish ones that are brought over are considered worth nothing. But you should not sell old silver in Sweden because they pay at least a half dollar or around 1 *riksdaler* 45 per *lod*[47] here. Besides we have a goldsmith called Troil[48] from Hälsingland in our congregation who works every day on things like that and does the best work that can be done, so we can get even more for it. But new silver that is prepared in Sweden doesn't sell here for any more than the old because it is not in fashion now. And as for taking along persons to work for you, I wouldn't advise you to take along anyone on the condition that they should repay their traveling expenses by working here, for there are many who made agreements like that with people, just to come over and seek their earthly fortunes, but as soon as they came over to this free country their promises were forgotten and they went their way. Those who paid their way have put out their money in vain, for it is like a miracle if anyone gets his due, for here they soon forget what their condition was in Sweden. And it has gotten so that there are hundreds of people around this country who we have both bought clothes for and paid their way all the way from Sweden, and some of them have stayed somewhere along the way out here and a lot of them have left us here. And all of them have become our worst enemies and persecutors by spreading terrible lies, not only through letters to our home country but also here among the people of this country they have talked, the one more unreasonable than the other.

Widén, *Amerikaemigrationen i dokument*, 59–60.

*Jonas Wallengren, a pastor's son from Skåne, describes his Atlantic crossing:*

New York, 23 July 1856

While there is the opportunity, I wish to inform you that I have, successfully and in good health, reached the great city of New York. We left Gothenburg on 30 May and arrived here after a sea journey of seven weeks and two days. The journey was very hard: five children died on the crossing and many were sick, though no more than two were left at the hospital here. A sixty-seven-year-old woman and a young man of around twenty-two years, together with three crew members, were left there, and one seaman was lost overboard. During the entire journey I was in good health except for two days when I had a bad case of diarrhea mixed with blood, so that I was afraid I had dysentery, but I took a strong dose of sealing wax which stopped it. Because there was so much sickness among the crew, four of us had to serve as seamen for over three weeks' time, but several of us caught cold because we had to go wet day and night. We had very bad weather with storms and rain during the whole crossing. Half of the foremast was carried away on 26 June, the same day the sailor lost his life; he fell from one of the highest spars. I, Nils, and Mattis, and some of the others, were not the least bit seasick, but otherwise they were generally all sick; many of them never left their bunks. We were quartered above decks so that it was quite healthy for us, but those who were below decks were full of all sorts of vermin, for people from all kinds of places were mixed together there.

We lay at anchor from Monday until yesterday afternoon, when we were put on a steamboat and taken in to Castle Garden, where we were lodged free in a large, former opera house that has been made over just for emigrants,[49] and here we are mixed together with Englishmen, Dutchmen, Irishmen, and all kinds of people, so we must be on our guard. It was so hot here on Friday that ten persons died in the streets of sunstroke. We will probably leave here for the west this evening if we can only get our letters of exchange cashed.

Here is the finest view you could find. Staten Island and Brooklyn lie on either side of the approach to New York. Everything is built with taste. The harbor is so filled with vessels that if Sweden's whole merchant fleet were collected together, it would not come to so many ships. Every house is a palace. Yesterday evening we heard the first sermon of one of Pastor Hedström's assistants, named Nyman. He is about forty-five years old. He helps us and advises us on what is necessary.

I have much to tell you about the journey, but time will not allow it. I will write more and in greater detail when I get a little peace and quiet, and therefore I will now end these lines with the heartfelt wish that you may be in good health and are well, and if I may remain in good health I shall soon write to you. Greet all my acquaintances. I gave away my medicine, at least most of it, and the provisions held out well, though we were afraid of the salted food toward the end. Farewell, dear parents, brothers, and sisters. God grant that when I receive news from you, it will be good news. May all go well with you, wishes your loving son

Jonas

P.S.  We have just now had matins and the New Testament is sold here in both English and Swedish for 1 *riksdaler* 24 *skilling* Swedish money. Swedish is on one page and English on the other page, and many spiritual tracts are given to emigrants in the Swedish, English, and German tongues. The Swedes have religious services here three times on Sundays and meetings during the week. Often they meet every evening. Again, greetings to you all from

J.

Sture Bolin, *En skånsk prästson i Amerika* (Lund, 1960), 45–47.

*Two years later, Wallengren writes an undated letter, evidently written on 30 June 1858, from Lyons, Iowa:*

Brother Janne,

Thanks for your letter of 4 May, which I now have the pleasure of answering. I am in good health and am feeling well and hope that you too are in good health. I see from your letter that you must be quite stout and that this fat is giving you trouble, but I will give you good advice on how to get rid of it. It is simply: come out here and be in the sun for a while, and I believe you will thin down all right. At least, I have not been at all bothered by overweight since I came here. I have put it on solidly enough in the winters but when summer comes I have usually lost it. Now that I am mostly out in the hot sun, I am, as Americans usually are, thin as a skeleton, and I believe I come close to the truth when I say that my face and hands are like an Indian's. I have a beard just about like yours, but a bit thicker. If I remember rightly, you had a rather thin beard. But your teeth, I would think, are whiter than mine, for mine are almost pitch-black from smoking and chewing tobacco. I would think, though, that because I have always drunk a lot of coffee and tea, and used a large amount of sugar in it, that has been a large part of the reason. The Americans always drink coffee and tea with their meals and feed milk to the pigs because they think milk is not healthy. I have taught them to drink milk, though, here where I am now, so they are almost worse than I am about drinking milk. . . .

The reason the President is negotiating with Brigham Young is that Salt Lake is so far away that it costs the Union an enormous amount to keep troops there. The Mormons have left and moved further out, at least the women and children. Certainly it is true that slaves and Mormons ought not to exist. But you should not say this to the Americans, for the Northern states are doing all they can against slavery. Still, as you know, it is the people of each state who make the laws and the slaveowners are the richest. And when it happens that they get a president who is on their side, he gets more votes sometimes than there are people in the place where the voting is held. That the Swedes are working to get rid of religious constraints shouldn't have anything to do with slavery or Mormonism. But it is nevertheless certain that the greatest difference between the slaves in America and in Sweden is color. Most of the slaves, at least those who are somewhat manageable, are much better off than many of the so-called free *husmän*[50] or day laborers at Ljungby. Slaves are necessary because of the burning sun in the South. I think Sweden's noblemen would gladly see slavery introduced into Sweden, if only it were in their power. Greet Broms, Lundberg, Eurenius, and all my other acquaintances for me. I have no news to tell, so you will have to be satisfied for this time. When you write, use the same address as before. . . .

J. M. Wallengren

*Ibid.*, 74–76.

*Mary Jonson, some of whose subsequent letters are given below under her married name, Stephenson, writes to her parents in Edshult parish, Småland.*

Mount Pleasant, Henry County, Iowa, May 7, 1859

Dearly beloved parents, brothers, and sisters:

In the first place I wish to thank you for the welcome letter which I received from you on the 24th of February, in which I learned that you were blessed with good health. I am in good health, and I hope these simple lines will find you in good circumstances. You write that you miss me very much. That is not to be wondered at, because nothing lies closer to the heart than the love between children and parents. But, pray, do not worry too much about me. I got along well in Sweden, and this being a better country, I will do even better here. As my plans are now, I have no desire to be in Sweden. I never expect to speak with you again in this life. . . . I am sending you my picture as a remembrance, and with it another picture which I am certain will be welcome, because it is the likeness of a man who is to become your second son-in-law sometime this fall. Perhaps I am in somewhat of a hurry to let you see it, but the opportunity to send messages with Swedes who are returning to Sweden comes but seldom. This letter is sent with a man who is going to Sweden to receive his inheritance on Öland. . . . The young man whose picture you will see came from Södra Vi parish. He has been here ten years. One who has been here that length of time is acquainted with the language and customs of America. . . .

> Your loving daughter unto death,
>
> Mary Jonson

George M. Stephenson, trans. and ed., "Typical America Letters," *Yearbook of the Swedish Historical Society of America*, vol. 7 (1921–1922), 54–55.

*A party of Swedes on their way to the California goldfields passed through Salt Lake City, where one wrote the following account, dated 12 October 1859, for the newspaper,* Hemlandet.

Yesterday evening we arrived at Salt Lake City and are now in the midst of the Mormons and their wives. In the morning we will continue our journey to California. We have a two months' trip before us, making the duration of our entire journey five months. We praise God that thus far we have met no misfortune. We have forded hundreds of rivers and for five weeks have traversed towering mountains. Our poor oxen are tired out and lean; they have had poor pasturage in the mountains, but we hope they will hold out until we arrive in California. In order to lighten the load for the oxen we have walked the entire distance and we will have to do likewise on the road to California.

Salt Lake City is a pretty town. The houses are built of brick and surrounded by large gardens. The town lies in a valley, surrounded by towering mountains. The large Salt Lake lies below the town; the water, however, is so salty and bitter that there are no fish and nothing grows on the shore. We are camping in the center of the town. We are all Swedes in our company, which now consists of four wagons. We have pitched our tents in the street and made a fire on the square to cook coffee, fry meat, and bake bread. We are besieged by hundreds of persons who offer to sell milk, butter, eggs, onions, etc. Sugar and coffee are very expensive, and people buy as much as they can afford. Brown sugar costs forty cents per pound, and coffee is just as high.

It is said that there are many Swedish and Norwegian girls here; but as we intend to be on our way today, I will have no opportunity to visit them. There are also many Swedes who have three and four wives. The president has ninety wives; and the high priest has thirty. There are many women, and most of them are attractive. Last evening I saw several men out walking with their wives, and some had five or six, others ten or twelve. . . .

George M. Stephenson, trans. and ed., *"Hemlandet* Letters," *Yearbook of the Swedish Historical Society of America*, vol. 8 (1922–1923), 109–10.

*After some years in the Swedish army, Oscar Malmborg served during the Mexican War in the United States Army. In 1854 and 1861 he went to Sweden as an agent of the Illinois Central Railroad to recruit settlers for its territory. The following letters, in his somewhat uncertain English, are from his second visit. In the Civil War he served as a colonel in the Union army. He eventually returned to Sweden.*

Wrigstad, Sweden, Feb. 17th, 61

A. E. Burnside, Esq.
Treasurer Ill. Cent RR Co.
New York.

My last to you was from Wexjö 15th inst. I left there in the afternoon following day for the inn of Starhult in the parish of Hjelmseryd where I arrived at midnight last night. I wrode up to the church early this morning, which large as it is, sitting over 2000 people, was soon crowded. After service among other notices mine was also read, as usual from the pulpit. By farmers hence to Wexjö at the fair it had already spread that I was to be there today and after service the parish hall was not only so crowded that I could scarcely move my arms but a still greater number had to remain in the yard. Several of these farmers had already sold their farms and during the next two weeks auctions will be held for the sale stock, implements &c; others are preparing to the same. I will get a few families hence and some intend to go to children or friends in Minnesota. This has been one of the best meetings I have had in Sweden and my article in the Wexjö paper has contributed to it in a great measure. I left for this place at 3 p. m. & arrived here at 10; yet would drop you these few lines. Tomorrow I shall visit the people around here, but understand I must not expect much here & if so will leave tomorrow night for Wernamo & neighbourhoods. If there is no mail will next write a line from Gislared.

I am very Respectfully
Your Obt. Servt.
Oscar Malmborg

A. A. Stomberg, ed., "Letters of an Early Emigrant Agent in the Scandinavian Countries," *Swedish-American Historical Bulletin*, 3 (1930):24.

9 March 1861, Gothenburg, Sweden

. . . In general character of country there is but little resemblance between Sweden and Norway, but climate, kind and quality of soil is nearly the same in both. But Norway enjoys the advantage of having neither a hereditary nor a so called landed aristocracy. The Diet have long ago abolished the former and the mountainous nature of the country, affording but small patches and far between fit for cultivation, has made impossible the growth of the latter.

Miserable, economically considered, as the norwegian farmer nevertheless is, he is at least not like the small farmer in Sweden, where as yet there are plenty of both of those kind of aristocracy, subject to their ruinous influence. Especially is it the object of the large gentleman farmer to annex the small farms in his vicinity to his estate. Of the three classes of actual farmers—the peasants—it is the poorest who are gradually being reduced from being owners to become mere laborers. Such a one who for instance owns from 25 to 50 acres, of which from 4 to 6 acres cultivable, though generally very stony land, a little timber and the main portion brush, slough & rock in all worth from $1500. to $3000. cannot in the long run, after the heavy taxes are paid, support an increasing family. One failure of crops causes his ruin at once, and in ordinary seasons he is but gradually approaching the same end. (The first cause of this evil is, however, a law passed by the Diet a few years ago allowing farms to be parcelled out in ever so many small pieces) He gradually becomes embarrassed by the "assistance" of the large landholder, who at length, and for a mere trifle, realizes the long contemplated annexation at the same time reducing the poor man and his family to work for nothing more than food, without hope of ever gaining a competency. But by selling out before he becomes too involved, generally all of them will have more than sufficient to establish themselves independently on at least a 40 acre lot of the Company's lands.

Familiar with these facts, I have taken particular pains in my intercourse with this people, as also by means of an article I had published (and of which I have sent copies) to show them the vast difference between farming in Illinois & here; consequently this class of farmers naturally look upon the advantages the state of Illinois offers, as real blessings. The greatest number of emigrants will come from among this class. The middle class of these farmers are the most contented. The third—the wealthiest—being economically independent, strive to become so socially, but then they meet the strong, and too often successful, opposition of the aristocratic classes. Finding himself thus hemmed in within his narrow sphere, he, also listens with interest and gratification to the representations of the fruitful soil of Illinois and the unbounded field that state opens to every branch of honest industry; of this class also a good many will come out.—Indeed, even some of the larger landholders (gentlemen farmers) think it worth the while to try farming in the prairie state; and I expect three or four families with me.

But from the policy pursued by the gentlemen farmer towards the poor peasant, it will & truly be inferred, that as a general thing, he is opposed to emigration, as he not only wants his land but his labor also, and the more of it the better, because the cheaper. In the governorship of Kalmar is the stronghold of these gentlemen especially. They have taken advantage of the feeling produced among the people by the misfortunes which years ago befell so many emigrants from that region, to make them remain. But they went too far by circulating stories among the peasantry about the fate of the emigrant, one more absurd than the other; as for instance, that those who ship for New York are instead "taken to Siberia or the Southern Am. States and sold as slaves" &c. I have this from farmers themselves who frankly admitted that "such tales were too much to be believed even by a poor peasant."

During my visits in that district I was shown a little poetical article in "Barometern" of Kalmar, written by one of those gentlemen with reference to the same subject, emigration, but in a very moderate way and without saying anything against the Company or their agent here. Yet I considered it my duty to answer it, and did so on my arrival at Kalmar. . . . The public authorities and the press are neutral on the subject of emigration, but at the same time willingly admit, in substance the same as did the governor of this province on my arrival last summer, that, while they cannot encourage emigration, the arrangements the company have made for the safety of the emigrants and the advantages they offer them on their arrival, is a blessing to them and therefore these facts should be made known.

Thus supported by the authorities, the press and people at large, I feel that the opposition of a few individuals, especially as their motives have been unmasked, instead of serving them, are effectually aiding the cause of the Company.

*Ibid.*, 32–34.


10 June 1861, Gothenburg, Sweden

Since nearly three months, when the press of these countries first began to circulate dispatches regarding the intestine troubles in the States,[51] I have constantly had to answer most anxious questions, verbal and by letters to all directions; as to their probable result and effect upon the prospects of the newcomers in america; but I believe, that, in nine cases out of ten, I have done so satisfactorily, and in this much facilitated by public opinion in these countries[52] which is very strong against slavery. But since the news received that the south are authorizing and encouraging piracy, a sort of panic seems to have taken possession of the minds of the emigrants and their friends regarding their safety across the Atlantic. And were it not for the liberal reasoning of the press, partly owing to my explanatory letters to editors in the country, and conversations with those at this place, the whole emigration might have been suspended at once. As it is, many have postponed their departures, especially among those who at the receipt of the news had not made their final arrangements. Even merchants at several ports, who have had the american trade for a number of years, are either delaying the departure of their vessels, or sending them elsewhere. As most of the norwegian emigrants had left or disposed of their property earlier, it will make very little if any decrease in their number.

*Ibid.*, 48–49.

*A pioneer pastor writes from Minnesota in 1861:*

. . . There are many wrong ideas among you there at home. Some believe that if they could only come to America they would live like lords and in a few years become well-off, even rich; but they deceive themselves for one has to work hard and sweat for what he gets here. Others, meanwhile, find too much fault with this country, and since they have heard that it has gone badly for some one or another who has come here, they believe that want and misery must be everyone's lot. That is also wrong. Say what you will about America, one thing is certain, and that is that those who wish to and can work can escape from want; for work and earnings for both men and women are not lacking here. The Swedes in this area are not prosperous; but this is not to be wondered at; for when they came a few years ago, there was complete wilderness here and you surely know that new land cannot be broken, fenced, and made into fertile fields quickly, nor buildings put up for themselves and their livestock; and therefore it is not surprising that we still have very poor houses and that things are far from what we would wish; but they get better each year, so that some already have quite comfortable homes. . . .

Albin Widén, *Vår sista folkvandring* (Stockholm, 1962), 54.

*From a small Swedish settlement in Illinois:*

Henry, 10 June 1862

Dear Pastor Jonson,

The Swedes around here humbly beg you to be kind enough to come to us, for C. A. Carlsson's wife has had two children, a son and a daughter, Olof Petter Nellson has a son, so there are three Christian children. We are sixteen Swedes, we will pay ten dollars for the trip, for it is very hard to travel with the small children. If you could come the first Sunday after Trinity, it would be real fine for all of us if we could hear a sermon on Saturday, but if you can't come on Sunday you are welcome the week after any day you want; but now we are waiting for an answer as soon as you get this letter. We will meet you in Henry, whatever day you set out we will meet at three o'clock. You come by train from Johnson to Henry, we will meet it with a wagon at three in the afternoon. God's peace be with us all.

signed by S. Nelson

My address S. Nelson, Henry, Marshall Co., Illinois

Widén, *Amerikaemigrationen i dokument*, 126.

*A minister in Minnesota later recalled his first church and home there.*

It was a little building about sixteen feet square, made of rough logs, which, when the pastor arrived in 1855, lacked floor and windows; the latter consisted of two small openings. That little house was used for the congregation's services up to the summer of 1862; however, a lean-to of boards was added to the north side in 1858. The lean-to had bare earth for a floor and posts were driven into it, on which boards were laid for benches. In an old sketch you can see the benches, lectern, the table with the parlor organ, and the organist. The two small window openings did not let enough light into the room, and if anyone outside stood against the opening, there was almost a complete eclipse, as happened one Sunday in 1857 when the minister was preaching. A man from Jämtland came with a group to look at the settlement and had a large leather sack on his shoulder. Most interested at having come across a divine service, he stuck his head and half of himself together with the leather sack through the opening and submitted everything and everyone inside to a detailed examination. The eclipse came so quickly that the minister nearly lost his place, but all were pleased to get several such sturdy fellows for the settlement. . . . Meanwhile we got along well in our little shack; we put up wallpaper over the boards, put a cheap carpet on the floor, bored holes into planks for tables and chairs, and tried to make it as cozy as possible. The worst part was getting food. We had nothing on the place except sometimes when we managed to catch a fish in the creek. It was fifteen English miles to town, there was often nothing to buy anything with, and no transportation to start with. It was also hard for my wife, for I had to be away from home much of the time. Indians still wandered around and made things uncomfortable, even if they did no harm. . . .

Widén, *Vår sista folkvandring*, 104–5.

*A. C. Warberg was one of a number of Swedish career officers who volunteered for service in the Union army during the Civil War. With a clear literary bent, he first describes a reception at the White House, then a bloody encounter with the Confederates during the Richmond campaign in 1864.*

October 1862, Washington, D.C.

. . . A few days ago, the President and his wife gave a great reception, and it has been claimed, though perhaps with exaggeration, that the visitors that evening amounted to the impressive number of some six to eight thousand persons.

From both stories of the White House, as well as from the portico with its four Ionic columns, under which the carriages drove up, there streamed forth the brightest illumination onto the cypresses in the surrounding park. Around nine the line of carriages and the number of those arriving on foot under the torchlit, vaulted canopy of foliage seemed at its peak. One entered the vestibule, carpeted and luxuriant with tropical plants. All the doors leading into it were wide open for the ever-surging stream of people, whose unusually mixed character would certainly have captivated even the eye most dazzled by our European regal pageantry. People came and went as they wished and individuals from all classes of society had equal entrée on this occasion. Exemplary orderliness, attentive behavior, and manifest respect for that kind of human worth that is not worn on one's coat were notable features at this gathering. There was no sign of any order of rank observed at the doors. A member of the Senate had no greater prerogative in paying his respects to the President than a greengrocer; the orator from Boston knew that his less exalted colleague, the "knight of labor" and tribune of the people, who stands on a barrel on a street corner shouting and stirring up the passions of the mob, would also be there and have the right to shake the President's hand.

Members of Lincoln's cabinet and their families jostled good-naturedly with the humblest employees of their respective departments; the foreign diplomats, in their ornate uniforms resplendent with gold braid, bowed and scraped alongside that son of nature innocent of all etiquette, the tall, powerful, sun-tanned, and long-bearded Kansas farmer; senators and representatives from the farthest states of the Republic, with their families (who had hardly had time to learn of the latest Paris fashions), mixed in the whirl of the capital's finest society. Here were the prominent New York lawyer, the prosperous Wall Street banker, the Boston philosopher; there the gold digger from the mines of Colorado, favored by the goddess Fortuna, with well-filled purse and flashing jeweled rings, paying his court to a siren from New York's "high life." Here yesterday's general, who had been an agent for a petroleum company the day before; there a railroad president from Pennsylvania's coal region. Here a beauty from Baltimore, who with Mediterranean blood and Grecian profile complements perfection of figure with grace, suppleness, and form. . . . Here in a group one finds some members of the Supreme Court; there some learned men (in the world of the abstract) for whom science is *living* and its practical application is not, as with some of the heroes of the world of thought and research on the other side of the Atlantic, buried in the darkness of that medieval night which there so largely envelops certain universities. Here a journalist, discussing "burning questions" with a young "lady of fashion"; there the prominent scientist, the respected Professor Henry, conversing with the brilliant orator, Senator "Billy" Wilson from Massachusetts, with his legal training, who time after time has been called away from his cobbler's awl and last to serve as general of militia, chief of a Zouave regiment, and chairman of the celebrated committee to investigate the reverses of the war; here the governor of Rhode Island and the mayor of Washington, making room for a crowd of soldiers in from the street, who wandered around in their simple, coarse, and threadbare uniforms, criticizing the battle of Antietam to an attentive newspaper reporter.

The President, dressed as usual in simple, black clothes, stood inside the door to one of the outer reception rooms, to receive and shake hands with each and every one in the order in which he entered, and his private secretary, standing right beside him, had the task of moving each one on, saying unceremoniously, "Pass the crowd on."

Anyone the President did not know was immediately presented by those around him or by the secretary, and since many mistakes were made which were corrected by the person in question, there was unconstrained merriment, which was further heightened by the hearty grin, quip, or short appropriate anecdote which the illustrious host always has ready at hand. . . .

[A. Carlsson Warberg], *Skizzer från Nordamerikanska kriget 1861–1865* (Stockholm, 1867), 114–16.

James Army, 10th Corps Headquarters, Encampment before Richmond, Virginia, October 1864

. . . Butler's scouts had meanwhile reported the evening before that the enemy was preparing to attack next morning, which was to involve nothing less than throwing us back against the James River in order to bring about our destruction in its waves. I cannot deny that at first things looked quite promising for our enemy, for although all the troops had been notified around midnight and necessary orders for all eventualities had been issued, they still seemed with their usual over-confidence to abandon themselves to a pleasant *dolce far niente*, which in consequence meant that the enemy, who attacked our cavalry in considerable force, had by daylight already thrown it back in complete disorder and thereby seized all eight cannon and a large number of prisoners. At the first report that came in with the *ventre-à-terre*, fleeing cavalrymen, the different corps were behind their earthworks ready to receive the enemy, who, it must be said, shortly thereafter attacked our right wing, with unusual rapidity, strength, and an assurance which showed how well he knew our position, from two directions with two infantry divisions and twelve field pieces. The enemy skirmishers rushed forward like tigers over a very wide field, obstructed by thickets and fallen trees, after which the main force, unshaken by any hindrance although they were being heavily bombarded from the flank by no less than four batteries of six guns each, stormed forward toward our breastworks amidst the wildest yells. Nothing seemed able to stop this mighty force, these heroes born in the moment of attack. The sight of it was truly gripping, for one saw how predatory lust burned in their eyes, as they, despite the murderous fire of repeating rifles, hurled themselves with lusty shouts over the ditches and low earthworks upon our soldiers.

I cannot hope to describe the wild tumult that followed, in the midst of thick smoke from unceasing rifle fire on all sides, any more than I can give you an impression of how the enemy soldiers looked. Clad in gray, like our military prisoners, with plumed, broad-brimmed felt hats pulled down over the forehead, ragged, gaunt, and browned by the sun like Indians, with flowing hair and wild beards fluttering in the wind, on weather-beaten, hardened features, these heroes of the South with antique valor in their breasts give an outward impression of the brigand bands of the chief of the Abruzzi, the cruel and indomitable Rinaldo Rinaldino. . . . Through powerful and well-executed dispositions from our side, the enemy was soon driven out of those points in our earthworks where he had penetrated, and the attack repulsed with the help of our reserve, after which by noon we forced him into a full retreat, following a morning long as a little eternity, marked by the usual horrors of war. . . .

I cannot end this letter without satisfying a long-nurtured wish, to convey to the old, beloved fatherland a greeting from some of its many sons who with ancient Swedish valor are fighting here in the ranks of the American army.

It is with pride that I can attest to the distinction with which all our comrades from the Swedish army who are employed here are serving, and it is altogether true that the officers from no nation have done their fatherland so much honor in the ranks of the American army as have ours. . . .

*Ibid.,* 311–13.

~~~~~~~~~~~~~~~~~~~~~~~~~~~~~~~~~~~~~~~~~~~~~~~~~~~~~~~~~~~~~

*It was hard to stay in Iowa when there was gold to be dug out west.*

Glendale, Jefferson County, Iowa, February 22, 1864

To Jonas P. Zackrison.

The grace and peace of God be with you all, beloved parents, sisters, brothers, relatives, and friends. We thank you for your welcome letter.

In the first place, I will let you know that we are all among the living and enjoying good health. We are grateful to God for the goodness he shows unto us daily. We are very sorry that we are unable to send money to our venerable parents. As you will see by the enclosed newspaper clipping, it is impossible to buy exchange on Sweden. At New Year's, to our great joy, Jonas August, his brother, Sven Peter, and Samuel Sandahl from Andover visited us; and then through Sven Peter it was arranged that the money he has coming to him in Sweden should be paid to our parents, with the understanding that we should reimburse him. Sven has written about this to the proper parties in Sweden; and if our parents have not seen that letter, read this letter to them.

We must let you know about the good fortune of Jonas August. He has been mining gold in the Idaho territory, and has in cash four thousand dollars (sixteen thousand *rixdaler*)[53] over and above all expenses. He made all this last summer. It sounds unbelievable, but it is true. I counted the money myself. He intends to return the last of this month. His brother Sven Peter will accompany him. . . . Jonas Peter, Johan Gustaf, and I have decided to join their party, if we are in good health. We have set the 29th of this month as the date of our departure. The journey is no pleasure trip, but full of danger, not because of its length (1,800 miles) but on account of the wild Indians, who are as rapacious as wolves. They kill the gold seekers at every opportunity, and one must be on the watch constantly while traveling through the wilderness where they have their haunts. But we hope the Lord will protect us on the journey. Remember to pray for our protection. If the Lord prospers us, it is not our intention to be selfish; we intend to share our good fortune with our nearest ones, our dear sisters and brothers.

It may be of interest to know how much expense is involved in mining gold. I submit the following items. We have bought four mules for $600, harness for $68, a wagon for $80, covering for the wagon, tent, bed clothes, provisions, etc., amounting in all to $950.

You ask if we hunt wild game. Yes; we certainly do. Wild turkeys, prairie chickens, partridges, geese, and rabbits are everywhere. Rabbits are smaller than the species in Sweden, but there are myriads of them. You may be sure the boys are good marksmen. We trap partridges, but they are smaller than those at home. Prairie chickens are exactly like the partridges in your country, and,they are so numerous that the prairies are literally covered with them in spots. We seldom fish. There are no lakes in Iowa, but fishing is good in the large rivers. There are no large streams in this vicinity.

Carl Magnus and Lawrence will husband the farm during our absence so there will be no interruption. We put in fourteen acres of fall wheat, which yielded 267 bushels, i.e., 66¾ *tunnor*. In addition we harvested ten *tunnor* of spring wheat. We sowed eighteen bushels of fall wheat and four bushels of spring wheat. You can estimate yourselves how large the returns were. I have sold wheat to the amount of $225 and hogs to the amount of $130. If it had not been for the ravages of the cholera, I would have realized double the latter amount. I lost thirty hogs and now have only thirty left.

John Z. Sandahl

Stephenson, "Typical America Letters," 71–73.

*In New Sweden, Iowa, Maria Jonson, whom we have already encount-
ered, met and married Olagus Steffansson, who had come from Småland
in 1849. They now called themselves Oliver and Mary Stephenson. The
latter writes:*

New Sweden, Iowa, August 2, 1864

Dear parents, brothers, and sisters:

My heartiest wishes for your spiritual and material welfare!

In the first place, I wish to thank you for your welcome letter. It is a
great privilege to be able to converse by means of letters, and it is a
still greater joy to know that we may meet our dear ones with God on
high. We are very grateful for the present you sent us. It was most
unexpected. I know and confess before God and man that my conduct
at home was not always what it ought to have been, for I have searched
my heart and confess that I was unworthy of your love. But it is a great
comfort, separated as we are by such a long distance, to feel that in
your ardent parental love you have forgotten everything. I do not know
how to repay you. I can only pray God that he may bless you spiritually
and materially. . . .

We certainly would be very happy to see you, but it would not be
right to insist, because the war has brought so much sorrow. We do not
know how long we shall be allowed to live in peace, because a rumor
is abroad that the enemy is coming to Iowa. But I am not greatly worried; if the horrors of war are in store for us, we are to be punished for
our sins. Whom the Lord protects need not fear. It is very noticeable
that the side reserved for the men in church is sparsely occupied, while
the women's section is full. At assemblies of young people the girls out-
number the men five or six to one. The number of killed and wounded
is appalling, and there are no prospects that the war will end very soon.

Our new home has many advantages over the old one, and I like it
much better. We have a good level road to church, and the distance is
no greater. I sell butter and eggs to a man who calls every other week.
I believe I have sold twenty dollars' worth of eggs, besides considerable
butter. We have four cows. We sheared six sheep. I have twenty-four
pounds of wool. I have begun to spin, and I intend to weave thirty
yards of cloth warped with wool. A yard is equal to one and one-half
*aln.* Cotton yarn is ten dollars per skein. . . .

I thank you for keeping us informed about our relatives and friends. . . .

Uncle Sandahl and Jonas Peter are in the goldfields, but they are not mining much gold. Uncle is bothered with backache. They write that they are coming home this fall. Our brother-in-law Alsin, who is married to Oliver's older sister, is there also. He makes wheelbarrows and earns six dollars per day.

In conclusion your children and grandchildren send cordial greetings.

Mary Stephenson

*Ibid.*, 76–77.

*In 1864 Måns Hultin served as doctor aboard the Swedish steamship* Ernst Merck *when it took a group of contract laborers to America. In the first excerpt from his travel account, he discusses the attitudes of the emigrants on board toward their new homeland. The following selections show what view of the Yankees his short stay in New York gave him.*

. . . They seldom speak of America and never of Sweden. It appears as though they lived only to eat, drink, dance, sleep, and gape at passing ships, but I have spoken more closely with one or another about their prospects in the new land and I have found them all full of hope and faith. Their conceptions of the land and fate they are going to are naturally highly obscure, and they are most obscure regarding themselves, but the goal which basically, it seems to me, they are expecting and hoping for is not any fresh and newly formed object, unlike all that the past has offered them, but rather is simply the old and well loved in a new and improved edition. It is old Sweden idealized, it is the past, sometimes regretted and deplored yet always inescapable, which now no longer will be painted over and gilded as best one can, but will be rebuilt from the ground up and will be the first step toward a promising future. And it is clear that it could not be otherwise, for what is to be expected no one can judge except from what he has seen. . . .

Måns Hultin, *Resa till Amerika 1864 med emigrantskeppet Ernst Merck*, ed. Erik Gamby (Helsingfors, 1958), 58–59.

A rascal among Yankees is to be sure no polished rogue; but he is a fine rogue, and finesse is just that quality which is his greatest pride. This is, however, no elegant, kid-gloved Parisian finesse, who with taste and grace to the fingertips spirits the wallet from the breast pocket of his duped fellow man. On the contrary! A Yankee stands there in front of you, ugly, scraggly, unpleasant, and gangling, makes no compliments at all, behaves so that it is altogether impossible to like him, and he dupes you even so. It is precisely herein that the finesse lies. . . . An American's idea of a rascal is not the same as our own by a far cry. If we should apply our views on this matter in New York, I fear the Yankees would be declared scoundrels to a man. . . . "If I find someone who is dumb enough to let himself be tricked, it is his own fault!"—this is the Yankee's fixed maxim in all his affairs. "If I meet someone who is so weak that he lets himself be taken in and fleeced, that is his own fault too!" . . .

*Ibid.*, 146–47.

One of our firemen on the *Ernst Merck* went out one evening and did not return. About fourteen days later we received a letter from the same man, postmarked Washington. He recounted in this letter how he had fallen in with a couple of Swedes who pitied him for having to do hard work for poor wages. They could surely get him a better job if he wished. He was encouraged and invited them for a drink. They invited him to fifteen, and the world in America shone forth in rosy hues. He agreed and was put on a train, then in a coach, and then a steamboat, traveling by many twists and turns. As a seaman, he was not without a sense of direction and followed the course as best he could, and felt at the journey's end that he was not far from New York. He later learned that he was in Jersey City on the other side of the river. He was taken up to an office and given a contract to sign. It concerned his employment on a large steamboat at a hefty wage, said his good countrymen.

The contract was in English and the fellow naturally did not understand a word, but his countrymen were helpful and must surely be honest people, so he signed. He was then given five hundred dollars in cash, but his friends became even more kindly and solicitous toward him. They said he could easily be robbed, unused as he was to this country. He ought therefore to give them his money, so that they could put it in a safe place and come back after a couple of hours. So they got the money, shook hands with their friend, and disappeared.

When they were gone, an official in the office opened a door and made signs for our fireman to be so good as to enter. When he seemed to hesitate, he got a push from behind, after which the door was locked after him. When he now looked around, he found himself quite unexpectedly in the midst of an honest company of sergeants and corporals, who all wrinkled their noses at his sooty fireman's uniform. He had to take off his clothes, got a jacket with shiny buttons, a peaked cap, and a pair of blue pantaloons. He did not quite like how he looked in this outfit, but before he could study himself in the mirror too long, he found himself again stuffed into a wagon and on his way. When he wrote to us after fourteen days, he was already posted outside Petersburg, in the face of the wildest artillery fire. He implored us for help, poor fellow!

*Ibid.*, 158–59.

PART TWO: The Great Farmer-Land in
the West, 1865—1889

# Background

The end of the Civil War in the spring of 1865 opened the flood-gates of European immigration to America, which now reached unprecedented levels. There can hardly have been more than 25,000 Swedes in America at the beginning of 1865, yet in the years that followed annual immigration from Sweden frequently exceeded that figure.[1] The American census of 1890 showed a Swedish-American population of 776,093.

In accounting for this phenomenal increase, both "push" and "pull" factors must again be considered. The first great impetus from the Swedish side came from the three successive crop failures in 1867, 1868, and 1869, which caused widespread misery and ruined large numbers of smaller independent and tenant farmers. Emigration jumped from 5,893 in 1867 to 21,472 in 1868 and to 32,053 in 1869. It thereafter fell off with the return of better harvests and the American depression of 1873, which continued until late in the decade. By the later 1870s, however, Swedish agriculture faced a new crisis in the form of competition from cheap foreign wheat. Railroads and steamships now made it possible to import into Europe vast quantities of wheat from Argentina, Australia, and North America (where a growing share of the crop was being produced by Swedish farmers in the Midwest). These imports drove down the prices for home-grown cereals. During the 1880s Swedish emigration thus rose to new heights, reaching 46,252 persons in 1887, its overall peak. Noneconomic factors now played a smaller role. Religious sects outside the state church were tolerated after 1860, though social and political discontent remained a contributing cause of emigration.

The pull from across the ocean meanwhile became far greater: America was suddenly much closer and its resources more accessible to more people than ever before. This was due above all to free or cheap land, improved transportation, pro-emigration publicity, and the growing numbers of Swedes already in America.

In 1862 Congress passed the Homestead Act, granting a quarter section (160 acres) of free public land to any American citizen or person declaring an intent to become one, who settled on the land for five years, built a house, and cleared five acres. Well-located homestead land was quickly taken up. Meanwhile, to encourage the opening up of the West, the United States government made large land-grants to railroad companies, normally alternate sections on either side of their projected roadbeds. The westward extension of the railroads made more homestead land accessible while the railroad companies, anxious to provide themselves with future traffic by promoting settlement along their rights of way, offered their land for sale at low prices and easy terms.

Transportation became faster, cheaper, more reliable and comfortable with the rapid spread of railroads in both Sweden and America. The American railroads often provided the further inducement of reduced fares for immigrants moving out to their respective areas, often on special immigrant trains with Spartan but adequate accommodations. The greatest change, however, was brought about by the rapid shift from sail to steam in the Atlantic emigrant traffic. Steam packets had indeed been in regular service since the 1830s but were virtually limited to carrying first-class passengers and mail. The predominance of American sailing vessels in the emigrant traffic was broken by Confederate commerce-raiding during the Civil War, while British and German shipping firms, liberally subsidized by their governments, took the opportunity to construct large numbers of steamships specially designed for carrying passengers. Anders Larson noted in 1873 that his voyage from Stockholm to Chicago in 1846 had taken him 93 days, including 74 days at sea, "a trip which nowadays can take place in 20 days." In 1867 J. V. Swenson crossed from Liverpool to New York on the Inman Line's *City of Baltimore* in nine days and six hours, "the fastest crossing to that date." If traveling in the steerage class could still be a harrowing experience, it nevertheless was, as Mary Stephenson claimed in 1868, "a pleasure trip compared to what it was in former days."

Steamships traveled on regular schedules, little disturbed by wind or weather, making it possible to announce in advance both departure dates and set fares, which now became much cheaper than before. A new basic route for Swedish emigrants evolved by the mid-1860s: from Gothenburg to Hull, England, on the Wilson Line; by rail across to Liverpool; thence via the Anchor, Cunard, Inman, White Star, and other lines to New York; and from there on to final destinations by rail. Smaller numbers of Swedes traveled by way of Christiania (Oslo), Copenhagen, Hamburg, or Bremen, usually also to New York.

Active promotion of emigration in Sweden came from several sources. The American railroads campaigned actively, both inside the United States and abroad, to attract settlers to their lands. As we have seen, the Illinois Central, even before the Civil War, had twice sent Oscar Malmborg to Sweden to recruit emigrants. Other companies took up this practice after the war, most notably in the case of Hans Mattson, who himself had emigrated in 1851, had been a colonel in the Union army and secretary of state in Minnesota, and who now served as an agent for American railroads in Sweden in 1868–75. The railroads widely disseminated advertising literature, in part by encouraging Swedes in America to send it to friends and relatives at home. A number of states likewise sought to attract settlers. Once again Hans Mattson played a leading role through his efforts on behalf of the Minnesota Immigration Board, both by contacts with Swedes already settled in the state and by a visit to Sweden in 1869. A former American consul and later minister to Sweden, W. W. Thomas, went over to recruit settlers for Maine, as a result of which the colony of New Sweden was established in that state in 1870. A number of states published promotional literature which was widely distributed to emigrants on both sides of the Atlantic.

The greatest publicity was soon undertaken, however, by the large steamship lines, which were most heavily dependent upon the emigrant traffic and were initially in fierce competition with each other. These companies established permanent agents in the principal Swedish port cities, supported by a network of subagents reaching into the most remote parts of the country, often in collaboration with one or another of the American railroads. The subagents, usually local tradesmen, distributed promotional literature and made out tickets for steamship and rail transportation to any American destination, on a commission basis. Prospective emigrants who themselves undertook to recruit others, like August Andrén in 1872, were given reduced fares or free passage. Particularly effective use was made of Swedish Americans who returned home to visit and were granted rebates or free transportation depending on how many of their countrymen they could take back with them.

Finally, the more Swedes there were in America, the greater was the attraction for more to follow. For more and more people there were now direct contacts with America, a destination to go to, the possibility of help and guidance in adjusting to the new land. The question may well be asked whether emigrants from the Swedish countryside to the farmlands of midwestern America faced, in this period of rapid transition at home, greater dislocation of their accustomed ways of life than those compelled by circumstance to move to Swedish cities and take up unfamiliar industrial employments, or even than some of those who stayed in their old localities. Many of the emigrants left disintegrating communities at home for reintegrating communities across the ocean, consisting largely of relatives, old friends, and neighbors. Swedes in America meanwhile gave financial as well as psychological support to emigration. Year after year they sent what money they could spare home to their relatives—sometimes a single, crumpled dollar bill, sometimes bank drafts for considerable sums. Such remittances helped raise the economic position of many families and made emigration possible for increasing numbers. And even more direct stimulus to emigration was provided by prepaid tickets, which could be purchased through numerous steamship agencies in America and sent to relatives at home.[2]

These new circumstances brought about significant changes in the overall character of the emigration and of the emigrants themselves. Because of improved and cheaper transportation, emigration could be undertaken much more lightly than before, often from a sheer sense of adventure by persons who, like August Segerberg in 1884, wanted to see something more in life than "the bed and the cupboard." It was now relatively easy to return to the old country either to visit or to stay, and increasing numbers of Swedish Americans did one or the other. Emigration no longer represented an almost irreversible commitment.

Meanwhile, people from progressively poorer elements of society emigrated. Technological improvements and competition reduced transportation costs, evidently by over one-half between 1865 and 1890, while wages for agricultural workers and others increased by more than one-third in the same period.[3] Group emigration for mutual support along the way and in the new land was no longer necessary. The majority of the emigrants were now young unmarried men and women, traveling singly. Such persons were often forerunners for others in their families. Having established themselves, they would send home money or prepaid tickets for others until often, with the emigration or death of elderly parents, the old crofts at home lay abandoned and in ruins, and cows grazed or the forest grew back over the rocky patches of ground from which numerous families had once eked out a precarious living.

The great majority of the emigrants in this middle period were still farmers and settled in the farmlands of the Midwest. As increasing numbers arrived with nothing but their bare hands, however, it was necessary for them to work for others to raise money. Many of the men worked on farms as regular hired hands or followed the harvests. Large numbers toiled on railroad construction gangs, prompting the railroad tycoon J. J. Hill to boast, "Give me Swedes, snuff and whisky, and I'll build a railroad to Hell!" Others cut timber in the great northern forests, which resounded to the "Swedish fiddle" (the timberman's saw) and where the great logs were manhandled by "Norwegian steam" (sheer muscle power). Some never got further than a drifting life of casual labor, although almost all aspired to own, and probably most eventually succeeded in acquiring, farms of their own. In America a person had to be prepared to do a little of everything, and it was no disgrace to do so. The emigrants constantly wrote home with pride, and sometimes surprise, at how well they were able to take things as they came. As the Swedish-American journalist, O. A. Linder, humorously put it in the 1880s:

> Some days there are when you are rich,
> The next day you are broke;

> You now and then aesthetics read,
>  And sometimes fences paint.
> At times, to make a living, you drive
>  Oxen at a lumber camp.
> And then you are an editor,
>  And in between, a tramp.[4]

It has often been held that emigration and adaptation to the new land required greater sacrifices from women than from men. Surely this was often enough true of married women with families. Yet for young unmarried girls the situation could be quite different, for this was the era of the Swedish maid. Middle-class town families usually kept domestic help and Swedish girls were in great demand. In America, these former country girls found to their delight, they were not expected to do outdoor work, had certain hours of the day and days of the week free, had rooms of their own, and were paid weekly. They were generally treated like members of the family and if they were not satisfied they could quit at any time and easily find jobs elsewhere. They could dress just as fancily as their mistresses and they found that American men treated "ladies," themselves included, with unaccustomed consideration. By the time they married—usually to Swedish men—they were enthusiastic apostles of American "gentility" and played an important part in the Americanization of their group. Swedish men often envied them their ease in finding work and the lightness of their duties, grumbling that it did not take long in America before they began to put on airs.

The immigrants' letters show significant changes in this middle period. They now reveal greater sophistication as the School Law of 1842 had increasing effect on Sweden. Grammar and spelling became more correct and consistent. Style was increasingly affected by newspapers, popular literature, and the appearance of letter-writing guides which gave appropriate examples for proper correspondence of all kinds. Thus the letters were more polished but at the same time rather more hackneyed and cliché-ridden, losing something of the pith and substance of the letters from the pioneer generation. Letters became more frequent, shorter, less formal in tone and painstaking in organization as mail traveled faster and postage rates went down, though C. F. Bergman could still write from Brooklyn in 1879 that "the worst thing is the postage money, but I can surely borrow it."[5] The letters also show their writers' greater prior knowledge of America. Their reactions upon reaching the new land were, if basically similar in nature, less naive and powerful than those of earlier immigrants. Or, if not really so sophisticated, the new arrivals made greater efforts to appear so. They now reveal more realistic and modest expectations, and are more frank in admitting hardships and disappointments as emigration required lesser commitments.

In 1865 most Swedes in America were concentrated in settlements in the upper Mississippi Valley: in northwestern Illinois, eastern Iowa, and east-central Minnesota. In Texas there were the beginnings of a colony near Austin, centered around the former seaman, S. M. Swenson, who had settled there as early as 1838. A Swede, J. E. Forsgren, was among the first Mormons to reach Utah in 1847, and by the early 1850s the first parties of Swedish converts had begun to arrive in the New Zion. During the next quarter century the area of Swedish settlement greatly expanded, in large part through the westward movement of Swedes from the older settlements: what George M. Stephenson has called the "swarming of the Swedes."[6] Swedish colonization around Lindsborg, Kansas, was for instance largely carried out through the First Swedish Agricultural Company in Chicago and the Galesburg Colonization Company, organized in the later 1860s by Swedes in Illinois. In due course a Swedish Colonization Company was founded in Lindsborg itself to establish further colonies in western Kansas. The Swedish communities in western Iowa and Minnesota, Nebraska, Colorado, Oregon, and the Washington Territory were for the most part founded by settlers from Illinois, eastern Iowa, east-central Minnesota, and eventually Kansas. The farthest outpost at this time was Kingsburg, California, settled by midwestern Swedes in the later 1880s. An interesting example of this kind of stage migration is provided by the people from the Knäred region of the province of Halland, who around 1850 established the Bergholm colony (later Munterville) in southeastern Iowa, a number of whom later moved out to the Skagit Valley, around La Conner, Washington Territory, from 1871 on.

As many left the older settlements for points west, their places were largely filled by fresh arrivals from Sweden, many of whom, after acclimatizing themselves and earning some money, themselves moved on. As new Swedish communities formed farther west, they too were joined by increasing numbers from the old country. Meanwhile, immigrants direct from Sweden settled in new locations farther east. The New Sweden settlement of 1870 in Maine has already been noted. A considerable colony of Swedes, mainly from Skåne, began to develop in Worcester, Massachusetts, around the same time. Jamestown, in western New York, where a few Swedes had settled before 1850, attracted growing numbers after 1865. By the 1880s Swedes were coming to northern Michigan to work in the iron mines. Increasing numbers of Swedes now lived in the cities, especially Chicago and Minneapolis-St. Paul, although among them there was often a sizable floating population of unmarried men who spent much of the year following the harvests, on railroad section gangs, or in lumber camps.

There has been much speculation as to why the Swedes settled where they did in America, it often being maintained that they naturally gravitated to localities that resembled their homeland. On the whole, however, it seems that practical considerations took precedence: the ready availability of good land, free or cheap on favorable terms; the location of relatives or friends; the enticements of state authorities, railroads, and land companies. If Minnesota eventually attracted the heaviest concentration of Swedes, this surely had more to do with the determined efforts of Hans Mattson than with the soughing of the wind in the pine tops. When C. F. Bergman wrote in 1896 that the area around Elgin, Texas, was "beginning to get like Sweden," he was not referring to the general appearance of things. Indeed, many of the most "Swedish" communities in America—places like Andover, Illinois, Lindsborg, Kansas, or Stromsburg, Nebraska—were located in highly un-Swedish surroundings on the rich, open prairie.

Building on modest beginnings from the pioneer period, Swedish religious and cultural institutions developed rapidly after 1865. A new religious denomination was added in 1885 with the forming of the Evangelical Mission Covenant Church by Swedish Mission Friends. In 1875 the Augustana College and Seminary moved from Paxton to Rock Island, Illinois. Soon other regional conferences of the Augustana Synod were anxious to have their own colleges. Gustavus Adolphus College, earlier a preparatory academy, was established in 1876 at St. Peter, Minnesota, Bethany College in Lindsborg, Kansas, in 1881, and Luther College, now defunct, in Wahoo, Nebraska, in 1883. There were short-lived Swedish academies in Minneapolis and Moorhead,

Minnesota. The Swedish Methodists founded a theological school in 1870 at Galesburg, Illinois, which continued in Evanston from 1875 until 1934, when it became Kendall College. The Swedish Baptist Bethel Academy in St. Paul, Minnesota, established in 1871, eventually became a college. In 1877 the Swedish Baptist Theological Seminary began its migratory career in Chicago. Such zeal is impressive, but unfortunately the old Swedish admonition to "match one's appetite to one's lunchbox" was rather lost sight of, and Swedish-American education long suffered from the intense rivalry of more institutions than the traffic would bear. As time passed these colleges became less theologically oriented. Increasing numbers of students prepared for nonclerical careers. In 1885 the first women were admitted to Augustana College.

Journalism too developed dynamically, with a large number of Swedish-language newspapers established between 1865 and 1889. Many, like Ernst Skarstedt's *Kansas-Tidningen* in 1879–1880, quickly folded, while others, like the liberal *Svenska Amerikanaren* founded in 1876, for which Skarstedt was a well-known contributor in the 1880s, or *Nordstjernan* in New York, established in 1872, enjoyed large followings. After many vicissitudes and mergers, *Svenska Amerikanaren-Tribunen* and *Nordstjernan-Svea* are still in operation at this time of writing. There was fierce rivalry between church papers like the old *Hemlandet* or the Methodist *Sändebudet* and the new secular newspapers. The latter were put out by a colorful group of bohemian intellectuals like Skarstedt, O. A. Linder, Magnus Elmblad, and others, who characteristically had left Sweden in revolt against worn-out conventions and social constraints, and who therefore were strongly influential in forming a sense of specifically Swedish-American—as opposed to Swedish—identity among their countrymen in America.

Along with newspaper publishing there appeared periodicals, mainly for religious denominations or social organizations, and books, both often printed by newspaper presses. Indeed the books were frequently offered as bonuses to subscribers to the newspapers. A landmark in Swedish-language publishing was the establishment in 1884 of the Augustana Book Concern in Rock Island, followed by other, shorter-lived enterprises. Although much of the material published consisted of devotional works and reprints of items from Sweden, there also developed a considerable Swedish-American literature, both poetry and prose, which to date has not received the attention it deserves, either in this country or in Sweden.

Swedish clubs and lodges of every description flourished in this period: for mutual self-help through sickness and burial insurance; for aid to newly arrived countrymen (and to send relief to Sweden in times of disaster and hardship there); for promotion of temperance; for the natives of various provinces; for social conviviality, sports, and choral singing. Naturally such societies were most accessible to Swedes in the cities. In general they were regarded by the religious denominations with a suspicion and mistrust that revealed a mounting concern over the increasing numbers of Swedish immigrants—ultimately the majority—who no longer sought formal affiliation with any Swedish church.

Finally, Swedish Americans in this middle period showed a growing interest in national affairs and, in proportion to their numbers, naturalization, and geographic concentration, they were able to make their weight felt in both local and regional elections. In Minnesota especially a Swedish name early became a political asset. The first Swedish American to serve in Congress, John Lind of Minnesota, was elected in 1887; after that time a number of others became congressmen, state legislators, and governors, including John Albert Johnson of Minnesota, who before his untimely death was a potential Democratic candidate for president in 1908.

# Letters and Documents

*The tribulations of Swedish immigrants arriving in New York just after the Civil War are described by the Augustana Lutheran pastor Andreas Andreen in a letter to* Hemlandet:

New York, September 5, 1865

Dear Brother:

Grace and peace!

. . . Every day since Brother Esbjörn left I have had to work among the immigrants. A great many are lying ill on Ward's Island; some have died and two women have given birth to children. One of them is reported dead, but I have been unable to visit her, as I live six miles away. The father is out west, and on Ward's Island there is said to be a deserted boy, who runs about dirty and full of vermin. At Castle Garden there are between twenty and thirty persons without a cent, who tug at my coat and tap my shoulder, crying: "Get me away from here so that we may escape the poor house." Last Friday I succeeded in getting a family to Chicago for eleven dollars, the regular fare being twenty-six, and today I persuaded a company to transport another by offering their effects for security. Some ask for bread, and I have been compelled to give what little I have until the supply is soon exhausted. I also write to their friends—for those who have them. I have at least two miles to Castle Garden, and when I return home in the evening I have to write to various people in behalf of these poor people. I have received about three hundred dollars in exchange from different relatives, the greater part of which has been disbursed to the proper parties. But all too few receive aid. . . .

Now a few suggestions regarding the work among immigrants, which

I believe of first importance, at least at present. In the first place, a home must be purchased for the missionary, preferably a small house in one of the suburbs, Brooklyn or some other place. . . . In the second place, a small office near Castle Garden is needed, but for a while we can continue to use the office of the Pennsylvania railway. (Yesterday I baptized a child there, who was born on the ocean.) But if we tie ourselves up with one railway company, and the others find out about it, they will probably brand the missionary as a "runner"[1] for that company, and in consequence he may be excluded from Castle Garden. In the third place, the above-named company ought to employ a Swede, who could converse with the immigrants and assist them. When a group is about to leave, I must assist them to purchase tickets, exchange gold, have their effects taken from Castle Garden, weigh them, and see that they are provided with food on their journey. . . .

A. Andreen

Stephenson, "*Hemlandet* Letters," 127–28.

*Upon arrival, beware the well-dressed gentleman with the glib tongue!*

Virginia, September 3, 1865

Dearest Cousin Olof, Swede Bend, Iowa:
    I will now write a few lines to you, my dear friend and cousin, and in my loneliness tell you how I am faring.
    I thank God that I am in good health. I have at last come to America after strange experiences. We arrived at New York without a penny, and I knew of no way to continue our journey, as there was no employment in sight. But then a Swedish gentleman put in his appearance and offered us employment. He was well dressed and extremely kind and offered to accompany us and find employment for us at a place three, and at the most four, hours' journey from Iowa (Iowa was my destination). Accordingly, it would be an easy matter to get there. Instead of keeping his promise he brought us to the southern states. We arrived

first at Richmond, where the war had wrought devastation, thence by canal for forty miles, to our destination. In New York he had promised that food, lodging, bedclothes, and a physician's services would be furnished free of cost in addition to monthly wages of thirteen dollars for myself and eight dollars for my wife. But instead I received ten dollars and my wife two. We are twelve Swedes, including men, women, and children, and receive less than twelve cans[2] of buttermilk per day, corn meal for pancakes in place of bread, and a small amount of pork. This is our daily allowance. We work hard all day, at night sleep on a hard brick floor, and an hour before sunrise begin work. Yes, the slaves are freed, but we are treated almost like slaves. I do not see any possibility of myself and mine holding out until I have earned enough to leave. I fear that before that time comes I will be unable to stand on my feet, even if I should be alive. Now, dear cousin, I pray you, if you possibly can, to do something to help us out of this precarious misery, fraud, and slavery. Help us, my dear friend, if you know of any way.

Yours truly,
Olof Brink

Address: Richmond, BenLemond County, Goochland, Virginia.

*Ibid.*, 130–31.

*Mary Stephenson writes home to Småland, where the end of the war in America aroused fresh interest in emigration:*

New Sweden, Iowa, June 15, 1865

Dear parents, sisters, and brothers:

I will again write to you and thank you for the welcome letter which we read so eagerly. The week your letter came we were in anxious expectation, as I dreamed many times about Sweden and about you. I always dream about you before your letters arrive. You may rest assured that your letters are read with eagerness, and it is with joy that we learn that you are in good health and are prospering. I am a little disappointed that sister Sophia does not come—we would have happy times together. But this prospect has faded since her fiancé doesn't want to leave. Now I am in hopes that Johanna will get the "America fever."

Oliver speaks a great deal of moving to Sweden, but I don't favor it, as I have things as good as I could wish. The only thing that could induce me to go to Sweden is the pleasure of being with you. Uncle and Aunt say that we may expect you, but we do not want to insist. We will soon make our decision, and we wish you would write as soon as possible whether you have any thoughts of coming to America. In our next letter we will inform you of our plans, but I do not believe that I can leave this place until death takes me away. We live better than the people in Sweden, and we are not wanting in spiritual food. When I compare conditions here with those in Sweden, we are fortunate. We have good bread and wheat flour and as much beef and pork as we desire for each meal. We have all the butter, eggs, and milk we need. Last summer I sold twenty dozen eggs every two weeks. Last fall we made a barrel and a half of good sugar syrup for cooking fruit. Last summer I cooked cherries in syrup. . . . We have an abundance of various kinds of apples. In fact, we have so many things that make for comfort and happiness that, when I compare Sweden with this country, I have no desire to return. But, on the other hand, when I think about Sweden's healthful climate and how pleasant it would be for us to be together, I confess that I am a little dissatisfied, especially since Gustaf passed away. It is a joy to see my brother-in-law and sister-in-law, but they have sold their farm, and it is hard to say where they will move. Oliver's younger sister Christine married an American last fall, and they moved to a town called Pella.

I will write what we are doing. Oliver is plowing corn, and I am busy sewing dresses. I intend to spin soon. We have about thirty pounds of wool, half of which I am going to have spun by machine and the remainder I am going to spin by hand. I am going to weave clothes for Oliver, and I intend to sell some cloth. Last fall I sold cloth to my nearest neighbor for two dollars per yard. She expected her daughter and son-in-law last summer, but the daughter and her two children died on the journey. . . .

The early part of the winter was severe, but after Christmas the weather was fine. We have just had a good rain, and everything looks fine.

I will close this letter with cordial greetings to my father and mother, brothers and sisters, and relatives.

Mary Stephenson

Stephenson, "Typical America Letters," 78–79.

*The first Swede to settle in Texas was S. M. Swenson, who arrived there in 1838 and eventually persuaded other countrymen to join him. In 1867 his nephew, Johannes Swenson, came to Texas with a group of some hundred young immigrants. Johannes's account, written in 1917 on the fiftieth anniversary of his arrival, gives a good picture of ocean travel in the early days of the new emigrant steamship lines.*

A beautiful summer day early in the morning of June 12, 1867, a large crowd was gathered at the railroad station in Forserum, a village in central Sweden. The occasion was that Daniel Heard and family were going to America for the second time and with him a group of about one hundred young men and women, all with few exceptions from fifteen to thirty years of age. Many people were gathered to say a last farewell to their relatives, and many fathers and mothers, their voices stifled with tears, gave utterance to "God be with you, my son, my daughter."

But we cannot stay here any longer as the locomotive is sputtering and the conductor is shouting "All aboard." When we were all on board, the engine gave a powerful jerk and our trip to America had begun. Soon we arrived in Jönköping where additional travelers joined us. Many friends were gathered to say a last farewell. The next stop was Falköping, our train being a special train from Forserum to Gothenburg. Here there was another great addition to our party from places in Skaraborgs province. The next time our train stopped we were in Gothenburg, where we arrived the same day, June 12. The next day we were all out sightseeing in the city. In the afternoon we called at Mr. Lyon's office as he was the agent of the Inman Line with which we were going to travel. Here we received our tickets and our Swedish money was exchanged for American dollars, but there were not many as worldly goods were rather meagerly represented in our party.

In due time, on the fourteenth we went aboard the steamer *Hero* which would take us from Gothenburg to Hull, England. We said farewell to many friends who had accompanied us to Gothenburg and shortly before sundown the S.S. *Hero* lifted its anchor and steered out into the Kattegat. We were all on deck as long as we could catch a glimpse of our beloved fatherland, which many of us would never see again. The next morning we were in the North Sea. There was a cold wind and high waves; with few exceptions all were seasick. From all quarters one heard groans, "I am so sick I believe I shall die! . . . Would that I had stayed at home instead of dying in this misery," and other similar expressions. As stated, the waves were running high, but the *Hero* was a good little steamer and made progress in spite of the waves.

On the afternoon of the sixteenth we caught a glimpse of the English coast and in a couple of hours we were in the harbor of Hull and went ashore. Here an emigrant agent met us and we were stowed in a hotel. I say "stowed" as it lacked ordinary conveniences. It was Saturday when we landed in Hull and our trunks and other luggage remained aboard the steamer until Monday. On Sunday most of us looked over the city and early Monday morning we were on the steamer's deck to see that our belongings were in good order and to arrange for the transfer to the railroad train which would take us to Liverpool. It was a special train, exclusively for emigrants.

The countryside around Hull had great natural beauty in its summer attire, a more glorious picture one could not ask to see, but it did not last long and when we approached Liverpool the entire stretch was that of a huge factory town—high chimneys and from all dense smoke columns rose to the sky.

Finally we arrived in Liverpool and after leaving the train, the three baggage cars were switched to another track and we were hustled off to an emigrant hotel with Mr. Lyon and Mr. Heard at the head, a policeman on either side, and one in the rear so that no one would get lost. The emigrant agent who met us was a half-blood Negro. There was a frightful commotion when our luggage was to be transferred from the railway to the S.S. *City of Baltimore* as a carload had disappeared and could not be located. What should we do? All our possessions were in these freight cars and no one would leave Liverpool without his belongings. We were compelled to go aboard the *City of Baltimore* and Mr. Lyon assured us that our effects would be located and shipped to New York. However, just as the Atlantic steamer was lifting its anchor we saw a small boat dart out between the larger ships and approach our steamer at high speed. All eyes were fixed on the little boat and as it came closer we recognized Mr. Lyon in the bow waving with an object in his hand. In a few minutes it was alongside and soon everything was on board and the *City of Baltimore* was gliding out of Liverpool harbor on the afternoon of June 20 with about one thousand passengers and a crew of one hundred twenty-five.

About the city of Liverpool there is not much to tell as I saw only a little and that did not make a good impression. One saw ragged, half-naked and dirty street boys by the hundreds, large gray houses, and filthy streets and alleys. But it was a trip to America which I was to write about, not cities and scenery, so we return to the *City of Baltimore*.

As already stated, the anchor was lifted and our course was steered to Ireland where a large number of sons and daughters of the "Emerald Isle" came aboard. Then our course was westward and we were soon again in the Atlantic Ocean. The weather was beautiful, the sea was calm and the *City of Baltimore* made good headway. The food was good and the treatment by officers and crew, all one could desire.

Occupation aboard varied greatly. Many read and sang songs while others danced to the music of an accordion; others engaged in finger-pulling and wrestling and many other pastimes were devised, more than I can name. The weather was beautiful the whole time we were in the Atlantic and the days were all alike.

On the morning of June 29 the lookout shouted "land." There was a terrific rush to get up on deck as all wanted the first sight of our future homeland. Soon we could see the Goddess of Liberty.[3] As we approached at good speed we could clearly see her as she stood with the torch extended as if to welcome us. Now we are directly in front. The *City of Baltimore* fired a cannon as a salute and all heads were bared. Shortly before sunset, Saturday, June 29, the *City of Baltimore* cast anchor and we had arrived in the highly publicized Land in the West. The voyage over the Atlantic from Liverpool to New York was made in nine days and six hours, the fastest crossing up to that date. We remained on board the steamer until the following Monday. The banker S. M. Swenson and the missionary Hedström came to see us on board the steamer. On Monday morning, July 1, we went ashore at Castle Garden and underwent medical examination. Here too the missionary Hedström met us and handed out tracts and New Testaments, both in Swedish and English. How the party as a whole fared during the stay in New York I know very little as I and a few others were taken by Mr. Hedström to a boardinghouse. After two days we moved to Mr. Swenson's home on Atlantic Street, Brooklyn. Now we had the opportunity to look extensively about the city. On the fourth of July with the banker Swenson as leader we took a street car to Central Park, but to describe all we saw there is impossible. After dinner at a restaurant we went to Barnum's museum. Among the remarkable displays were also General Tom Thumb, his wife, and baby.[4] Later we went to Swenson's home for supper. In the evening we visited Brooklyn Heights where we saw the grandest fireworks we had ever seen.

Saturday, July 6, we all boarded the steamer bound for Galveston. The name of the boat I have forgotten, in the event that it ever had a name and, with the reader's kind permission, I will include the captain, the ship, and crew in one bundle and call it all trash. We were all aboard the steamer and steered out into the Atlantic Ocean. The weather was beautiful and the sea calm, but a severe storm came to meet us and the waves struck our boat with terrific force. There was a creaking and a crashing, the mast and the entire ship trembled, and a cry came from the engine room that the ship had sprung a leak. In a rush the pumping equipment was put in motion, but it consisted only of an old wooden pump operated by hand, heavy labor which required many hands and which continued without the slightest interruption for two days and two nights. Fortunately there were many strong men on board so that we could change places, otherwise all would have gone to the bottom. The old pump spurted a stream of water continuously four inches in diameter, requiring three men at the pump handle.

Another unpleasant incident added to the difficult situation. The first mate quarreled with the cook and shot and killed him. With the prospect that at any moment we might go to the bottom we arrived at a harbor in North Carolina. If I recall correctly it was named Smithville. Here the damage to the ship was repaired after two days. We saw a little of the destruction caused by the war due to a battle between a

Northern fleet and Southern troops. Many destroyed ships lined the water's edge; on the shore were long breastworks and behind them the graves of the fallen warriors.

Our next stop was Key West where we arrived on July 18. Our food had been bad and insufficient. We spent two days there unloading cargo from New York and took on a cargo of coconuts and bananas. In the tropical heat some of our party took a good salt sea bath but forgot that we were under a tropical sun, so their backs were sunburned, something that caused a great deal of discomfort for the remainder of the trip.

We hoped to get more and better food as the captain had been ashore to get provisions, but we were greatly deceived as they became worse daily. Shortly before sundown on July 19 we left Key West. All the sailors were drunk and a bloody fight arose among them. All left their stations and the ship drifted aimlessly before the wind and waves. About midnight the crew sobered up so that our course was set toward Galveston, where we arrived July 22. The last days on board we subsisted on a few potatoes, a few drops of molasses, and some hardtack. The per capita allotment of drinking water was about one quart daily. However, we thought if only we get to Galveston all will be well, but upon arrival there we were placed in quarantine and kept there three days on account of the yellow fever. Our food remained the same as before.

When the quarantine was lifted we boarded the steamer that would take us up the Buffalo Bayou to Houston. Here we got the first good meal since we left New York. We left Galveston and steered into Buffalo Bayou shortly before sunset. It was a beautiful moonlit night. How delightful it was to stand on deck and let the leaves of the trees on shore pass between the fingers. About midnight the ship stopped to take on wood. I shall never forget how glorious it felt to put the feet on solid ground again. It was also the first time on Texas soil. After the wood had been loaded the ship continued up the bay and at four in the morning we were in Houston. Here we were met by Gust and Wilhelm Forsgard and Mr. Wettemark who was in Texas to collect insects for a museum in Stockholm, also some other Swedes who had arrived in Houston a year earlier. Some of our party were invited to Mr. Forsgard's home about a mile south of the city limits, which I learn is now in the heart of the city. In Mr. Forsgard's home we had a hearty reception and stayed a few hours. Then again to the city and at one o'clock we were on the train bound for Brenham.

Houston at that time appeared to be no larger than Round Rock is today. The railroad between Houston and Brenham was very bad and it jolted as if we were sitting in an old farm wagon. Especially defective was the bridge across the Brazos River. The train moved very slowly and it creaked and cracked so that I expected that we would fall into the watery deep.

Late in the afternoon we arrived in Brenham where S. W. Palm, Otto Swenson from Austin, also Johan Israelson and a wagon from Mrs. Parson met us. We took our baggage from the train and loaded it on the wagons whereupon S. W. Palm and Otto Swenson announced that supper was ready, which we shared together. Next morning we were up early. Some of our party remained with Mr. Forsgard in Houston, namely fifteen manservants and two servant girls,[5] and here in Brenham the rest of the party separated, some bound for Manor and Austin, others to Brushy in Williamson County.

After a good breakfast our caravan started. All the men had to walk as the wagons were heavily loaded with our baggage and the women and a few children who were with us. We now had a warm struggle ahead. To walk in the deep sand in Washington and Lee Counties was no small matter. But we went ahead steadily although the sweat poured in streams down our cheeks and backs. We soon found that our old Swedish clothing was too heavy in this warm climate; however, we plodded bravely onward and perspired.

Finally at eleven o'clock on July 31 our party came to a halt at John Palm's house in Brushy, the present Palm Valley.[6] We had reached our destination and many of the Swedes who lived in the neighborhood came to extend a welcome.

This ends my story. I am convinced that none of my traveling companions had the remotest thought that we should live to see the splendid results now manifest in the large and beautiful Swedish communities which have sprung up in many parts of this great state. God's will has been done, a miracle before our eyes.

Johannes Swenson, "A Journey from Sweden to Texas 90 Years Ago," trans. Carl T. Widén, *Swedish Pioneer Historical Quarterly*, 8 (1957):128–35.

*After trying his hand at one thing and another, August Andrén from Halland led a mixed gang of Scandinavians to the area around Fort MacPherson in western Nebraska to cut railroad ties on contract in 1867. Here he reminisces about encounters with the Indians.*

. . . We still had not seen any Indians although we knew that we were in the Sioux Indians' territory, but we were not sure of our scalps and one evening as we were sitting around the campfire, we heard a rustling some distance away which gave us a real fright.

"Put out the fire!" Schwartz commanded.

"Get rid of your pipes," whispered the Knalle.

"God damn it, be quiet," urged Olle.

I, for my part, looked for my revolver, but Rundbäck considered this much too reckless and pointed out, those are not Hallänningar[7] you have to deal with, and when I aimed at where the rustling was still coming from and asked if it was friend or foe—now he would have to look out for himself for I would shoot—the Norwegian grabbed a chunk of firewood and said that if I could not keep my mouth shut he would help me, for here it was no use to show one's daring but rather to commit oneself to the care of the Almighty and act friendly, for we could not manage a fight with the Indians. Well, there we sat and listened to the rustling in the dry leaves and did not know whether it was Indians or wild animals, but later at night it became quiet and sleep overcame us. When we woke up and investigated the place, we found a very large rat that had made off with a hunk of pork, and had made all the noise in the leaves, and then had finally eaten itself to death on it.

Fort MacPherson lay in the northwest part of the present state of Nebraska and in those parts there seldom used to be cold winters, but at the end of 1866 and the beginning of 1867 there was severe cold and much snow, so we had to build a cabin for the winter, and this we put up in the old Swedish manner with a rooftree, with a large fireplace at one end and a window opening in the roof and a place for a bed over the door. The work force had been increased by the younger Peter Jansson, who had found where we were, and a good-natured Smålänning,[8] Johannes Blomberg, and we had provided ourselves with two teams of oxen and the cutest little Indian pony which we used as a riding horse, and which for speed could compete with the antelope.

Odel had gotten a Copenhagener, Jens Rasmusen, for a partner in driving one of the ox teams.

During the winter everything went smoothly, but by spring the redskins began to get restless. One day a German came and asked for work, and we let him eat his fill and sent him farther up into the woods where a Frenchman was camping, and there he got work; but a few days later he was no longer. One night a man came riding from the Frenchman's camp at a hard gallop and cried that the Indians were murdering and plundering, and urged us to flee. Since we had chosen a good location for our dwelling with only a narrow access road to the ravine and were well armed, we had no fear of being overrun but we posted a guard and kept watch the next day. In the Frenchman's camp the savages had been on a real rampage and among the dead was the poor German, who had been scalped because of his fine hair. A detachment from the fort was sent out to pursue the Indians, but only a few of them returned. The Indian creeps up on his prey from the bushes or silently shoots the poisoned arrow from where he lies concealed in the high grass. If they see they are in a position to win, they charge in a mass like a whirlwind, giving a war cry—the Indian yell—which makes the blood freeze in your veins, and it is quite impossible to manage a horse in a fight against them.

One day in the spring when we had made camp on the prairie, five miles west of the fort, to have the timber inspected which we had driven down during the winter, a scene unrolled before us that aroused alarm in the camp. The whole plain, as far as we could see, was covered with red warriors, and that they were on the warpath was shown by their painted faces and by the fact that not a squaw or a papoose was with them. Immediately I jumped into the saddle and rode off to Morén's ranch and told Mr. Morén to ride out to meet them and find out if they intended to attack us, for in that case we were determined to sell our lives as dearly as possible, and they would not get by unless they promised peace. Morén, who was the government's paid interpreter for the Sioux Indians, immediately raised the flag as a sign that they should stop until he could talk with them, which then took place.

When he came back he said that they had indeed prepared to fight, but first they wanted to find out from the commander at the fort if their promised support was not forthcoming, for in that case they intended no harm, but if this did not work out, no one would be spared.[9] Thereafter, the whole swarm passed by at some distance from us, for we had entrenched ourselves as well as we could, and had our guns at the ready. Later in the afternoon they came back from the fort and then they were so contented that there was no danger at all; you had to shake hands with the most important of them and they asked for "pappiehes" (money), "killikineck" (tobacco), and "minniaka" (liquor). Minni means water, minnioka is coffee, and minniaka is spirits. They were big, powerfully built fellows, almost all of them, with prominent cheekbones, crooked noses, and strong chins. Their features were hard and determined and their gaze bold. Their hair, which was bristly and pitch-black, was worn high on the top of the head, with several turns of woolen cloth wound around it, into which several large eagle feathers were stuck. I threw my jacket onto a pile of timber. A large Indian rode over on his pony intending to appropriate it, but I hastened to put it back on. He gave me a long look and looked toward the sun, beat his breast and closed his eyes and pronounced the word "socko." By this he meant that when "socko" (the sun) had gone down, it would be nice to sleep under the warm coat. The cook, William, put a kettle of dried apples on the fire. A very old warrior sat down by the fire and was going to try the tobacco he had begged, and then he pointed at the simmering kettle and made it known that it would be good if he could taste the fruit. "Take off the pot and give the old man a spoon," I said to William, and therewith began a meal that lasted as long as there was a bit of apple left. It was really a pity about the old man, for he did not know that the apples would later swell up and probably burst his stomach, but he was so old that his time was up, although that would hardly be a pleasant way to go.

Somewhat later in the summer, the Indians pulled up the railroad tracks and when the train derailed, it was attacked and plundered. One of the passengers, who later came to out in the grass, found he had been scalped but found his scalp which had been dropped in the confusion and took it with him down to Omaha and exhibited it there, the newspapers claimed. After this attack on the railroad, the government saw fit to negotiate with the Indians. General Sheridan together with a number of officers and troops came to North Platte and called both the chiefs of the Sioux tribe to a meeting. The elder of them, Spotted Tail, was the more accommodating and demanded only that since the white man's advance into the West had spoiled the hunting, the government should compensate him and his people with clothing and grain, as well as three dollars per month for every male, and this the general promised on the government's behalf. I stood and listened to this agreement and almost shuddered when I thought of how the government commissioners would keep for themselves a large part of what the Indians were to have, and how the latter in rightful indignation over this would attack and take out their grievance on peaceful settlers who had never done them any harm, for the Indians' outbreaks of violence are often the result of broken agreements.

The younger of the chiefs was called Red Cloud and he did not look mild on that occasion. He spoke briefly of how the palefaces had forced the red man farther and farther westward and that it had most recently been agreed that the northwestern part of Nebraska and Wyoming Territory, together with the Black Hills, should form a reservation for the Sioux Indians:

"And now, in spite of this, the palefaces come creeping like swarms of ants into their area and cut down their forests, and they have got a machine going that rushes along and says puff, puff, puff, and when the buffalo hear this they are frightened and run off. I have heard my brother, Spotted Tail, give the white war chief peaceful promises, and if his heart tells him this is right, he should do so; but my heart tells me that the white man wishes only to deceive and drive out his red brother, who owned the land when he came here, and therefore I have no choice but to fall like my forefathers for the right of my people. My decision, and my people's, is to fight to the last man. Red Cloud has spoken."

A long and bitter struggle followed between the Union's soldiers and Red Cloud's warriors, and if General Sheridan had not found and armed three hundred Pawnee warriors, it would have caused greater losses among the whites. Some days after this meeting, a group of Spotted Tail's people came accompanying his daughter, a red beauty of the first order. A warrior led her horse, which was saddled. Two poles with their ends crossed lay on the saddle and the large ends dragged on the ground behind. Right behind the horse a rug was made fast between the poles and there she sat wrapped in red blankets. She pointed at us and laughed, and I am quite sure that none of us found favor with her. She was then just in her golden age.

Already by the beginning of April, the thick snow cover had begun to melt and when a heavy rain followed, the ground was soon bare and before long clothed itself in the pleasant green of spring. From the fertile soil there not only grew luxuriant grass but the ravines were filled with wild grape vines, which twined around the slender cedar trunks, and wild plums, currants, and berries in great plenty.

This tract could rightly be called a little earthly paradise, with all its manifold blessings, were it not for the serpent; but this was present in the form of the Sioux tribe's twelve thousand red warriors, who to be sure were not on the warpath, but when they could catch a white man on their wanderings, he was no more to be seen. It often happened that when a man came alone, driving his load of timber, an arrow came whizzing through the air and plunged into his breast, after which the harness was cut from the horses, which were taken as a prize. For the summer, I and my companion had undertaken a delivery of beams and telegraph poles, and to manage that we sold our oxen and bought three teams of horses for fifteen hundred dollars, and we took room and board with a Swedish rancher, Conrad Eriksson from Värmland, who together with his family, wife, and three small daughters had come to this place during the winter and had timbered up his house right near the fort. Our gang worked out in the woods, but because we were so many and well armed—each man had two revolvers and a carbine and two hundred rounds at his disposal—the small bands of wandering Indians did not consider it wise to disturb us.

August Andrén, "Som emigrant i USA på 1860- och 1870-talen," *Halland och hallänningar, Årsbok 3* (Halmstad, 1956), 40–46.

*After his sojourn on the western plains, Andrén returned to Omaha. Here he gives a picture of social life in the Scandinavian colony.*

. . . The year before, the Scandinavians had held a meeting, called together by the Dane, Valdemar Nelson, and established the Scandia Society, of which Nelson became president, and this society, which I belonged to even while away, had grown considerably. That was not surprising, since before the church was founded the society was the only thing that held the Scandinavians together in the city of Omaha. The purpose of the society was to provide the opportunity for Scandinavians living in Omaha to gather in order to exchange ideas and debate questions, which each time were set up for discussion at the following meeting. Those of the society's members who so wished were also to be given the chance to practice singing under song-leader Hartman, and finally the society, in the event any of its less prosperous members became sick, was to pay for a nurse and also to pay the unfortunate up to eight dollars a week, and when immigrants came from Sweden, Norway, or Denmark, to provide them with advice and help, as well as economic assistance if needed.

The society had its meetings every Wednesday evening from six to eight, presided over by the president, vice-president, secretary, treasurer, and sergeant at arms; the latter had to go around with the ballot box, a box with white and black balls with which the voting was carried out. From this it will be seen that we had the same fine manner about us as our higher courts when they reach their decisions, and no one became a member of the society without first being sponsored by a member and then being voted on. The society was very careful of its reputation, so it happened that the black balls were often in the majority when such a vote was taken, and it was then entered with great solemnity into the minutes that N. N. had failed to pass the vote for membership. The latter then took his hat and the sergeant at arms opened the door, and the members looked around at each other for signs of repressed merriment.

Now and then the society arranged a ball on a Friday evening between eight and twelve. The admission for gentlemen was one dollar and twenty-five cents—supper included—and the ladies got in free, which is to say that no ladies came who were not invited. Some evenings before, one had to invite his lady and was told to fetch her at 8:00 P.M. It could then happen that one had to stroll up and down for half an hour on the sidewalk and see the shadow of one's partner for the evening against the blinds on the second or third floor; the cold could be so great that the walls creaked and one's mustaches turned as white as an eighty-year-old's before the door opened and a lovable little voice exclaimed: *"You will excuse me, my Dear, for I happen to let you wait on me?"*[10] And so one would have to be prepared to reply through half-frozen lips: *"Of course I do,"*[11] but the words *"of course"* can also be a meaningless phrase, for it would be much more natural that one were ready to give vent to his feelings in reproaches for having had to serve as a sentry out in the cold. But how many truths must not be passed over in silence to avoid hurt feelings, and when one's lady took off her hat and wrap in the wardrobe, and came down into the ballroom radiant and happy, one was expected to say: *"O! what you look beautiful this evening!"*[12]

After such a little compliment to his lady, Ket Lundvall, my friend Andrew Borg came to me and said: "Here you have to go and be polite because you had to get frozen through waiting for the soldier's daughter[13] from Ystad to get the flowers in her hair to sit just right." Borg was the son of a prosperous farmer from Jönköping *län*[14] and thought it was going too far to have to make much over a soldier's daughter. But Ket was seventeen and very pretty and worked for a rich family, whose ways she had taken on, and since she was not yet inclined to marry, Borg was often sorely tried when she felt like playing with his feelings.

The Scandinavians in Omaha could show a collection of pretty girls at their official functions. No thought was given to what their parents had been. Old Man Lundvall had been a soldier and had come out to America as a Mormon, but once in Utah, Lundvall was too much a genuine Swede to be able to stomach the Mormon prophet Brigham Young's humbug, and he therefore left both the Mormons' country and their faith and settled down in Omaha, where he rented lodgings on Bowery Place and mended shoes for a living. His daughters, Betty (Bengta) and Ket (Kerstin), worked for fine families in town and got eight dollars a week and were free every Wednesday and Sunday afternoon.

*Ibid.,* 48–50.

*On a visit to Sweden, an Augustana Lutheran pastor writes back to* Hemlandet *in Chicago:*

Kristdala, July 11, 1867

. . . Everywhere I am overwhelmed with questions about America. The upper classes and the ministers think it is entirely bad; the peasants think it is wholly good. The truth lies midway between the two extremes. I wrote an article for *Wäktaren,* and the editor made the stupid comment that what I wrote applied only to those who were "entirely at home in the English language." I made no reply to this. *Hemlandet* may explain the situation, if it sees fit. . . .

G. Peters

Stephenson, *"Hemlandet* Letters," 139.

~~~~~~~~~~~~~~~~~~~~~~~~~~~~~~~~~~~~~~~~~~~~~~~~~~~~~~~~~~~~~~~~~~~~

*A Mr. Sahlström sends advice for prospective emigrants to the newspaper* Nerikes Allahanda *(reprinted in* Hemlandet, *19 November 1867):*

From New York we traveled west by rail. . . . It was distressing to us, who were accustomed to see a legion of well-dressed employees at the stations and on trains, to see none but ordinary people dressed in working clothes in charge of everything, and so few in number that we, mindful of the poverty of Sweden, were driven to the thought that America must be insolvent if it had to be so economical with servants. . . .

This year . . . the crops are so promising that now, during the dull season, competent farmhands are paid as high as four dollars per day. Now you people at home must not get the impression that if you were in America you could earn four dollars per day the year around. And don't say to yourself: If I could only get to America, I would get rich— and similar thoughts. No one should come here in hopes of this. . . . Change of food and climate constitutes a kind of "new birth"; but it is alleged that those who are taken sick and recover are in better health than before. Whoever comes here must adopt new manners and customs. In many cases this is done too soon. The least attractive manners, disrespect and rudeness, are aped; religion is not taken seriously and is even held in contempt; an unbridled freedom and conceit reigns; and this state of mind sometimes brings a man to a point where, when reverses come, he curses and frets and blames the country for his own foolhardiness. . . .

In Sweden it is customary to enhance the price of an article purchased or sold by indulging in a drink of liquor; this is never thought of here even if the bargain involves hundreds of thousands of *riksdaler*. In Sweden it is the custom to serve guests at least coffee, tea, or the like; in this country it is also customary to serve the very best, but only at meals. In Sweden every person bears the stamp of his profession or occupation, which can never be mistaken; here it is difficult to distinguish a banker or a grocer in a group of working people. In Sweden even a man's life is taxed, if he possesses nothing else taxable; but here the person himself is not taxed. Instead rather heavy taxes are assessed on land and necessaries of life as well as on expensive furniture and vehicles. The latter form may have certain advantages, but probably does little to discourage luxury. . . . I do not write this to wound or to defame, but with the sincere wish that my dear native land either might become one of the American states or that America's laws and advantages, its good customs and manners, might be grafted onto Sweden.

*Ibid.*, 141–42.

*Mary Stephenson writes her family:*

Mount Pleasant, Iowa, June or July 1868

Dear parents, brothers, and sisters:

The peace of God be with you!

We send greetings to you all. Oliver has just finished writing his letter, and since he did not have space to write everything he intended, I will add this supplement.

Dear Brother-in-law Carl and Sister Johanna, you ask how you can put your money to the best advantage. You cannot buy a farm, because land is too high priced, but you can get a start by renting a farm. Renters get ahead much faster here than in Sweden. Those who want to own land go farther west, where the land is free. If you settle in this community, however, you can soon get started by buying colts and calves and harvesting fodder. Livestock develops rapidly, and it will not be long before you can realize on them. Oliver says he will help you all he can. You will not regret coming here if you do not encounter misfortunes—and misfortunes are met with in every country.

Day laborers are able to save money here—an impossibility in Sweden. I know of many who own farms who didn't even have gruel in Sweden. I am reminded of Jonas Peter, whose possessions on his arrival consisted only of his clothing. Now if his property were converted into money he could buy a good estate in Sweden, and this in spite of the fact that he married a poor girl, suffered misfortunes, and had no one to help him. But he is industrious and has a good wife. There are many similar cases. A housekeeper has few worries, because food is so plentiful. There is no necessity for begging.

A few weeks ago seventeen emigrants from Nydala parish arrived and made their headquarters with us. We housed and fed them, as they had no relatives or acquaintances. One family is still with us. The husband has been engaged to work two months for an American for twenty dollars per month, his wife and two children staying with us. She assists me in various ways. People are arriving from Sweden and from other countries and sections in large numbers; but do not worry over the danger of overpopulation, as Iowa is as large as Sweden and only half settled.[15] Then think of the other states! People come and go constantly.

I want to warn you that the voyage is trying, and some become seasick. I escaped that. Now, however, the voyage is so brief that it is a pleasure trip compared to what it was in former days. The sooner you come the better.

Addressing Sven and Christine, let me say that, accustomed as you are to the ways of Sweden, I doubt that you would be satisfied here, unable to understand the language of the country. But you would do well by your children, and Christine would no doubt have things better.

Now a few words with my parents. We are glad to know America is in your thoughts, but I am sorry that Mother is so reluctant. One of you will have to yield, and that of course will be difficult. But whatever you do, don't separate; if Father came without Mother, he would be so lonesome that he would see the dark side of everything and finally return. An old man who left his wife in Sweden came with Peter Gustaf. In this community there is a lonesome and dissatisfied man, making his home with his son, who left his wife. who in spite of the most urgent letters refuses to join him. He cannot return to her because they lived unhappily and had little in common. I advise you to come together, and I believe you will spend a happy old age here.

It may be that you are afraid we will expect some recompense from you, but that has never entered our minds. Don't let that worry you. If in the providence of God sickness should come upon you, we will perform our duty as your children and care for you. It is doubtful if Sven and Christine will stay at Bredagård until your days are ended. If you think it desirable, you might rent your farm and order the money sent to America in case you need it. But you know what is best, and it is hardly necessary to lay plans a hundred years ahead. I am sure that you will get along better here; you will not have to grind and cook and bake. Weigh the matter carefully. I am sorry for Mother if she is persuaded to go against her will. If Johanna is in the party, she can be of assistance in case of need. I hope what I have written will be taken in the right spirit. I do not want to take the responsibility of causing you to undertake something for which you will be sorry.

Our son thanks his grandfather for the present . . . and I thank you for the yarn. Our little daughter is the best baby I have ever seen. She is growing fast and, although only five months old, sits alone. I have a great deal of work, but my health remains good. We get ten gallons of milk from four cows. We sold a cow two weeks ago. I got over thirty pounds of wool this year.

I close with greetings to all. Write soon, and we will reply immediately.

Mary Helena Stephenson

Stephenson, "Typical America Letters," 91–93.

*It was not only in America that the emigrant was plagued by sharp-dealing "runners," according to this complaint in* Hemlandet *from a Chicago Swede back from a visit to Sweden.*

Chicago, October 25, 1868

. . . At the stations in Sweden we were grievously beset by lieutenants of emigration agents, and in Gothenburg the situation was deplorable, to put it mildly. What a fine thing it would be if this nuisance were done away with! I want to warn everybody who intends to emigrate not to take any stock in these agents, who talk and make promises as though they were angels of light, but do not know the least thing about what they promise. . . .

A. Hult

Stephenson, "*Hemlandet* Letters," 146.

*Heavy emigration during the poor crop years in Sweden between 1867*
*and 1869 more than doubled the Swedish population of the United*
*States, creating serious challenges for the Augustana Lutheran Church,*
*as explained by Pastor Hasselquist at the seminary in Paxton in a letter*
*to his colleague, Pastor Peter Wieselgren, in Sweden:*

1 April 1869, Paxton, Illinois

. . . Emigration this year is without doubt going to be terribly great
and will consist for the most part of people hostile to the church. We
must prepare ourselves for them here and maintain ourselves against
both Christian and un-Christian enemies of the church, to keep them
from inundating our congregations and blowing them apart. We are
at present suffering considerably in many places from itinerant, self-
appointed preachers, mostly of the neo-evangelical type, who see true
freedom in the dissolution of all order. We expect nothing but still
more bitter struggles. And yet, everything possible should be done to
win over the new arrivals for the church and the regular congregations,
and to place them under the influence of the holy and sanctifying
Word, so that as many as possible may be saved, both for the church
and for heaven. I have a suggestion to make, though I thereby only add
new concerns and perhaps expenses: in Gothenburg a "Word of Farewell" from the fatherland and its church should be put into the hands
of *all* who depart on the long sea voyage. I need not say what this
"word" ought to contain, but I believe that it could, with God's grace,
do much good. It should be serious, yet loving in tone, and should
make it a matter of conscience for the emigrants to maintain that for-
bearance which holds promise of deliverance in the hour of temptation,
even in the hour of death. The "Word of Farewell" could be and
remain a moving message of revival. I shall try to prepare a "Word of
Welcome," which could meet the emigrants in New York or Chicago,
or along the way. Norelius,[16] who because of his chest ailment cannot
preach but can and wants to write, will, I hope, take the authorship
upon himself. The unfortunate thing is that we do not have capable
and gifted workers to send among them right away. Right now many
should presumably be open to the gospel message, since the dangers of
the voyage and the sicknesses and difficulties that here await them, as
well as unexpected reverses, tend to soften people's attitudes; but after

a few years the doors to many hearts are closed, not only through death, but also through love for the things of this world and agnosticism, which now seems to be growing among the Swedes, a false belief. We have six or eight candidates here who are more or less ready to enter their calling at the next synod, but they cannot fill half the positions already vacant in the congregations. O Lord, send, according to thy promise, workers in thy vineyard!

In Germany they *prepare* crowds of candidates for the ministry to serve the Word in America; we have to work on our own. If this is a complaint, it is not directed against any of our brethren who share with us our concerns as though they were their own. May God reward them! But our work is heavy, at least for some among us. . . .

Gunnar Westin, ed., *Emigranterna och kyrkan. Brev från och till svenskar i Amerika 1849–1892* (Stockholm: Verbum, 1932), 224–25.

*Pity the poor Swedish postmaster!*

Kristdala, Sweden, August 24, 1869

To the Editor of *Hemlandet*:

The undersigned, superintendent of the post office at Kristdala, hereby requests the editor to urge through the columns of his paper emigrant Swedes to send their correct addresses to their relatives here and also to address letters to Sweden so that they can be forwarded to the right parties.

The addresses on most of the letters from America are in all respects so obscure that they cannot be delivered to the right parties. To take one instance among many: "Nils Persson, Sisala, Swerget."[17] This letter is first sent to Kalmar and Cristwalla and returned. Then perhaps there are fifty persons in the parish bearing the name Nils Persson, and the letter must be opened to ascertain, if possible, the owner. If the letter is unsigned, it will have to go the rounds of the parish until it reaches the right party. . . . Addresses sent home read "Wod hul," or "Ward Hult," "Iellenogs," etc.[18]

The majority of emigrants cannot write Swedish, much less English. Notwithstanding this, certain emigrants, in order to advertise their proficiency in the new language to their relatives, put a good many English words in their letters; but as these words are incorrectly spelled and put together, the letters are unreadable to the recipient. He brings it to the preacher to have him read it. If he cannot, it remains unread.

Therefore, everybody who writes home, as they call it, is urged to consult somebody who is a good speller and who can write a legible address to send to the addressee and one to keep as a model when he addresses a letter. Do not use English words, because they do more harm than good. . . .

If the Americans would make the little sacrifice of having their addresses printed and sent here, their relatives could address the letters themselves, and it would not be necessary for them to go to other persons with blurred pieces of paper to have addresses verified.

Correspondence from America is not so small at this place. Fifty letters per week are not unusual. Correspondence on both sides seems to increase every year. For this reason I take it for granted that the editor will briefly point out the above indicated mistakes in his esteemed paper for the benefit of our dear countrymen who may profit by it. . . .

Yours respectfully,
S. M. Körling

Stephenson, "*Hemlandet* Letters," 151–52.

*A voice from the Great North Woods:*

1869 Jan. 1, Du-Luth, Minn.
Dear Mother,

I am now up in the woods behind a little town which is called Du-Luth but you can hardly see it in the immense pine forest.

There are only a few houses down by the lakeshore and Rice's Point. Came here as a bookkeeper for a logging company together with a friend G. G. Barnum. He is a bookkeeper for another company.

It is no fun, dear little Mother, to trudge in the snow up the high hills, all alone in the wild forest, with a lot of money in your rucksack, when you don't know from one minute to the next when a gang of Indians will creep out from behind the trees.

They are so threatening and terrible. They held me prisoner a whole day, jumped around and grunted. I don't understand their language. I thought my last hour had come. Then I got an idea, that if I gave them the large package of tobacco I had bought for the boys maybe they would let me go.

They became completely wild with joy and stuck big wads in their mouths. I was able to go right away to my destination.

But there I was nearly beaten up by the boys, for I had given away their long-awaited tobacco. The poor fellows were all out of that commodity.

I had no Christmas this year. In the wilderness no Christmas was celebrated, which I missed. Jonas is down in Vasa, Minnesota. He writes that there Christmas was celebrated in a Christian way with singing and God's Word.

I am just now waiting for P. D. Lindén from Wislanda and Anders Johan Blomquist from Blädinge to come here to me.

Your son
Anders Petter Nyman

Unpublished letter, provided by K. G. Gilstring, Linköping, Sweden.

*The disastrous crop years ruined many who had incurred debts during better times, among them Gustaf Lindgren, a large tenant farmer in Skåne, and his wife, Ida, people of background and breeding. In 1870 they emigrated to America with their five children, Ida's brother, Magnus, his wife, Johanna, and a small group of other Swedes. Here Ida in her travel diary describes their arrival at their first destination, the little settlement of Lake Sibley on the open prairie, two days by wagon from Manhattan, Kansas. Thereafter her letters to her mother and sisters tell of their pioneering life near Manhattan. In 1881 the family, except for one daughter, returned to Sweden.*

15 May 1870

What shall I say? Why has the Lord brought us here? Oh, I feel so oppressed, so unhappy! Two whole days it took us to get here and they were not the least trying part of our travels. We sat on boards in the work-wagon, packed in so tightly that we could not move a foot, and we drove across endless, endless prairies, on narrow roads; no, not roads, tracks like those in the fields at home when they harvested grain. No forest but only a few trees which grow along the rivers and creeks. And then here and there you see a homestead and pass a little settlement. The closer we came to Lake Sibley the more desolate the country seemed and the roads were altogether frightful, almost trackless. When we finally saw Lake Sibley, at twelve o'clock at night, it consisted of four houses, two larger ones and two small, very small, as well as two under construction. The rooms Albinson had written he wished to rent us were not available but we were quartered here in Albinson's attic. The attic is divided into three rooms but with no doors; I have hung up a sheet in front of our "door." When I immediately asked, after we arrived, to go up with the children and put them to bed, there was no table, no chair, no bed, *nothing*, and there we were to stay! I set the candle on the floor, sat down beside it, took the children in my lap and burst into tears. I feel about to do so now too, I cannot really pull myself together and the Albinsons appear quite uncomfortable every time they see me. The Indians are not so far away from here, I can understand, and all the men you see coming by, riding or driving wagons, are armed with revolvers and long carbines, and look like highway robbers.

The Albinsons themselves are quite comfortable in their rooms and have a very handsome organ, which Olga has already tried out.

Gustaf is out with Magnus and Albinson to look at the land he bought and to see if there is any that Magnus would like to have. . . .

Ida Lindgren, *Beskrifning öfver vår resa till Amerika 1870. Dagboksanteckningar*, ed. Gustaf Lindgren (Stockholm: AB Svea, 1958), 37–38.

[No date. Probably written in July 1870 from Manhattan, Kansas.]

Do you know what I miss here most in the way of food? Really good sour-sweet rye bread and a glass of fruit drink, for such things do not exist here, though I hope someday to be able to make them myself. We were a fortnight at Lake Sibley and do you know what we got to eat? Fried pork and potatoes, butter, bread, and coffee for every meal, *every meal!* Have you ever heard of such a thing?

One thing that is pretty here are the fireflies, they look so pretty in the evenings. They do not shine steadily, rather there are a couple of seconds between each time they flash, and when there are many fireflies and they fly sometimes among the trees, sometimes high, sometimes low, it looks so lovely, for it gets dark right away in the evenings here.

Ida talks so often about all of you and says: "You can be sure that Aunt 'Lifva,' Gerda and Ellen and Sandberg miss us." She is good but so terribly dependent upon me. Anna is talking quite a lot now but ever since we were at sea she will not eat any food, she lives only on milk. Claus and his wife lost their youngest child at Lake Sibley and it was very sad in many ways. There was no real cemetery but out on the prairie stood a large, solitary tree, and around it they bury their dead, without tolling of bells, without a pastor, and sometimes without any coffin. A coffin was made here for their child, it was not painted black, but we lined it with flowers and one of the men read the funeral service, and then there was a hymn, and that was all.

Oh, if only I could soon hear a good Swedish sermon, one like Gottfrid Billing often used to give; it was so good and so enjoyable to hear him. One Sunday in Lake Sibley there was a Swedish church service; that is, there was a Swede who spoke and a couple of hymns were sung. It was quite fun and good, but he was an uneducated man and he often made such strange comparisons that thoughtless people smiled. The intention was nonetheless good, but there was still something missing. It was so good on the journey to have all the dear books I got from Mamma, Sven, Aunt, Louise, Adèle, and Gottfrid. Farewell, my dear, my beloved ones, pray for your

Ida

Ida Lindgren, *Brev från nybyggarhemmet i Kansas 1870–1881* (Gothenburg: Riksföreningen för svenskhetens bevarande i utlandet, 1960), 18–19.

20 November 1870, Manhattan, Kansas

I am now back in Manhattan and sewing, I have been here about eight days and don't know when I will be going home. I am now getting one dollar a day and it is good to be earning something, so I will stay here as long as they want me and I will surely stay over my birthday. It will feel both empty and strange to sit among strangers that whole day and sew; surely more than one tear will fall on my work at the thought of bygone times, of other birthdays, when I had you with me. Oh, well, how things have changed. I can rightly say, *"tempora mutantur."*

One day they had a party here. All were invited for eight o'clock, I think about thirty people, but they had all eaten supper before they came. The ladies elegant, in silk with many frills, but the gentlemen in everyday clothes, coats and worn trousers, boots the same. It is good form for the hostess or the daughters of the house right away to take the gentlemen's hats and caps. When all had arrived, part of the company, or rather most of them, went out into the kitchen, a large, pretty room, and I could not understand what they had hit upon there, there was so much laughing and carrying on. And can Mamma imagine what? Yes, they were playing blind man's buff; I burst out laughing when I saw it, for it is to be noted that there were no children there at all; those who were in the house had already been put to bed so as not to be in the way, but these were married people and a few young people. They must have gone on with their blind man's buff for a whole hour and then they played "borrow fire." Then the daughter of the house came and gave everyone a plate and a knife, and after her came the lady and offered a piece of cake, and then the man with apples, one apiece, and with that the party was over, at ten-thirty. These people were from the town's finest noblesse, persons who own many thousands of dollars. What do you think of that?

They would never touch a glass of wine or anything like that, even if there is company for dinner, and it is considered very improper to take a dram for the appetite. I have met a couple of girls here, one from New York and one from Leavenworth, visiting here in the house for a few days, two very pretty, charming girls with a fine, good upbringing; they spoke both German and French; it was fun to see people who were as polite and attentive as fine folk in Sweden. I can't help it, it really bothers me to see their manners here, the men's especially. They sit and talk with ladies with their caps on and rock themselves on a chair with their feet on the table. Usch! I get really angry sometimes and would so much like to teach them other manners, but I believe it would be wasted effort to try; rather I will just gradually have to accustom myself to considering it fine and proper.

When I was last home for two days we slaughtered a cow. She was so fat and pretty, but I had never (despite all the animals we had slaughtered at Köpingsberg) helped out myself; so it was hard. . . .

A little while ago the oldest son in the house here, a gawky 16-year-old boy, asked "what could I write such long letters about," and I replied, "I am writing a description of you and your home, how 'gentlemen' sit and talk with ladies with their hats on." He got red in the face, snatched off his hat, but afterwards he gave me sour looks. . . .

*Ibid.,* 27–29.


5 January 1871, Manhattan, Kansas

Dear, beloved Mamma,

It is Twelfth Night today and only now have I had the first peaceful moment during the Christmas season to write; I had meant to write just at Christmas but didn't have time. But today I am all alone in the house with little Anna and Ida, and so I can, I hope, be left in peace, at least for a while. Mamma's last letter I got a few days after my birthday; thank you for it, dear Mamma, and a thousand thanks for your unfailing love!

It was so cold, so cold, the week before Christmas, that we never felt the likes of it in Sweden. We have a thermometer with us from Sweden which cannot show anything lower than minus twenty-five degrees, but it was below that; we don't know how many degrees, but Gustaf's watch, which was in his vest pocket in among his clothes, stopped one night from the cold; there you can see that it was cold. When Gustaf warmed it up again in the morning, it started to go again; it was terrible.

We kept the fire going the whole day through and sat around the fireplace, and still we could see our breath when we talked. We piled everything we could think of on top of us at night and I sat up until midnight to tend the fire and then Gustaf got up at three and built the fire up again, and still we were so cold we thought we would get the chills, and Ida and Anna had frost on both their faces and hands, poor dears! Yes, it was hard those days and we thought we would become ill, but, thank God, no one has been sick yet, and now it is not so cold any more; quite to the contrary, it has been such fine weather some days that the children can play outdoors without even having to wear a shawl. New Year's Day was a real summer day, so that we had the door open for several hours and we were all outside in the afternoon and played *"banka läder"* and all sorts of games, and finally a long "curtsy-polka" up to the spring to drink the water and then inside for coffee on top of it. It was plus fourteen degrees in the shade, so changeable the weather is here!

I must tell you about our Christmas! On "Little Christmas Eve," Sylvan (he had been in Chicago but came here to celebrate Christmas with us) and Tekla Littorin (she is employed four miles on the other side of Manhattan) arrived, then we all went over to Magnus and his family for Christmas Eve. They had everything so fine and cozy, three rooms downstairs and the attic all in order, and a Christmas tree of green cedar with candles and bonbons and apples on it, and the coffee table set, so it was really Christmas-like, and because of that I could not tear my thoughts away from you and from my old home and the tears kept welling up! Magnus played and we were to sing, but it didn't go too well. Then we had a few Christmas presents, the finest was a rocking chair which Magnus and his family gave us. From Gustaf I got two serving dishes, since we had none before, from Olga a rolling pin for cookies and three dozen clothespins to hang up wet clothes with when you do laundry, from Hugo a pair of woolen mittens, from Littorin a knitting bag, from Hedenskog material for a little sofa which we have made for the children to sleep on, from Carlson a pair of fire tongs.

I gave Magnus and the family a sofa cover, which I sewed last summer to exhibit, and a couple of pictures of Gustaf Vasa[19] which we had with us. Hugo gave them a pair of drinking glasses and Olga gave Magnus a pipe pouch and Johanna clothespins like those I got. Helge had himself sewn a little lamp mat for them. I gave Gustaf a pair of real coarse, strong gloves for working, and Olga, Hugo, and Helge had gotten together to buy him a hat. Olga and Hugo had earned the money themselves that they used for Christmas presents.

After we had eaten our rice pudding and Christmas cookies, we sang a few hymns and "Hosianna," and then we broke up, though we all slept there, all the bachelors in the attic, Magnus and family in the kitchen, Gustaf, the younger children, and myself in the bedroom, and Olga, Tekla, and their hired girl in the parlor.

We stayed until the morning after the second day of Christmas and then we went home. Tekla, Ida, and Anna stayed on there, and so instead we took their hired girl and their hired man to help us slaughter our pig, which we were to have for New Year's, when Magnus and his family were to come to us. After we had finished with the slaughtering, I got started with laundry while we had Johanna's hired girl here, for it had been so cold that we had not been able to do any washing for some weeks, so now we had so much laundry. *Washing* is the worst work I have to do, for my hands can't take it and they have been so miserable, swollen and raw, that all the knuckles bled, but now it is better.

Then on New Year's Eve, Magnus and family came, with the hired girl and man and Tekla Littorin. Sylvan was already here, and then just as we were sitting down Nelander also arrived, so that with the little ones we were sixteen persons. Can Mamma imagine how I could find room for them all? Well, all the men and boys slept in the attic and all of us womenfolk down here in our only room, and we had lots of fun. We had spareribs and potatoes, rice pudding and a kind of American cookies that are quite cheap but good.

On New Year's Day, another Swede arrived, a Smålänning, Carl Anderson, who lives a bit on the other side of Magnus's, so there were enough of us! Tekla stayed until today and Sylvan is still here, I don't know if he is thinking of leaving now after Twelfth Night. He is meanwhile helping out with a will, so he is earning his keep.

All my menfolk are out in the woods today to cut fence rails, they took lunch with them so I don't know how long they will be away. Helge is in school. We are going to dinner at Magnus's tomorrow but will come home in the evening.

Now, dear Mamma, I will end for today, for I must tidy up a little here in the room before they come back from the woods, since it is Twelfth Night, and then I must skin two small hares for this evening, and therefore farewell for today. I long for a letter to come out today with Olga, who is in town.

*Ibid.*, 30–31.


8 January 1871

. . . On Twelfth Night we were at Magnus's and they were visited by three old American ladies, three sisters and widows all three. They came riding and the two oldest ones sat together on one horse, they were 64, 66, and 68 years old, and the 68-year-old jumped up onto the horse behind her sister as lightly as if she had been a young boy; what does Mamma say about that? I said to one of them that it surprised me that people rode so much here in America after they have become so old. She replied: "Our mother was a good bit over 70 and was out and rode a fortnight before she died."

*Ibid.*, 32.


Manhattan, Kansas, 9 February 1871

Dear Sister Oliva,

Now we are bombarding you like mad with letters, aren't we? But now it is a month until your birthday and before that I wanted this letter to reach you with my heartfelt blessings and good wishes for your happiness and well-being. May the Lord be with you, dear Oliva, and give you much grace and blessing. May He give you health and joy for many years together with all your dear ones, may the Lord give you everything that is best for you.

You will perhaps laugh at me for sending a couple of such simple collars such a long way, but since I so wanted to send something and just now had nothing to buy anything with, I decided to sew a couple of everyday collars, one for Mamma and one for you, out of some pieces I had left over from a couple of little aprons I sewed for the children for Christmas. And I don't think you will spurn them, but will wear them sometimes for my sake. Both Lindgren and Olga think I should not send such trifles, but I *feel* that one is made happy by every little thing from those one loves, and so I am sending them with this hope; another time maybe I can send something better. I had thought of sewing one for Ingrid, but since they think here that they are so simple, I don't want to, but if I knew it would please her I would certainly send her one.

It is so soon since I wrote that I almost don't have anything to talk about today, I am afraid. But I can at least tell you that I am sitting and writing on top of the stove, for since we do not have more than one table and Olga is ironing on it, I did not know where I should put myself. For I had to write today, because I had thought of going to Johanna's tomorrow morning, and day after tomorrow the letter is to go into town. But then Lindgren came in and also had to write something, and he calmly sat down and put all his writing things on the stove, and so I thought, "Ah, I can sit there too," and so here I sit now, rather uncomfortably to be sure, but still it works, and if my writing is too bad I blame the stove.

Magnus was here for a while this morning, so I can send greetings from them. They are well, but their hired girl has left so that Johanna now has to do everything herself, as I do. With the difference, however, that they are only two plus their hired man, while we are ten to bake and cook and wash up for every day, and worst of all, to wash clothes for. There is not much time for me to sit and do any handwork. America may be good in many respects, but certainly not for having servants. For no matter how good they may be in Sweden, as soon as they reach America's free soil they become far from good and want instead to be gentlemen and ladies themselves, and would rather be waited on than wait on others. It is hard to get used to this and therefore I think it is better to be one's own maid, though one gets awfully tired sometimes in both the back and legs. And my hands will not really accustom themselves to these tasks; they are sometimes roses, sometimes burrs, but never lilies smooth as satin.

I must tell about something that will amuse you. The other evening, it was past nine and we all sat and worked; one of the men was sitting and mending a sweater for himself and I was just showing Hugo how to mend his overcoat, when—there was a knock on the door, and when we said "Come in," there entered no less than twenty persons in couples. Young girls, quite elegantly dressed, and young men, and they sat down and began first to sing and then to play games and we taught them various games, which they greatly enjoyed. They and our young people amused themselves until past midnight, then all went home. They had all come on one wagon, which stood a little distance from the house, with three horses hitched to it.

What do you think, don't they have funny entertainments? They called this a "surprise party." After they had gone their way, we couldn't help having a good laugh over the whole business, though it was of course really very friendly of them to come and make the best of how we had it. We had never seen some of them. They neither greeted us when they came nor when they left, but when I said as they were leaving, "Come again" (politeness requires that you say these two words), they answered, "Thanks, we would like to."

We have now gotten more or less used to wheat bread with all kinds of food, with both boiled and fried pork and yellow peas, indeed with everything, though I often think about good rye bread and really good sour-sweet bread, which is my delight. The yellow peas sold in the stores in Manhattan are very good. They are hulled and split in two, so that when you cook them they completely dissolve, almost like strained peas, and so good. But they are rather expensive, so that we cannot have them often yet. I think it will be nice to have spring and warmth soon, although it is nice not to have to see snakes during the winter, which I can never think of without a shudder.

You may be sure that the wolves[20] come very close. Day before yesterday, three of them went by here in the morning, only a couple of hundred yards from the house, but they run as soon as they see a human, so they are not easy to shoot. And last night, when we were going to bed, I am sure there was a wolf right by the stairway when I opened the door. It was so dark I could not see, I only heard something running away and it could hardly have been anything but a wolf.

Our cows are not milking at all now but for a while we will have milk anyway; for six weeks Hugo will go every morning for an hour to feed the livestock for one of our neighbors, and for this we will get three-quarters of a gallon of fresh milk a day, but skimmed. But it is good to have a little. When this ends, I hope there will be some other way.

Now, dear Oliva, farewell for this time! Greet Mamma and Sandberg and your little ones and Wilhelm and Ingrid heartily from me. I so often dream that I am home with you and I weep so much with joy that I awaken. Shall I ever be able to weep these tears of joy awake? Farewell, may the Lord watch over all my dear ones in the old homeland. May He bring us all together in His true homeland, there not to shed tears but to sing songs of joy. Oh, were we but there!

Your Ida

*Ibid.,* 35–37.

Manhattan, Kansas, 18 October 1871

. . . I was alone at home with the younger children, for Hugo had ridden over to Lindesfrid[21] in the morning to help with the corn picking there, and around noon there was such a smell and smoke from burnt grass that I immediately suspected there was a prairie fire somewhere. Suddenly the smoke was so thick and ashes flew around (it was blowing up a real storm and the wind lay this way), that I couldn't see the nearest hills. I believed then that the fire was right upon us, so I ran in and gathered up the silver and Gustaf's watch and a little money all in a bundle, and put Anna on my arm and took Ida by the hand and ran through the woods down to the river. Oh, Mamma, how my heart pounded! I felt I could do nothing else, alone as I was with my little ones, for I believed that with the force with which the fire was moving today, it would go across the cornfield and set off all six haystacks and then there would be no saving the house. And then the woods were close by and there are now so many dry leaves that I felt there was no

9. Emigrants' baggage taken to the ship in Gothenburg.
(Courtesy of Sjöfartsmuséet, Gothenburg.)

"Bort till det stora landet i vester!"

10. "Away to the Great Land in the West!" (Pen sketch by Olof Granström,
from Ernst Skarstedt, *Vid hennes sida*, Portland, Oregon, 1889.)

11. Swedes in Kearney, Nebraska, ready to move out onto the prairie, 1886.
(Folkminnessamlingen, Nordiska muséet, Stockholm.)

12. Swedish homesteaders outside their sod house on the Nebraska prairie in 1886. (Folkminnessamlingen, Nordiska muséet, Stockholm.)

13. "Per Svensson's New Home in America":

1. "As he imagined it."

2. "As it actually turned out."

(Caricature from *Förr och nu*, Nordiska muséet, Stockholm.)

14. "Life in the Big City." (Pen sketch by Olof Granström,
in Ernst Skarstedt, *Vid hennes sida*.)

15. Swedish lumberjacks near Isle, Minnesota, around 1880.
(Courtesy of Dalarnas museum, Falun.)

16. "The biggest load of timber ever pulled by six horses." Isle, Minnesota, around 1880. (Courtesy, Dalarnas museum, Falun.)

17. A Swedish society in Cloquet, Minnesota, buries one of its members. (Folkminnessamlingen, Nordiska muséet, Stockholm.)

safety there. No, only in the river, there must I fly; if the fire should come so close to us I would take both children in my arms and go as far out into the water as I could: that was what I thought.

But first we sat down on the bank; Anna did not understand the danger, but Ida cried so bitterly that I had to try to calm her, fearful as I was myself. I told them, "We should pray to the Lord that He protect us." And so I prayed as well as I could, and the children repeated after me, and last of all we prayed for rain—for it had now been dry for several months and everything was so dried out that the fire could range freely, and no autumn grain could be sowed either until rain came. We sat there a couple of hours; once I took water in a spoon to drink but could not for it was black with ash that had flown here. When I thought the smoke had become less, I had the children sit where they were and I went up onto a rise to look.

Behold, there stood our house and home and the six haystacks unharmed, but a few that were out in the field and were intended for the owner were burned up, and the fire flamed on the other side on the hills and dales. We then went home and when we came in we fell on our knees and thanked the Lord who had protected us and our house and home. A little while later Hugo came: they had seen the fire coming toward us and Gustaf had sent him to help me, and a half hour or hour later Lindgren came himself, for all danger was far from past. I now felt so calm and glad, but they had to be out with water and rags with others to fight the fire until late at night, when all danger was over here. How far the fire later continued, we don't know, but many, many people had their hay burned up and we also had two small stacks at Lindesfrid that were lost. At Magnus's no hay burned but a section of fence. . . .

*Ibid.*, 45.


Manhattan, Kansas, 25 August 1874

Beloved Mamma,

It has been long since I have written, hasn't it? I think so at least, but when one never has anything fun to write about, it is no fun to write, so if it were not for the cherished replies and seeing from them that you are all alive and well, perhaps I would cease writing altogether. But no, I would surely not do that either, for at times I have a real need to speak with you in this way and thereby to some extent lighten my own cares by so to speak burdening you with them instead, especially Mamma. Yes, it is this that I find so unfair and therefore I ought never to write, or to write (if I could) a pretty verse about how we wander here on roses, caressed by the balmy breezes of the south. But alas, the roses are dried up, the grass, the corn, everything is dried up and the balmy breezes are burning instead, as if they came from a frightfully heated-up steam engine, so that we cannot leave the windows open, but must close them and pull down the blinds to keep out the dreadful heat, which many days has gone up to forty-five degrees Celsius in the shade.[22] That is to say, we have the thermometer hanging on the north side of the house, if it had been on the south side it would well have been over fifty degrees.

We have not had rain since the beginning of June, and then with this heat and often strong winds as well, you can imagine how everything has dried out. There has also been a general lamentation and fear for the coming year. We have gotten a fair amount of wheat, rye, and oats, for they are ready so early, but no one here will get corn or potatoes. We have a few summer potatoes but many don't even have that, and we thought and hoped we would get a good crop of other potatoes, but will evidently get none. Instead of selling the oats and part of the rye as we had expected, we must now use them for the livestock, since there was no corn. We are glad we have the oats (for many don't have any and must feed wheat to the stock) and had hoped to have the corn leaves to add to the fodder. But then one fine day there came millions, trillions of grasshoppers in great clouds, hiding the sun, and coming down onto the fields, eating up *everything* that was still there, the leaves on the trees, peaches, grapes, cucumbers, onions, cabbage, everything, everything. Only the peach stones still hung on the trees, showing what had once been there.

They are not the kind of grasshoppers we see in Sweden but are large, grayish ones. Now most of them have moved southward, to devastate other areas since there was nothing more to consume here. Certainly it is sad and distressing and depressing for body and soul to find that no matter how hard one drudges and works, one still has nothing, less than nothing.

Don't you think, Mamma, that I could bear a little bit of *success*? I think myself that I could well manage a little, but the Lord sees best what we need and therefore He daily strikes and humiliates us, now in one way, now in another. But still He has not crushed our stubborn hearts. As burdened as I feel, my heart is still not weighed down, it still rises up from time to time.

Tomorrow is a church Sunday, when we hope to get in to the service. Oh, could I but hear really powerful and encouraging words then. Pastor Scheleen, poor man, has a very hard time of it. He has a little patch of land fifteen or sixteen miles from Manhattan and a small house, which I suppose the little Swedish congregation there built for him, although they are all poor Swedes. And he has only one cow and one horse and his wife is very sickly besides. They have no children but have adopted a little girl. The last time I talked with him, I don't know how it came up, but I said I had such a longing to see all my people in Sweden again. He said then, "Yes, I am sure my wife would get well again if we could go to Sweden. But it is no fun to go there so poor." Poor people, I felt so sorry for them!

Ida and Anna go every afternoon and read a little English with a woman a little way from here, a good mile. But today they got to ride there with Pappa, he rode on one horse and the two children on the other, so that Anna sat and held Ida around the waist. They are so happy to be able to ride and ride alone on our young horse, "Alma," who is so gentle and tame. But Anna is still a little confused about the reins, which rein she should pull on when she wants to go to the right or left.

I have not been quite well for a long while but am better now. Alas, it is no fun to be sick in America! In Sweden, even illness had its poetic side, at least for me. Everyone looked after you and tried to make it as nice and comfortable as possible, and then Mamma came and took special care of you. But here you must drag yourself around as long as possible and tend to all your many chores.

Greet everyone, everyone, from
Mamma's own

Ida

*Ibid.*, 61–62.

Manhattan, Kansas, 15 November 1874

. . . Would you believe it, Magnus is contemplating a great deal over constructing a flying machine! He claims he has it worked out in his head, if he could only have it put together that way. He wrote to John Ericson[23] about it once but did not get a very encouraging answer, except that he (Ericson) was so overburdened with all sorts of mechanical speculations and had so little time to spend on them. But I don't think Magnus will let it go at that but will write to him again and clearly set forth his ideas. If Ericson can then make something out of it—then Magnus will have made his fortune and made a name for himself throughout the world.

You once wrote that "we would perhaps come like birds of passage and land on your roof," and Magnus commented that maybe you were prophesying without knowing it. "For," he said, "it is not impossible that we will get into my flying machine here and land, if not right on the roof, at least in the garden at Hammenhög." Sometimes I am almost afraid of his ideas about a flying machine, but such flying speculations are in the air in America, for farming is poor now. . . .

*Ibid.,* 63.

Manhattan, Kansas, 1 July 1877

. . . It seems so strange to me when I think that more than seven years have passed since I have seen you all; it seems it could not have been a quarter of that time. I can see so clearly the last glimpse I had of Mamma, standing alone amid all the tracks at Eslöv station. Oliva I last saw sitting on her sofa in her red and black dress, holding little Brita, one month old, on her lap. And Wilhelm I last saw in Lund at the station, as he rolled away with the train, waving his last farewell to me. . . .

*Ibid.,* 70.

*From A. P. Ahlberg's school for lay evangelists near Vetlanda, Småland, a number of young men went into the Swedish-American ministry, either through the Swedish state church or, more frequently, through the Augustana Seminary at Paxton (later Rock Island). However, by the 1870s the Augustana Lutheran Church's pressing need for pastors aroused overly sanguine hopes among many of Ahlberg's students, as the latter writes to Pastor Hasselquist in Paxton.*

27 February 1872, Ahlsborg, Sweden

. . . I would now like to ask you to be so kind as to send me a few lines as soon as possible to help me to calm my poor, dear students, especially those ten of them who want to go out to Paxton to become pastors in America as quickly as they can. Most of these latter are not only very ignorant but also very untried (after one or two years' stay here) and they imagine they ought to be able to make good quickly if only they could get out there. You can well picture their level of knowledge since almost all when they arrived here were nothing but raw farm boys, who could not read a book, write their names, etc. Now they have begun to learn to read English, and so forth, and right away they believe themselves ready for clerical ordination. They think they can be good ministers if only they have strong lungs to preach a lot of tautology or meaningless words, without any kind of logical order, etc.

I do not want either this school or the seminary at Paxton to be put to shame by such new arrivals, rather I see the need for the young men in general to stay here for three or four years and get a good grounding in various things. By this means I can also form a basis to make a necessary selection among the candidates. I also know that this reduces your great expenses in Paxton. I have thought that they ought to go through a certain definite course of learning here to be recommended for Paxton, corresponding in the most important subjects (such as languages) to the fourth or fifth class at the public *gymnasia*.[24] Besides this, I have now for the first time been able to push them a little farther along in English, through writing and small exercises in speaking, and wish them to become familiar with the New Testament in English. When I speak of such things to them, they become upset, indeed almost rebellious, and maintain that they know as much as many clergymen in America, etc. It has even been rumored that if I do not recommend them to the Augustana Synod's seminary, they will turn to the Wisconsin Synod (which is more liberal, and so forth). I believe it would sober them considerably if you would write to me something to inform them regarding the need for good, thorough preparatory studies and generally for a stay here of three or four years for beginners. I nonetheless hope, either this summer or in any case a year from now, to be able to recommend to you one or another candidate who is fairly well educated and steady. Forgive my haste. May God, our steadfast God, strengthen and comfort you in all your labors and cares for God's kingdom.

Your frail but devoted brother,<br>P. Ahlberg

Westin, *Emigranterna och kyrkan*, 326–27.


*Pastor Hasselquist replies:*


Paxton, Illinois, 28 April 1872

Dear Brother Ahlberg,

God's peace be with you in your work! Two letters I have received from your hand and I should have answered the first long ago; you must not, however, take my failure to reply too hard, it was not indifference from my side but my multifarious work that takes up time and energy, and soon enough even enthusiasm as well. Your last letter too has lain on my desk for some weeks and the day and hour for answering it have been set aside time and again, but necessary duties have intervened and ruined good intentions. So it has gone until now and thus I must forgo the chance to go with the crowd to God's house this evening to stay home and at least begin a letter to you; otherwise the later letter might remain unanswered like the first. I am heartily pleased to hear that you have in your school a not inconsiderable number of young men who wish to journey over land and sea to serve our countrymen in need out here, and the need in truth is great; indeed it grows constantly and the resources we employ here do not suffice.

But dear Brother! One thing I beseech you, that you keep the young brothers as long as possible so that none of them may undertake the long journey without the most thorough introspection and clear assurance of his call for the important work here. I have discovered that this self-examination is not so easily done. Many believe they only wish to serve the Lord, and still other things are in the backs of their minds; or else they imagine the work out here to be fun, and yet it is only for him who will bear it like a cross, following Christ's example. They think that because of the great need very little must be required to be a pastor among us, and yet even more is required here than in Sweden. We must not only found congregations but put in order those that already exist, and this demands experience, firm character, a knowledge of conditions and of people, and the ability to accommodate oneself to them in such a way that one builds up rather than tears down. Therefore I again beseech you: keep the dear lads as long as circumstances allow and let none go without assurance of the existence of both inward and outward gifts, as well as of their education, as much as is possible. You would thereby be doing not only us a service, but also the young men, who thereby can be saved from particular spiritual dangers, which to be sure they do not suspect, but which you surely can understand. This is not to say that we would not welcome with open arms a good fifty well-tried and capable men if you could send them to us the day after you receive these lines. But rather none than untried ones and such as believe that no particular "learnedness" is required.

They can certainly learn some English, but I believe nonetheless that too much time should not be spent on it since the language is learned much more quickly and easily here. They should be able both to speak and write Swedish *correctly*, and they should have some acquaintance with Swedish history, too, for those who leave Sweden are often asked here about such things. It would also be well for them to be well grounded in other general subjects, both for their own necessity as well as for the cultivating influence they exercise. We cannot manage without German. If you have students of mature years who seem particularly suited to the duties of the calling but who because of their age cannot be required to learn the dead languages, they need so much the more thorough training in other subjects. We have, to be sure, sent out into the vineyard workers with quite limited qualifications when we considered them to have the proper spirit and reasonable outward gifts, but this has proven more and more impossible to continue in the long run. Such men often lose the confidence of their congregations and they are looked down upon, something they should have the means to prevent (Tit. 2:15 and elsewhere), since God's cause thereby suffers irreparable harm. We are constantly raising the requirements for those who are to be ordained. Exceptions still occur and should always occur, but it is for those who through many years of faithful and successful activity as colporteurs or, as we call them here, catechists, have won the congregation's and the Synod's confidence.

In the above I have naturally not sought to prescribe any courses of study for your school, but only to express a wish as well as what we consider the best both for ourselves and for those who feel the call to come over here to help us. As for the latter, I should like to enjoin them in love to be industrious and faithful in preparation for the Lord's service and await the hour when the call will come; then they can go their way *glad of heart,* but before that time they would not have the Lord with them, they would work without blessing and with uneasy conscience and under fear of the day of reckoning. Oh, we must have the Lord with us, but this we have only when we go where He sends us. If they are governed by the love of Christ, they will understand my words. May the Lord preserve them in fear of Him in these egotistical times, when each and everyone wants to go his own way and believes it alone to be right. . . .

But what of Sweden? What a struggle seems to be in the offing even there. The "free church" people strain against the bonds and *bite* them to pieces if they can; the state church people cling to all the old forms, as if a state church were the only thing necessary to the existence of God's kingdom. The *improvement* of the existing church is thereby obstructed and its ultimate dissolution is indirectly prepared for. But where are there not perils? May the Lord only keep us steadfast.

Now this is all! God be with you, dear Brother! Greetings from your former students here; they are well and all are promising.

Yours in the Lord,
T. N. Hasselquist

*Ibid.,* 335–37.

*Pastor S. J. Kronberg later recalled the early days at the Augustana Seminary in Paxton, giving a personal glimpse of the stern but kindly patriarch, Pastor Hasselquist.*

One fine day, right after morning prayers, Dr. Hasselquist told us to stay for a few minutes. "There is something I want to say to you," said he. We all listened and thought, what might he have to tell us now? He began thus: "It is well known to you that we have no gymnastics here at the school. You also know the reason, it is poverty. It is, however, necessary for young students to get some exercise, so much sitting is not good in the long run. I have therefore thought of a way to take care of this lack of gymnastic exercise in a gymnasium hall—and that is for you by twos to saw and split a cord of firewood each." And so he drew his hand over his mouth, chin, and beard and lightly slapped his knee with the flat of his hand, and so it was time for us to go. Some of us farm boys immediately followed his admonition and as soon as we left the classroom we went straight to the woodshed and sawed and chopped so that the wood flew around us. Soon several cords of wood were sawn and split.

A week after this admonition our dear mentor found to his great indignation and dismay that not everyone had followed his well-intended and good advice. He then told us again to stay after morning prayers. We awaited with eager curiosity what was to come. He begins now in the following manner, with some flush to his cheeks and a very serious tone to his words: "A while ago I reminded you that we did not have any gymnastics but that you need some bodily exercise. I therefore urged you each to saw up and split a cord of wood, but to my great sorrow I find now that most of you have not wished to follow my advice. This shows that you do not have the right spirit, that you do not want what is good for you. If you gentlemen think yourselves too fine, or if you consider that your strength will not bear up under it, come to me and I will help you with your cord. I was a pastor in Sweden for thirteen years, and when I came here to this country I sawed and chopped, for three years, all the wood we needed for the household. And I believe I am as good as any one of you." He did not mince his words. We who had sawed and chopped our wood smiled somewhat smugly up our sleeves and looked at those who had not done theirs.

The "Swedish students," as we used to call those who had come from Sweden together with Dr. Hasselquist, thought that for a student to saw and chop wood—that was something they were not used to and which they found it hard to accustom themselves to and accept in this promised land. One of them whispered to another and said, "Fie! That is un-Swedish"; the other replied, but in genuine American. If we remember rightly, they hired one of us farm boys to saw and chop up their cord. But not even this was satisfactory for H., for he wanted them to do it themselves. But some "natives," who had come so far that they were up in the Seminary, did not feel embarrassed to saw and chop wood, to work in the cornfield, milk cows, help with the dishes in the kitchen, and so forth, even right up to the year when they were to be ordained.

Now and then someone complained about the food, but it seemed to us that since we lived like paupers, lived on the bread of charity, we had no real reason to complain. Whoever thought the food was too scanty was free to go into town to a first-class hotel. If anyone ever complained of the food, he was quickly told by H. just what he could do, and this usually had its immediate effect.

Some of us "pietists" were surprised that H. permitted the boys to play ball, blow on brass horns, and so forth. "Be not pious in excess," it says somewhere in our Bible, and we should perhaps have reflected on those words. We held conventicle meetings sometimes, but it did not work out well. The thing was that they were not called forth by any need.

S. J. Kronberg, *Banbrytaren. Historisk skildring af nybyggarlifvet i Nordvästern under en tid af trettiofem år 1870–1905* (Rock Island, Ill., 1906), 106–8.

*An Illinois pastor reports on his flock to the Augustana Synod.*

Farmersville, 17 June 1872

In accordance with the Synod's resolution, I wish herewith to report on the condition of the congregation here. First, concerning the congregation's religious and spiritual condition I must say that it is to be sure not by far what one might wish and no particularly outstanding signs of spiritual activity have revealed themselves. During the congregation's five years of existence there have been unending conflicts, partly over the building plan for the church, partly over the provision of the congregation with pastoral care, and this has in my view considerably hindered the blessings of the preaching of the Word and has formerly kept many from attending the public services. This conflict has now been resolved and a notable outward unity prevails. Divine services are now well attended when not prevented by excessively severe weather. The Word seems to be heard with much attentiveness and it is not so rare to see tears, too, running down their cheeks. Some there are indeed who now and then find their way to strong drink and show their attachment to it, but such cases are rare among those belonging to my congregation.

Sunday school is well attended and the children's reading, both to themselves and aloud, is all one might expect, and in the case of not so few one might almost say it is all one might wish. Much interest has also been shown regarding a parish school and some results of this reveal themselves, as already mentioned, in the Sunday School. Concerning sectarianism, we hardly know such a thing exists except on occasion when we read about it in the newspapers. For the Mission and other charitable works, what has been done is more or less what might be expected in view of the number of communicants and the position of the congregation. Still, there is need here for more of what is called the spirit of sacrifice.

Secondly, regarding the congregation's economic situation, I can report: that the church is under construction, 30′ x 40′, with an addition on the west end 18′ x 10′ high, to be used as a sacristy, etc. The church is expected to cost "enclosed" around $1,850. Through subscription, which for the most part was carried out through the issue of legal notes, a sum of about $2,000 has been collected and from the sale of forty acres of land belonging to the congregation $850 will come in, thus $2,850 in all. And for this sum we hope to be able to complete the construction of our church.

There is no parsonage for the present other than what the pastor provides for himself. For ten weeks of school-teaching plus the pastoral duties in general $200 are paid in salary for this year, besides lesser amounts that have gone for the same purpose. That this salary cannot cover the necessities of life should be clear; still less can it cover travel expenses to synods and conferences, etc., even if health permitted going to them. May the Lord give me greater strength to work with the gifts and energies He has given me and to await my reward from Him, not in earnings but in grace.

John Johnson

Widén, *Amerikaemigrationen i dokument*, 129–30.

~~~~~~~~~~~~~~~~~~~~~~~~~~~~~~~~~~~~~~~~~~~~~~~~~~~~~

*After four years in America, August Andrén, whose adventures in Nebraska have been recounted above, went back to Sweden in 1869 and settled down. Three years later, however, he was persuaded to recruit a railroad gang which worked first in New Jersey and later in Wisconsin. Here he recalls the misadventures on the first lap of their journey. Andrén returned to Sweden for good at the end of the year and was a prominent figure in his community until his death in 1904.*

It was at the beginning of 1872. I had gotten several letters from a railroad entrepreneur named Thomas P. Simpson—he had twenty railroads under construction—and he wanted me to come over and take charge of a job that was being carried out 20 English miles (3 Swedish) outside the city of New York. He promised that if any emigrants in search of work came over with me, they would get work at a daily wage of one dollar and seventy-five cents.

Good earnings beckoned to me from across the ocean, but since I had both taken a wife and bought a farm, it was not so easy to follow the call. For some months I then had the chance to learn how one ought to go about convincing his better half that it could be advantageous to put the ocean between himself and her, and then to get her to take upon herself all the responsibilities on the farm. My wife is a sensible woman and has never been stubborn, thus she gave way, though the promise was followed by tears.

When there is a snowstorm here in Halland we know that the longest it can last is three days, but at the end of March 1872 there was a snowstorm that lasted a whole week. It began on Sunday and therefore both I and the forty-odd emigrants who accompanied me believed that the storm would be over before Thursday, when we were to go up to Gothenburg,[25] but the storm and snowfall continued both Thursday and Friday, so it looked bad. But then I got a telegram that the ship had postponed its departure until Saturday afternoon at 2:00 and that day happened to fall that year right on Annunciation Day. We decided to go up on Friday, but it turned out to be in many ways a difficult journey. The Flabäck road was snowed under and it was impossible to hire carts at the inns for either love or money. I then decided to have my horses haul our things up to Gothenburg and hired in advance some horses and sleds from farmers north of Kungsbacka for those of the emigrants who wanted to ride.

It was not manly to weep, I thought in my younger days, and therefore I put on a brave front when at the turn of the road near Joesberg I met the whole snow-plowing team for Wallby district, as I was accompanied a bit along the road from home by my mother on one arm and my wife on the other, amidst sighs and snifflings.

At the Glädjen Inn in Kungsbacka, the emigrants were to take leave of their friends, and as I feared the merriment might become too great I went to Innkeeper Petersson and asked him kindly not to serve the travelers anything but wine. He became ill-tempered and replied that he would "sell whatever they asked for" and had full right to do so; but since I knew that the way from merriment to the clink or to landing headfirst in a snowdrift was unpleasant, I went into the big room where the emigrants and their leave-taking friends had gathered and bade them share a few bottles of wine and drink a parting *skål*, and then to part from their friends and start on the way to Gothenburg, and they followed this admonition from me. But I was suspicious of the treacherous hip flasks, so at Skårby I again hired a farmer with horses and sled, and took the road toward Kungsbacka. Quite right, three of our emigrants had fallen behind, and when we met them, the road was too narrow for them. We took the old road from Ahlafors past Annestorp, for the road was filled with potholes, and when we neared the latter place I heard from the sleds behind joyful cries that there was beer to be had in Annestorp. "Aha," thought I, and hurried ahead to the general store and bade the girl there to say that they had no beer. When the emigrants arrived, they stormed up the steps and ordered several

dozen bottles of beer but received the answer that "there was none."
They were later surprised that they could find no beer there, and I was
to blame that the Lindome girl told a lie and wish therefore that it
should be a "white lie," since I had her tell it.

When we came to "Galgkrogarna" or "Kloera," as the people called
the southern suburb of Gothenburg, and caught sight of Police Con-
stable Börjesson on patrol there, the comrade in my sled began waving
his hand at the policeman and shouted.

"So long, you 'Svedis man,' I'm off for America now."

"Sure, go ahead," said the policeman, but then I came to think that
when we got into the city where the police did not know our comrade,
he would land in the "Sausage Kettle" (as the clink was called) for his
loose tongue, so I asked to change places with the farmer who was driving and climbed onto the runners in back. When we came to a large
snowdrift, I got off and overturned the sled. After I managed a while
later to fish my comrades out of the snow and deplored their misadven-
ture, the journey continued to the emigrant hotel without a word being
uttered.

Gradually the whole group assembled at the hotel. The last to come
was Johan Peter Bolin, driven from Kungsbacka by "Per i Hvarla," and
thereafter we had an enjoyable evening, for we had not always been
able to sit with our legs under a blanket but at times had had to wade
through the worst snowdrifts. There was no sleep to speak of that
night, partly because the emigrants had to make up for what they had
lost in Kungsbacka and Annestorp, and then too they had so much to
talk about. How, now, one of our comrades had managed to do it, he
had gotten hold of a whole bottle of *brännvin* on Saturday, even
though it was a holy day, and with this he remedied his hangover so
that he went completely wild. When we passed the city hall and were
to get onto the barge to be taken out to the emigrant steamer, I was
afraid the person in question might try some mischief which would
land him headfirst in the sea and therefore I hailed a rowboat and took
him along in it and told the oarsman to take us around to the stern of
the ship. When we then had to climb up the rope ladder, he stamped
and carried on so that I thought we would both fall into the sea. On the
salon deck at the top of the rope ladder an old, white-haired policeman
was posted and he had taken note of the trouble I was having, and
when we finally came up face-to-face with the policeman, he seized my

comrade by the collar and made as if to throw him overboard. I have seldom seen anyone sober up and become reasonable in such haste as did the comrade in question.

Andrén, "Som emigrant i USA pa 1860- och 1870-talen," 75–77.

*Among the Janssonists who came over in 1846 was Anders Larsson from Västmanland. Larsson soon left the group and settled in Chicago, where he became a leading figure in the Svea Society. Here he describes the aftermath of the great fire of 1871 and the flourishing Swedish cultural life which early made Chicago the recognized capital of Swedish America.*

28 November 1872, Chicago

. . . To write about Chicago and its rising again from the ruins after 8 and 9 October 1871 belongs altogether to the unbelievable. Much, much remains to be done. Where before there were ordinary brick and wooden houses, there are palaces all with marble fronts (a kind of sandstone) or cast iron. According to reliable statistics, between 31 March and 1 November a house, from three to seven stories high (some of them taking up a half or a whole block along the front) has been put up for every working hour, reckoned at eight hours in each working day (although this, for all who are unfamiliar with conditions here, sounds fantastic and unbelievable, it is still undisputably true). Thousands and thousands of wooden houses, larger and smaller, have also been built outside the so-called "fair limits"; but inside the fair limits no wooden houses may be built. The city authorities keep a close watch over this, but all wooden houses that were started before 1 April inside the fair limits may remain until they decay or burn down. (We also took the opportunity and built two houses on the lot at 89 Ohio Street which we got back in court; the case cost seven hundred dollars, but now the lot is worth thirty-five hundred dollars). . . .

Now I should say something about our own affairs. We have had bad luck but, thanks be to God, it has not been disastrous. Through the fire we lost over five thousand dollars and we have not yet collected any fire insurance, but we shall get seven per cent next month, and how soon we will get more is not clear. We exchanged the lot at 98 Ohio Street and got another lot in the same block opposite the lot where we live, but it faces 110 Ontario Street. But we had bad luck; we were going to build a brick house three stories high and when the house was half built, the contractor disappeared and all the bills for materials and labor were unpaid (the law here is that all who have claims for debts can within twenty days confiscate the house or whatever else and the owner must pay without recourse) and we had to pay something over three hundred dollars more than was in the contract. It was the same thing with the contractor for all the carpentry work. He was always drunk and impossible, and we had to get rid of him at a further loss of two hundred dollars. The house, according to the contract, was supposed to be ready by 1 November and some things are still not finished. . . .

In Chicago at least one or two murders belong to the order of the day, and this is not only true in Chicago where all the scum gathers; the situation is just about the same throughout the whole country. The Swedes are in general not among the least represented. Complaints come in from almost all the states that the death penalty should once again be applied more often and the governor's discretionary right to grant pardon revoked, for Lynch law (that is to say, the people take revenge into their own hands and without investigation or judgment hang the guilty) has been resorted to in many places, even in the more populated states. Here things have not gotten that far, but in the days after the great fire many suspected arsonists are said to have been lynched, though the newspapers were rather quiet about this. . . .

J. E. Ekbloms arkiv, Uppsala landsarkiv. (See also Widén, *När Svensk-Amerika grundades*, 113–15.)

10 July 1876, Chicago

. . . Now I should say something about America and the Swedes here, who in Chicago alone are around eighteen thousand, but strangely enough they have altogether too much of the hereditary sin, or in other words the Royal Swedish Jealousy. All the other nationalities, meanwhile, are, as the old saying goes, like peas in the pod. But all the attempts that have been made and are being made among us sooner or later go on the rocks. The Svea Society has nevertheless been doing its best for twenty years now, though often amid storms and winter winds. Dozens of Swedish societies under a variety of different names have been born and have died unmissed by the survivors; the reason must in some part be that Svea has had a good library. Before the fire we had over two thousand books, all of which disappeared within a few minutes, but now we already have not quite eight hundred. I have been the librarian for eight years and this is now actually my only occupation and amusement, which from my childhood has also been my greatest pleasure. We are now awaiting more books from Sweden and there are beginning to be plenty of Swedish books here, though they are expensive. There are many booksellers and lending libraries, besides the excellent Chicago Library, which in one year already has over fifty thousand volumes in all known languages, also newspapers in all languages. In Swedish there are 1,500 volumes and two newspapers. . . .

We could hardly have a bigger gang of thieves than under Grant's administration, but fortunately . . . many scoundrels have been discovered. Over one thousand millions have been embezzled during his time and it is presumed that when his time is up on 4 March 1877 he will be brought to trial as an accomplice to the swindles. He is already morally condemned. Thirteen of Chicago's leading men have gotten their light sentences and the old Swedish saying may be applied here, that big thieves, etc.; for example, Rheem has in two years robbed the city of over a million and he is to pay a fine of one thousand dollars and get six months in jail, and it is believed that Grant will pardon all the rascals.

The sad news has come in that an old, experienced general, Custer, thirty-six officers, and five companies have been killed and frightfully massacred by the Indians at the beginning of the month, at Big Horn, Montana Territory. Not a single man escaped from the whole troop. They are supposed to have defended themselves bravely but the Indians were ten to one, so now the flames of war burn again in all their horror and it will hardly end before the death of the last Indian; that is, with the exception of those who have accepted civilization. . . .

*Ibid.* (See also Widén, *När Svensk-Amerika grundades,* 133–35.)

1 March 1877, Chicago

. . . It would appear that the Swedes in Chicago have now gotten the urge to read, for no less than eight Swedish newspapers are now being published here in Chicago: namely, *Hemlandet, Svenska Amerikanaren, Nya Verlden, Svenska Posten,* and *Vid Aftonbrasan,* all of these for politics and literature; *Sändebudet, Nordstjernan,*[26] and *Chicago Bladet,* for religion and politics; as well as *Scandia* from Moline, *Folkets Tidning* from Omaha, and *Vårt Nya Hem* from Minnesota, all of these for politics and literature. Besides, there are some newspapers from Sweden as well as the American ones, so we certainly have access to the general news, although almost always the same things are recounted from the home tracts in Sweden. . . .

*Ibid.* (See also Widén, *När Svensk-Amerika grundades,* 139.)

12 June 1877, Chicago

. . . The Seventh Day Adventists have now, after several miscalculations, come to the sure conclusion that their ascent into heaven will take place next September, but nevertheless they are now building a church here on 22nd Street. . . .

*Ibid.* (See also Widén, *När Svensk-Amerika grundades,* 141–42.)

*In 1876 Pastor C. J. Nyvall of the Swedish Mission Friends traveled in the United States. He recounts from his visit to Kearney, Nebraska:*

. . . I heard to my surprise that some sixty or seventy Swedish immigrants, planning to settle in this vicinity, were to arrive by train from the East. My friend and I met the group at the station; among them were several whom I knew and they were happy to hear that they could gather around the Word of God the following day. Thus the next day the immigrants packed themselves into a house they had rented for the time being, where the women and children were to stay while the men were out on the prairies locating land and digging a hole or nailing up a shed of boards for a dwelling. I preached the Word of God twice for these pilgrims and it seemed that their hearts at this time were more receptive than otherwise. Among them I met several dear children of God and we had a very enjoyable time together in this strange land. The day passed swiftly and it was with real sympathy that I said farewell to them.

The prospects for these immigrants, whose number was obviously to be increased within a few days, were not very bright. When one gets to know through firsthand contacts what pioneer life in America is like, one wonders how people can endure it. It seemed to me, however, as if some have become so accustomed to living in these hovels that they are not very eager to improve their circumstances. It even happens sometimes that when a settler has finally succeeded in acquiring a comfortable home he sells out, if he gets a good price, and moves farther west to begin all over again. Even though the settlers may have plenty of food, may own several fine horses and other livestock, and perhaps from sixty to eighty acres of cultivated fields, they themselves live, as already mentioned, in wretched wooden sheds, in sod houses, or in dugouts. The settler's wife usually has fine clothing, hats, etc., while the man is ragged. Interior comforts are not pretentious. A visitor is happy if he is given a place in the same bed as the family. One may sleep comfortably enough on the floor of a sod house but in wooden houses, where the wind penetrates the walls, one cannot do so because of the cold. The furniture usually consists of one large bed, a table, three or four chairs, and a chest of drawers. Preachers who would serve the Lord in America by seeking out the scattered immigrants must be prepared for severe privations. When I compare the circumstances here with those in Sweden I am convinced that many of our itinerant preachers at home would become less demanding and more satisfied with their lot, so far as lodging and such is concerned, if they had been in America for a time.

Carl Johan Nyvall, *Travel Memories from America, Among Swedish Pietists in America . . . 1875–76*, trans. E. Gustav Johnson (Chicago, 1959).

*A Mission Covenant preacher recalls a prayer meeting on the prairie frontier.*

I could not see any road but Brother F. said he could see it. We recounted to each other how we had come to believe in God and F. spoke of the prospects for activity in that place. After several hours a light was seen on the prairie. F. said, "That is my home." We were met at the door by a motherly woman, who said in a cheerful and friendly way, "Welcome! Now you shall have something to eat and then you must sleep a few hours." Not a word of complaint because she had been up all night. Some hours' sleep. I looked out the window; up against the side of the house a large grocery box was set up. Round about were arranged wagon seats and planks, where a large group of people had gathered. I was told that some had come thirty-five miles. It was hot out under the blazing sun, for there was no shade. We sang and prayed and then Brother F. said, "Now the Covenant's youngest preacher will preach."

I then had to stand up on the box. Before me was a group of weather-beaten and deeply furrowed faces with that faraway gaze which is only seen among folk from the prairie. When I had preached for some forty minutes, I jumped down from the box, but then a thickset man said, "You ought to know, Pastor, that we have come a long way and that we don't have meetings so often, so please go and get up on the box again." There was nothing else to do. An equally long sermon again. Baskets and boxes were now opened. There was plenty of food. F. said, "We will go on with the meeting as soon as we have eaten." So, up on the box again. The Lord was with us. Oh, what an advantage to be able to preach for these people! When I had finished preaching, a small man stood up, who said in a hoarse voice, "Those were good, deep draughts," and then he prayed fervently to God. F. whispered to me, "That is Pastor G. Norseen." I became apprehensive, for it was said of him that he did not like young preachers. I warmly implored him to preach, but he said he would not. "No," he said, "you must get up on the box; there will not be more than four sermons in any case." There was nothing else to do.

Widén, *Amerikaemigrationen i dokument*, 132.

*From a Swedish Mormon in Utah to a friend on a proselytizing trip to Sweden:*

[1879]

Brother Anders Hansson, I wish to write a few lines to you and answer your letters which we have gotten. . . . Åke did not get hold of his sister before yesterday because they have been sick but she said she wanted to help someone to come here and even a little more. My children want to save up a little together, twenty-five dollars in all, but they say that they will not help anyone over unless they are Mormons. . . . I would like you to tell us who are the girls you have sent to us. We have tried our best to get something to send you but it looks like no one wants to. But we are sending you a dollar. Jensen and I both gave twenty-five cents, my son Peter gave twenty-five cents, Johanna Andersson who was living with the family gave twenty-five cents. Write as soon as you get this letter and we will send another letter as soon as we can, but write when you mean to depart from Sweden. We will do what we can, but we wish they could have faith enough to interpret the gospels there, for here there are so many wretches who try to mislead as many as they can. You wanted to know some news from Utah but it is as usual. President Hayes has proposed that polygamy should be abolished, but they could just as well try to take down the stars. . . .

*Ibid.*, 32–33.

*Another Swede writes home from Utah:*

Mount Pleasant, Utah, 14 December 1879

Dear Brother and Sister-in-Law,
    It is Sunday today and nothing outside interests me, for pietists, preachers, and apostles have now finished their interesting meetings

and sent each other to the worst places in eternity they can think of. The weather has now changed considerably since I last wrote so that today there is only snow and water wherever you turn; right after I last wrote it began to snow and has continued almost since then so that it is claimed that the snow in the mountains is already six feet deep, a good sign for next year's crops, for snow in the mountains is our summer rain.

Since today is the third Sunday in Advent, Christmas is drawing near and I may wish you a joyful Christmas and a good and happy New Year. These holidays, which are so much celebrated and so looked forward to by the young people in Sweden, are not much observed in America and are celebrated almost alone by Scandinavians and Germans. So if Christmas or New Year's Day comes on a weekday, you will see among the Americans that their shops are open the whole day and the miners and loggers go to work as usual, and the only change in their diet is a turkey and a drink of liquor. But what can you do about it? We eat wheat bread every day; pork, beef, chicken, eggs, butter, cheese, milk, and beer are everyday food. When we consider the old Swedish custom of living high, wide, and handsome for a few days, with fine bread, fish, and rice pudding, and then after two or three days going back to the usual coarse fare, that is just to play tricks on your stomach and appetite. The children here enjoy themselves as usual at Christmas, the youngest with a few small toys for Christmas presents and the older ones with snowballs and dances, sleigh rides, and so on.

You wrote to me that the sun never goes down in America. That is a mistake, however, as far as the United States is concerned, when you leave out South America, the British part, and Mexico, which have separate governments. The time difference from east to west is only four hours and thirty-three minutes. When it is 12:00 in New York, it is 9:26 in Salt Lake City and 7:27 in San Francisco, the largest western city.

*Ibid.,* 37.

*Ernst Skarstedt, the unconventional-minded son of a noted Lund theologian, was a leading and representative Swedish-American newspaperman and author until his death in 1929. He sailed to America in 1878 and, after knocking about Minnesota and Kansas as a farmhand and carpenter, made his first brief venture into journalism, which he here recounts:*

. . . and so I came up, when no other means of livelihood was to be found, with the foolish idea, which was encouraged by several of my friends, of publishing a newspaper.

There now followed a time of hectic activity for the intended newspaper. First and foremost there was the matter of investigating how much might be expected from the advertisements; prospectuses had to be sent to Swedish settlements in Kansas and Colorado; type, paper, an office had to be found, etc. The foreman at the *Svenska Härolden* in Salina, Emil Lundqvist, said he was willing to join my undertaking as a partner. He did not, to be sure, have much cash to put into it, but he was a skilled typesetter, a pleasant companion, a man with an optimistic, happy outlook on life, experienced in the newspaper business, used to speaking English and associating with businessmen, in brief, just the sort of man I needed. We estimated that if we could get together advertisements to the value of five hundred dollars for the first year, we should be able, with the subscription area available in a number of Swedish communities, especially in eastern Kansas, to get by fairly well. Our plan was to make the newspaper more liberal than *Härolden* and consequently to seek our support outside of its readership. In this way the two newspapers would not exactly have to get in each others' way. Even among the church people dissatisfaction here and there revealed itself with *Härolden's* one-sided, intolerant viewpoint, its vehemence against disagreement, and its constant, coarse attacks against all who did not favor its ideas on the temperance question. . . . The only person who openly expressed his disfavor toward our undertaking was Pastor C. A. Swenson. It was too costly could not possibly succeed, and so forth, and time would show that he was right. Meanwhile, it did not take me too long to get the five hundred dollars signed for on the advertisers' list, and with my own capital (nearly three hundred dollars), Lundqvist's contribution (about thirty dollars) plus a couple of prepaid subscriptions, we felt fairly secure for the future. . . .

After a good deal of trouble I was promised an office consisting of three rooms at a rental of twelve dollars a month, to be occupied at New Year's. On 15 December, type and paper arrived from Chicago and Kansas City. I moved up to Salina to help my partner put everything in order for the first number, which was to be printed there. I wrote the text for the number and began learning to set type. On Christmas Eve, the first number was printed. The newspaper was called *Kansas Stats-Tidning*. It had four pages with seven columns on each page, and the subscription price was $1.50. The first number, for the setting of which we had the help of a couple of American typesetters of the roving sort, who never have any goal higher than a "general drunk" in view, was above all distinguished by numerous typographical errors, a situation not alleviated by the fact that the letter *ö* was missing and was throughout replaced by *o*. This lack was, however, soon made good. The Salina Swedish paper, the editor of which had solemnly promised me not to pick any quarrel, began immediately to deride the newborn, and before long an altercation developed between Wenngren and myself which never would have come about if he had kept his promise. Instead, it now became so much the fiercer and sometimes degenerated into scandal-mongering on both sides, not least my own.

Our publication was delayed until New Year's Day, thanks to the carelessness of one of the printers. The latter, whose name was Willis, often used to disappear and in time return drunk and impossible as far as work was concerned. The other printer disappeared and never returned. Sometimes I had to go out in town looking for Willis and then had no small task to drag home the prey. His greatest pleasure, after drinking himself full, seemed to be to lie backward on a chair and experiment with propping his legs up against the hot stove and letting them come crashing down on the floor every fifteen seconds or so, threatening to bring both the stove and the stovepipe down with him, all the while regaling us with more or less (especially the latter) edifying stories from his past. We thus got to know that he had murdered three men (highly unlikely), financially ruined his old mother (very likely), set fire to the jailhouse in the little town of Brookville (quite true, according to what we later found out), never met another printer who could match himself in skill and industry (a complete untruth, according to what we daily saw proof of), and so on. . . .

On 2 January 1880 the *Kansas Stats-Tidning* and its personnel moved to Lindsborg. Already that morning Dr. Rundström came up to Salina for us with both a buggy and a farm wagon. Onto the latter we loaded type cases, a part of Lundqvist's household utensils (the rest was fetched the next day), and on top L. esconced himself with wife and baby, as well as Willis, who had promised to better his ways if he could come along to Lindsborg. Arriving there, we moved into the place I had rented—the newspaper and I in the two small rooms facing the street and L. and his family in the big room in back. I tried at first to spend the nights on my old seaman's chest, with my head resting on my only chair and my legs dangling on the floor. But this position was just too uncomfortable. I found it impossible to sleep lying in this fashion, especially as it was cold and I had nothing to wrap up in. My purse was empty, some of my earlier hotel bills were unpaid, and I did not want to run up new debts. To rent a bedroom or buy bedclothes was thus out of the question. Instead, I arranged with my friend, the druggist Lindström, to sleep in his apothecary shop, sometimes on the counter, sometimes on three chairs, always with the big pharmacopoeia for a pillow and my coat for a cover. Some nights could be mild enough, but most were bitter cold. When my nose froze more than I could take, I pulled the coat over my face, a while later, when my legs began to ache, I pulled it down over them. Thus the nights passed for the next two months. I still freeze at the very thought of it. It happened not infrequently that I was frozen so stiff when I awoke in the mornings that I could not stir from the spot until Lindström's brother Charles, a former seaman, who lived with L. and cleaned up the shop in the mornings, pounded me a while with his fists.

The worst was that there was nothing that gave me any hope of improving my situation. The few dollars we were able to take in for advertisements and subscriptions did not cover much more than the newspaper's expenditures for paper, printing, and so forth. We (I ate with my partner) barely managed to have food in the house. Willis did not indeed demand much pay but caused various problems by his inability to read the letters in my manuscripts, for which reason his proofreading could scarcely show a correct line. We dismissed him when a young Swede made known his wish to learn the typesetter's trade. It was agreed between him and ourselves that he need not pay us anything, but that he should cost us nothing either. We could not possibly have exchanged Willis for a youth completely unfamiliar with the trade under any other conditions. But later I learned how easily, when one fails to put contracts in *writing*, one can be duped, even by so-called religious folk. Thanks to this circumstance, I later had to pay sixteen dollars for the boy's board for the time he worked for us.

I experienced besides so many proofs of undependability, callousness, arrogance, and humbug in this community, so much vaunted and admired as Christian *par préférence*, that my disposition, which was naturally affected by the sheer physical discomfort to which I was constantly exposed, became more and more embittered and the basis was laid for the mistrust, not to speak of anything worse, which I have ever since felt toward anything having to do with church people, social reformers, and apostles of morality. It would have been unnatural if this frame of mind had not also put its stamp upon what I wrote. . . . Under such circumstances, I decided to swim against the tide no longer. And after I had entered an agreement with *Svenska Amerikanaren* in Chicago, according to which that newspaper was to be sent to our subscribers for as long a time as they had paid for, I let the *Kansas Stats-Tidning* die.[27] Its last number, the tenth, came out on 25 February 1880. In my poverty and deep depression, I still experienced a feeling of happiness in the knowledge that I had, despite all, maintained my independence and had not let myself be tempted to dance to anyone's whistle or to turn my coat according to the wind.

Ernst Skarstedt, *Vagabond och redaktör. Lefnadsöden och tidsbilder* (Seattle, 1914), 66–67, 69–73, 78.

*The brothers Carl Johan and Fredrik Bergman came from a poor torpare or tenant-farmer family near Linköping in Östergotland and emigrated in 1879, when they were twenty-one and seventeen years old. At first Carl worked as a cigar-maker in Brooklyn, Fredrik in a factory in Bridgeport, Connecticut. In 1884, together with other Swedes from Bridgeport, they moved to Travis County, Texas, and took up farming, eventually acquiring other businesses as well. Their letters—written by Carl until his death in 1903 and thereafter by "Fred," as he came to call himself—cover close to half a century, down to 1928.*

New York, 21 October 1879

Dear Sisters,

A third letter to you and still no answer to any of them, but it is possible they did not reach you. I don't have anything to write about except what I wrote about in the other letters. Whether you have gotten them I don't know. We have our health and are feeling quite well, but earnings are quite small the first year. We can hardly earn enough for food, so our pocketbooks are not bursting you may be sure. I put my pocketbook under my pillow every night, for if thieves come then I don't have to be afraid; there are a lot of thieves. Here they murder people almost in broad daylight. There have been two murders since we came here, one on the same street where we live, and here they hang people who have done something wrong. Here there is also a fire every day so it is nothing unusual. The other day some Swedes came here where we are living in the boardinghouse. They had come on a boat that belonged to the North German Line. The boat began to burn when they came out to the middle of the ocean it was terrible, cries of distress were heard from all sides. It began burning at eight in the evening, at four in the morning the fire was put out. The captain on the vessel passed out; the fire had been started by an infernal machine someone had packed among silk goods to get high insurance. How little a human life is valued here. It is dreadful; in good old Sweden you know of nothing but good. Here you cannot enjoy life, people don't know what that means here, to earn money is their pleasure. It is still so very warm here. It is not as warm in Sweden at Midsummer when there is a warm year, but you have to get used to everything. In this country the womenfolk are masters over the men. You don't even dare look at a women for fear of being reported to the police. But here live very fine folk. Here you can see big houses that are ten stories high. The railway goes above the city so there is so much noise. Now I want to ask how you have it there at home in Sweden. Is Algot Cederholm's store still open? Write soon, it is so sad to wait a long time for letters. Once a month we will write to each other. It is such fun to be able to write to you, but the worst thing is postage money, but I can surely borrow it. . . .

Karl and Fredrik

Otto Robert Landelius, ed., *Amerikabreven* (Stockholm: Natur och Kultur, 1957), 33–34.

Brooklyn, 9 March 1880

Dear Sisters,

Many thanks for the letter we got with Nyberg; he has now come to us and is living with us until he finds work. I was completely surprised when he came. He came ashore or to us on Sunday the 7th. He found his way quite well though he had no knowledge of the language, but it was chance that things went so well. . . . We have a lot of fun because we almost feel at home. I am teaching him what English I can. He couldn't even say yes or no. It was so strange; he was standing and resting right across from the house where we live. An American was also standing in the same place. Nyberg then took out the letter and pointed to the number. He showed him across the street; there he met some girls I am acquainted with. They took the letter and came up to me. They told Nyberg he should go up, but he didn't understand them, then they waved to him and he understood that it was right. This time I don't have anything to write about. Almstedt sends greetings. Please greet our friends. Warm greetings to you from

Carl and Frigge

*Far well!!!!!!*[28]

P.S. (Don't show this to anybody.) Poor Nyberg, he didn't have any money, he almost cried when he came to us. He didn't want to tell Almstedt how things were for him. He bade me from the heart that we should help him, which we did. He was quite starved and one foot hurt him. He cried with joy that he found us; he can now live together with us. We will try to find him work. I am very glad he was able to find his way for it hurts me to see a countryman cold and hungry. It is a serious matter to come to a foreign land with no money, not knowing the language. Nyberg is happy now. He greets you.

*Ibid.*, 63–64.

Brooklyn, 6 December 1880

Dear Sisters,

Thanks for your letter dated the thirteenth of November. We got it on the fourth of this month. It is fun to hear that you are well; we are also well. Well, now we have come a good bit into winter, it has been cold for about a week, but now it is mild, also there has been a little snow but not so that sleds could be used. Well, now it's getting on toward Christmas. Oh, how lovely Christmas used to be compared with how it is now. It is celebrated here of course, but it is almost like a Sunday. We now wish you all a merry Christmas and a happy New Year. It is very sad that we can't sent you any Christmas present, but what could we send you that would be suitable. We don't know what you want for you must have everything in abundance? Frigge's thought was to send his photograph as a Christmas present, but since it can't be arranged he will have to send it after Christmas. He expects it will be just as welcome.

It was funny Hilma and Karlson couldn't locate us. Certainly it is fun to see acquaintances coming direct from Sweden, but for the most part you have more trouble from them. It is all right when they have money so that they don't come broke like Nyberg, for we don't have anything more than we need ourselves. Nyberg lived with us for a long time. As you know he had pain in one foot. What could we do with him? We couldn't kick him out into the street. He then got fifty dollars into debt to us. He has paid back fourteen dollars, that's all, so there are still thirty-six dollars left. Now he scorns us, we have even gotten various words we didn't deserve from him. We have never demanded that he should go and act humble because we helped him, therefore we think it is sad to be treated in such a way when we treat people politely. Don't mention this to anyone because we don't want to hurt him. Don't do that! If there is anyone who asks for our address, give it to them and we will gladly help them with what we can. We have still not registered as American subjects. . . .

So, my old fiddle is lying there and cracking? He must be doing that in anger because he didn't get to go along with me to America. But let him crack, it can't be helped. . . .

*Ibid.*, 79–80.

Brooklyn, 1 June 1881

Dear Sisters,

. . . Whew! So hot it is, the sweat runs off of me as I write. You may be sure it is warm enough so we don't have to blow into our hands any longer. Now we have to blow on them instead. . . . I ate strawberries on Sunday, that was out with an American family; they live in the same house as we do so we are together a lot. He is a mate on a boat that goes on the river; I have supper almost every Sunday evening with them, for we play dominoes with them, and so they ask us to stay for supper. I believe that no other nation is as hospitable as the Americans, but they will not stand any ceremony. They will invite you just once and if you stand on ceremony you then have to take the consequences. . . .

*Ibid.*, 88.

Manor, Texas, 6 August 1884

Dear Sisters,

It gets longer and longer between every time we hear from you. The reason must be that we are still farther away from you than we were before, or maybe it is largely our fault for being neglectful, but if that is so, forgive us, for often when we have the chance to write we are either tired out or not in the mood.

It is terribly hot here, so that one even suffers from the heat, and sometimes dreary, for everything is so strange here compared with what we are used to. The houses are generally very bad, so bad that when it rains the water runs in on us. Right now we are very busy with carting out in the fields. Farming is very different here from in Sweden.

We raise corn and cotton. We are farming together with an old farmer from Sweden. He was an estate manager there. I think I have mentioned them before, for they were the same family I stayed with when I was in Bridgeport, Connecticut.

Thank you for your last letter, I just got it now. We are glad to see that you are all well. You wonder how I can manage with farming. It is hard for I am not so strong, but I hope that when our resources improve it will be easier for us, for when we have money we can hire help for a lot of things we have to do ourselves now. The harvest looks good at the moment, it could happen that if we have a good one we could make ourselves around five or six hundred dollars by fall, you know, Fredrik and I on our part, and that's not so little.

You think we have had a hard time—it is true that we often did in the beginning, when we first came to America. For me it often would have been hard if Fred hadn't been so good. I know when I needed money for food or rent, he gave me all that he had and that he had thought of using for clothes for himself, for the need of getting them was great enough for both him and me, but he helped us both. Then better times came, we learned the language, and everything began to look rosier and for the present our situation is quite good. We have enough clothes. I still have my good Swedish overcoat, almost as fine as when I came over, and even my gold ring, so you may be sure I am still a bit Swedish. The shirt buttons, also of gold, I still have too. We both have watches, though not such expensive ones. Fred also has a gold ring. Each of us has a violin, worth from twenty to twenty-five dollars, we have an organ, worth seventy dollars, a team of oxen, worth seventy-five dollars, and in cash, though loaned out, one hundred seventy-five dollars, not counting some unsure debts to us which we will probably never get back. Nyberg has not repaid the fifteen dollars he owed, we will certainly never get them. Well, in any case our situation, as I say, is pretty fair and we hope that it will get better hereafter, for there are good prospects here, if you only have your health, and thank God, we have had it up to the present. Though we have sometimes not felt so good it is nothing to speak of.

I wish I could describe Texas for you, but that would be much too hard, for many things are still strange to me. When it begins to rain it usually lasts for long periods, and the same when we have dry weather, it also lasts for long periods. Swedes who have been here a longer time say there was one time when it did not rain for eighteen months; there was a terrible drought and lack of water. That was naturally something unusual, maybe it had never happened before and is not going to happen ever again. The ground here is such that when it rains we can neither drive nor go on foot because it gets so soft, so then you have to stay indoors a long time. Or if you have to go out, you have to ride. Winter here is changeable, sometimes warm and sometimes cold. We don't have any winter before Christmas.

I haven't been in any town now for seven months and maybe four or five months more will go by before I will go there. But it's all the same, I don't miss it. It is eighteen English miles from here, that is not quite three Swedish miles. Fred and I have slept out on the porch for over a week, for it is so warm in our room that we can't be there, and we will have to sleep there all summer, for it will get warmer still. July, August, and even September are usually so hot that you can't go outside in the middle of the day, but later it gets a little cooler.

I don't think you would recognize us if you could see us now, for we are so brown and thin. You asked if we don't have any sweethearts yet. Who dares to think about women? There are so few of them here, and besides we still have not met any who have made our hearts beat any faster than usual. But how is it with you? Aren't you thinking of marrying? Hurry while you have time. But I don't mean it that way; you are wise enough not to marry before you find someone who suits you. It would be better to stay unmarried your whole life through than to get someone no good, whether a man or a woman. Farewell for this time with many hearty greetings from us, your brothers

C. and F.

*Ibid.*, 109–11.


Manor, Texas, 21 July 1886

Dear Sisters,

It is a very long time since we got any letter from you, we have not had any since Christmas. We have written two letters, but have not gotten any from you, which gives us reason to believe you are not well. We meanwhile hope that is not the case. We are as usual in good health and are working day in and day out in the terrible heat we have here, but we are now so used to it that it does not bother us much. You may be sure that you get thin, for the whole system is so weakened that you lose your appetite. Drinking is the only thing you feel like and fortunately we have good, cold water. We have more than enough milk, for we have three cows which are milking quite well. Since we can't keep the milk because of the heat, for it turns sour from morning to afternoon, we just have to drink as much of it as we can, and the rest we give to the pigs and the dog.

On 19 June we had quite a bad storm accompanied by hail, so that a large part of the crops were damaged, indeed almost everything was ruined, but luckily it did not hurt us. We had hail, but not so much or so large, they were like small hen's eggs. In other places, however, they were like when you put both your hands together. That seemed big enough, but they had still bigger ones in other places. It sounds unbelievable but I don't doubt it, it must be true in any case: they weighed seven pounds and then you must believe they must have been big. Our house came near to being blown apart. Fred was inside when the storm started, he felt how the house began to give way in the wind and tried to get out but the doors wouldn't open because of the way the house was leaning, therefore he had to jump out the window. I happened to be out in the outhouse, so I was not afraid. In other places the hail went right through roofs and in many places livestock was killed. As I say, we did not suffer so much from the storm as many others did.

The cotton crop seems for the present very promising and is now beginning to ripen fully. I am sending here a Mexican stamp to the Wigander sisters. Maybe I can get more in the future. Forgive me, Sister, time will not permit me to write the paper full.

Fond greetings from your brothers

Carl and Fred

*Ibid.*, 119–20.

Manor, Texas, 28 September 1888

Dear Sister,

Many thanks for your letter, which we received long ago though we have not had time to answer it before. We have now gotten into our harvest time, so that is why we are so busy. The harvest promises to be good this year, prices likewise, for which we feel well contented. It was really fun to get a letter from sister Hanna. We have now written to her, but I don't think the letter has reached her. It would certainly be fun if all four of us sisters and brothers could meet one more time, here in this life, but it is not to be thought of. To be sure we could go and look in on you, but it would cost us too much, therefore we never think of it. Now I don't know what I should write. I have nothing new to talk about, so it will be a short letter you will be getting this time. Finally, many hearty greetings to you and the others. Your brothers

Carl and Fred

*Ibid.*, 129.

∽∽∽∽∽∽∽∽∽∽∽∽∽∽∽∽∽∽∽∽∽∽∽∽∽∽∽∽∽∽∽∽∽∽∽∽

*Newly arrived in Nebraska, C. F. Carlsson writes enthusiastically home to Dalarna:*

Clarcksville, Merrick Co., Nebraska, 1 February [early 1880s]

. . . Much I have seen, heard, and experienced, but nothing unhappy, no shady sides. To be sure I believed when I departed from home, from the fatherland, from family, friends, and acquaintances, that everything would at first be rather unfamiliar. But no, strangely enough, everything is as I wished it should be. The country is beautiful, if any land on earth deserves to be called so. And if you compare conditions here with Sweden's, there is no similarity at all. The soil consists of a kind of dark loam over a layer of marl on a clay base; your finest plowlands at home cannot compare with the rich prairies here, where golden harvests grow from year to year without having to be manured or ditched. No stones, no stumps hinder the cultivator's plow. If you add to this that one can almost get such land as a gift or for an insignificant sum compared with its natural value, you soon have an idea *why* America *is* truly and undeniably better than old Sweden. But here is another thing, taxes do not consume the American farmer, they are extremely light. America maintains no *expensive* royal house, no inactive armies, which undermine the people's welfare; such things are considered here as superfluous articles and *extremely* harmful. Never has a freer people trodden, cultivated, and tended a better land than this. Hundreds of thousands of persons have found here the happiness they vainly sought in Europe's lands.

The greater part have come here without means, many even with debts. But with good will and an unshakable will to work they have within a few years gradually attained sustenance, prosperity, indeed quite often wealth. And still there is land for a hundred million people, as fabulous as this may sound. In twelve years the population of Nebraska has increased from thirty thousand to four hundred thousand; no other place in America can show such rapid growth. Swedes number around fifteen thousand in Nebraska. All are getting along well, and when you are getting along well you are not likely to long for what was not pleasant; even homesickness is fully cured. And as far as food is concerned, there is such great abundance here that one would be amazed, even if he were the greatest gourmet. To list everything here would surely be too long; let me therefore say that it is unfamiliar to us Swedes. Now someone may perhaps believe that there are bad persons and dangerous beasts here, but there is neither. When we arrived we heard from everyone's lips, welcome, heartily welcome, and they showed by their actions that they meant what they said; they invited us to eat as though we had been their nearest relatives. My traveling companion has bought eighty acres or *tunnland* of land for around fifty dollars. The climate is remarkably fine; nothing stands in our way except the language. We cannot understand their speech, but it is possible for us to learn as well as others have done. I see after this first short time that it is going well. And therefore you can understand that I do not regret the journey, other than to regret that I had not made it before. But better late than never, as the saying goes, and I agree.

There is no forest here in Nebraska to speak of, but there is so much corn that it is used for fuel instead of firewood. Corn is also given to the large pigs which are raised for sale. Rivers flow through the land in all directions, railroads also cross it in all directions.

I have recently finished with my job; I also worked for a railroad company, where at first we got one and a quarter, but at the end one and a half dollars, and we paid three and a half dollars per man a week for room and board. But a family can live on three dollars a week, no matter how large the family may be. We had to quit our job because the ground froze, but we will begin again at the end of February when the weather turns milder. They start sowing and driving out onto the fields at the end of February and the beginning of March. I am doing fine and I expect to do better when I can learn the language. I shall now go to school and learn English for five or six weeks, which anyone can do gratis.

Björn Hallerdt, ed., "Breven berättar om dalfolk i Amerika," *Dalarnas hembygdsbok 1966* (Falun, 1968), 47–50.

∿∿∿∿∿∿∿∿∿∿∿∿∿∿∿∿∿∿∿∿∿∿∿∿∿∿∿∿∿∿∿∿

*Finding himself at loose ends again, this time in Chicago in the early 1880s, Ernst Skarstedt, one-time editor and publisher of the ill-fated* Kansas Stats-Tidning, *turned to a fresh expedient:*

. . . at the end of May there was nothing more for me to do there. I then tried my hand as a book salesman, in that I went from house to house in those parts of the city inhabited by Swedes, offering books for sale. Of everything I had tried up to that time, this was the worst. Some did not want any books at all, others—as for instance an old woman whose library consisted of three Bibles, three collections of sermons, and a hymnal—considered that they already had too many books. One man did not want to buy *Kellogg's Handbook for the Home* because he did not intend to become a doctor; another borrowed for examination *Ask Me About Anything,* but returned it because it was not a "Lutheran book."

Tired of this, I packed a trunk full of books and betook myself off to Missouri, where, with a mighty burden of spiritual fare upon my back, I wandered through a new Swedish settlement—with the same result as in Chicago. Almost everywhere I was regaled with the choicest remarks. But then it should be noted that I had landed right in the very heart of Swedish-American Waldenströmian pietism.[29] Daily I was asked if I had been "born anew." Only at *one* place I was greeted without questions, with the assurance, "He lives in Jesus, that fellow, since he wants to spread God's word." (Among the books there was also the new translation of the New Testament.) A woman received God's command—so she maintained at least—to call me back after I had left. And from her I received, besides quite a good dinner with several glasses of milk to sustain me, a long spiritual disquisition about how she had lost a little girl since she had loved the child more than Jesus, but that she reached the point where she could joyfully lose both her remaining children and her husband, if God so willed. Indeed, filled with joy, she could cry out, "Come, dear God, and take what Thou willst, take my husband or my children; I shall not grieve." The poor man sat there quiet as a pike and listened to the woman's prattle. At another place, I met an old, unpleasant crone who assured me that when she and her husband had come to America six years before they had brought with them all the books that I could possibly have. When I modestly remarked that I had books which had come out since then, she replied wisely, "Yes, I know, of course, that they give out new editions, with changes and corrections."

Ernst Skarstedt, "Vid hennes sida" (unpublished but privately duplicated, Portland, Oregon, 1889), 29.

*J. S. Olsson came to America in 1883 and worked on railroads in Wisconsin and Minnesota before his tragic death in the mountains near Albany, Oregon, where he became lost and sick, in 1900.*

Gaylord, Michigan, 16 June 1883

Brother Alfred,

I thought of writing several times but was too lazy. I have always been well although the greater part of them were sick at sea. Two died and were buried at sea, and one child on the railroad, but I have always felt well. The Swedish group has broken up, only the people from Lagga, and Hattman and Selin, five households in all, have stayed, since the promised conditions according to the circular have not been fulfilled. Everyone can get railroad land for five dollars per acre covered with old, virgin forest. The timber pays well so it will go all right if there are companies they can work for in the summer. At present I am working at laying track and have room and board plus a dollar and a quarter per day; the food is real good, three to four dishes and different kinds of dessert, doughnuts and pound cake standard fare for every meal, but as for beverages tea has taken its place as the beverage. Twice we have had peas. The best thing I could wish for would be salt herring. The work is hard enough but not worse than it used to be in Sweden, though there are some heavy lifts now and then. Working hours are from six to twelve, one to seven, and we always ride on the locomotive to go for our food. But in five days I believe we will reach the place where there is going to be a station, and then I am going to start on woodworking, for I want two whole dollars, otherwise I will go to Detroit or Chicago. There are just about enough mosquitoes so it is hard to hold still and write, for you get more tired out from them than from the work. Also it is very hot here but it is possible it could be as warm as this in Sweden sometimes. The days are shorter and the nights are darker and cold. The soil is sand and three inches of humus but the crops look good. My money or notes which you took, take and put them in a bank so that they can be drawn three or four months after I write and don't let them out in any other way. You can tell everyone in Solvalla that I am here in America and am well. I had others I should write to but my notebook, where I had several addresses, was stolen from me. The people are very friendly here but no trust should be put in anyone. The best thing here is health and I also wish you good health. If you want to write to me use this address

Mr S. Olsson

North Amerika          *Gaylord*
Poste Restante          Otsego co
                        Michigan


Best wishes to you all from
J. S. Olsson

Unpublished letters of J. S. Olsson, 1883–1900.

Bradford Lake, Michigan, 28 July 1883

Brother E. A. Olsson.

Since I have not yet been long enough at the place I have now moved to, I can't yet determine so well how I have it with the pay, but I am hoping for the best, for when I took the job I was alone without an interpreter and could not understand the conditions. But here there are twenty-one Swedes before me, of which half have worked here for several years at the same place and have always been handled properly and treated fairly, which is not always the case here. Meanwhile I am as safe here as in Sweden from either attack or robbery, for if anyone loses a single day from drinking he is laid off. Just this week one of the best foremen had to quit because he left his work for half a day. He is going to be missed a lot by us Swedes although he was a Yankee. Meanwhile I am working at a place where there is a big steam saw and all kinds of planing machines and am getting along very well as long as I have my health. I don't regret at all that I came here. Although those Lagga people so far as I know did not choose the best place for farming we are not far from each other.

If Filipsson's hired hand, August Åberg, would like to come to America, tell him or write to him that he can well come over in the fall, for it would not be more dangerous for him than for others since there are Swedes here who will go home to visit this fall, and if he is then in need of money you can give him what he needs out of mine with the agreement that he returns or repays in Swedish money. You should also tell him to take along as few personal effects with him as possible, not over 105 Swedish *skålpund*, not counting his food box and bedroll. Besides I will write to Solvalla that I can find him work hereabouts. He can easily repay the journey twice over by spring if he stays healthy. In the meantime he should be prepared with at least 200 *kronor*[30] and get work immediately when he gets here.

Have you heard or do you hear anything about J. Jönsson at Solvalla *boställe*?[31] Write to me and tell me what sentence he is getting for burning off the land there. Or if you know any other news that could interest me, tell about it in the letter I am expecting from you five weeks from this date. It is very good here, in my opinion, so that I regret I did not come here several years ago. There are newspapers in Swedish here, *Nya och Gamla Hemlandet* and *Svenska Tribunen*, which are available for us to read. Presumably my last letter has reached you but I have asked in Gaylord a couple of times in hopes of hearing something from you, but in vain. Now I urge you to write immediately. And wish you all good health and greetings from me to you and to all the acquaintances, and tell them I am well to date.

Signed, J. S. Olsson

*Ibid.*

*In 1884 August Segerberg, a young estate inspector from Dalsland, went to America, hoping to become economically independent, and left behind his fiancée, Hertha Schedin, a governess at a nearby manor. His letters to her describe his years as a farm laborer and railroad section hand in Illinois, and as a miner in Colorado, until he returned to marry his Hertha and bring her back to Denver in 1889.*

Gothenburg, 11 July 1884

My eternally beloved Hertha,

Warm and heartfelt thanks for your dear letter, which I received yesterday morning.

It is now the last morning, yes, the last hours that I find myself within that land's borders which for me enclose all that is dear and sacred.

No wonder, then, that I should wish to send one last greeting, upon departing, to my very dearest, my deeply and truly beloved Herta. Dear Herta, when this letter comes into your hands I will find myself already a good distance from this strand and will with tearful eyes cast my glance in the direction where last I saw the coast disappear, and will send with the wind a final greeting to you. Next time the morning sun rises he will not hallow Swedish soil for me.

I go to a foreign land to meet an unknown fate, but with trust in God and in myself, I hope they will favor me. I know besides that you will always pray for my well-being for it will at the same time be your own, and with assurance I go calmly and securely to meet my future. That which most disquiets me is that you cannot be as calm as I had hoped but perhaps grieve more than you can bear. You must promise, my beloved, that you will banish all worrisome thoughts and will feel a calm confidence in the future, and like myself hope for a speedy reunion. How lovely may this reunion not be when we shall no longer have to part. What a reward for what we now must suffer!

Oh, how I would wish once again before I depart to be able to whisper words of consolation into your ear and brush the tears from your eye. Be assured that I nonetheless do this in my heart. Time is flying, I have time for no more, therefore farewell my beloved Herta, a warm and heartfelt farewell. We shall meet again soon, and think meanwhile with longing, not with sorrow, of your

Eternally faithful

August

Georg Harnell, et al., eds. *Dalsländska emigrantbrev* (Mellerud, 1963), 72–73.

Galesburg, Illinois, 28 September 1884

. . . Your guesses and speculations over the reasons for my America journey are not so far off. I readily admit that the desire to see something more than "the bed and the cupboard," as they say, was perhaps the greatest reason for it. That you cannot "cut gold with a whittling knife" here either, I knew just as well when I was home as I do now, but it never hurts to have seen "more than a pot and a stove." If I should return tomorrow I would consider that the little experience I have already had was worth the money it cost to travel here and back.

I still have too little experience of this country for me to give any definite judgment of it. What I nonetheless believe I have observed is that he who in Sweden must slave for others for his food does better to come here, for he can do it more easily here. But he who has known better days and does not wish, and perhaps cannot or lacks strength, to take up any sort of menial work whatsoever, he would be wisest to stay on his fathers' soil and work the turf that they broke. For here one must clear one's own way on ground where not only strength and an unbending willpower are needed, but also courage and self-denial. This at least during the early period.

The daily wage I now have on the railroad is among the lowest one can get, no more than one dollar and thirty cents a day, and half of that goes for room and board. Railroad workers are generally paid the worst of all for the reason that they get plenty of those who as a result of their ignorance of the language cannot undertake anything else. You may be sure that there are many who have been here seven or eight years and do not know a bit more than I do now, that is to say, nothing.

As I have mentioned before, I am not going to continue much longer with the work I now have, presumably not more than fourteen days more, then I will quit. We have now been in Kewanee for a while once again but will move tomorrow to another town fifty miles west of Galesburg, which is called Corkford. What I think is such fun is that we get to move so often and see more than one place.

Here in America a bitter struggle is going on between the two parties, the Republicans and the Democrats, in connection with the forthcoming presidential election. Both have naturally put up their own candidates and are now seeking by every possible and impossible means to win votes for same. Almost every evening one or the other has its meetings and then it is usual for them to march back and forth in the streets to rousing music, dressed up in fantastic outfits and with burning torches, to attract attention to themselves and get people to listen to their speeches about the necessity of voting for their candidate. Yesterday evening, for instance, there were several hundred men, all carrying torches and brooms and dressed in red capes and gray hats, who moved along in marching order, preceded by a brass band consisting of some twenty young girls, also dressed up, and who blew quite well. The whole thing looked quite droll and amusing.

There is really a very great political liveliness among the American people, including both the millionaire and the poor workingman. All work with both hands and feet to get the party they belong to on top. In this, just as in a thousand other ways, there is a world of difference between here and old Sweden, where at least as far as the lower classes are concerned an extreme indifference to all matters of state prevails. That is surely altogether natural, for while in Sweden it is only the money-magnates who have a voice, here the day laborer's and the multimillionaire's vote weigh the same on the scales, when they are otherwise empowered to vote. . . .

*Ibid.*, 105–7.

Avon, Illinois, 18 October 1884

. . . We had a lively discussion at the table this evening, you may be sure (you see the hired hand eats at the same table with the family). I was asked about everything possible in the old country, among other things if we had such pretty girls there as here, and whether I was thinking of getting myself a Swedish "lass." I gave an affirmative reply to ' oth questions, which surprised them not so little, for they thought that "poor little Sweden" could not measure up to America in this case. I tried the best I could to convince them of their great error and told them that only with the noble Swedish maidens can one seek for true love and faithfulness, those in whom there is no guile or egotistical calculation.

Yes, you may be sure that things get lively when I get into discussions with the Americans. I like the American people in general very much and much prefer them to my own countrymen who have been here a few years. The latter I find hard to take since they are usually less accommodating and always regard with a certain pride and contempt the newcomer who cannot speak as well as themselves. They want to condemn everything Swedish, and are almost ashamed over being from Sweden.

It is deplorable but this is really how it is with a large part of them. Naturally, there are many shining exceptions. You also have to over-look a little in their case, for those who are that way are always persons without the slightest education and cultivation from the mother coun-try, and when they then come here and have seen better days than they had in Sweden and seen something of fashionable ways, they consider themselves such "swells" that no one in Sweden can measure up to them. I have already had many a hot dispute with such men. . . .

*Ibid.,* 111–12.

Ironton, Colorado, 25 September 1887

. . . I must relate an occurrence that can help somewhat to give an idea of conditions and the civilization of the people hereabouts. A little over a week ago a Negro who was employed as a cook at a hotel in

Ouray, during an argument shot one of the waitresses at the same place. He was naturally arrested immediately and put in a little out-of-the-way shed which was used to throw drunk people into. The following night around two the shed was doused with kerosene and set on fire, and the Negro was roasted to death in the sight of a cheering crowd of some two hundred persons. The remarkable thing is that although there is a kind of regular jail which could not be burned without causing greater damage, the Negro was still put by the authorities in this shed which was accessible to the mob. Reflections suggest themselves. By way of comparison I can point out that some time before this another man shot down a person in cold blood, but the latter—is still at large on a few hundred dollars' bail, and his sentence, if he ever gets any, will probably amount to a couple of years in jail. That is the difference between those who have money and consequently friends as well.

Although the act of burning a human being to a cinder concedes nothing to the barbarism of heathendom, there is still one thing that justifies it in some degree and that is the lawlessness that prevails here, that any gross crime at all can be committed as long as one has money to bribe his judge with. One thus has to overlook it to some extent when the citizens themselves seek to punish wrongdoers. But why not be consistent? Why not do the same for all? . . .

*Ibid.*, 132.

*A young girl writes home about her job with a family:*

Minneapolis, 10 April 1888

Dear Sister Lotten,

May you be well, that is my wish! Thank you dear Lotten for the welcome letter I got from you, in which I see that you did not get my letters which I wrote to you. I am very sorry about that. I have written two letters to you since I came here but have not gotten any answer. I don't know how I should do now. I think I will send this letter home and then they can send it to you. It is sad when letters don't get there. The last one I addressed to the place where you moved to last fall. You say that I should tell you about every thing and I did that, I wrote real long letters too, but what fun is it if they don't get there? I must now tell you that I have health and get along real well here in this new land. When I first came here I came to Nordens' and I was there for five days, then I found a job and I am still working at the same place. They are very proper and kind folks, they are English and have three children. We are two girls. The first two months I was what we call at home a chambermaid, then I had to clean house and wait on the table the best I could. It was not so good you can be sure as long as I couldn't understand what they were talking about but then I had a Swedish girl as a comrade so she could interpret. She was kind to me and talked for me as good as she could. A little while before Christmas she left and then I had to take her place and I have had it since then. I am now glad because I believe the worst time is over. I can now soon understand almost everything they say, for it is hardest the first half year as long as you can't manage with the language, but if you only can happen to find decent folks to work for it goes well and good humor is something wherever you go. I must tell you now what my work is, it is to cook food, wash, and iron. I wash clothes every Monday and Tuesday, then I iron, and also Wednesday I have to iron sometimes, and bake on Thursdays and on Fridays I only have the cooking.

I wonder if you have to iron anything? Now I will tell you that I have to iron as much as I want, I have two starched shirts to iron every week. At first I was so scared they would be ruined but now I shine them up so that they are like a mirror, you may be sure, dear sister. I wonder if you are thinking some about America now, you have never mentioned it. I think it would be so much fun if you came here. I don't think you would be homesick for I at least have not been homesick the slightest bit since I came here. I think that it is here like in Sweden, but better, because I would not earn more in Sweden than I get here. . . .

Eric H. Andersson, ed., "Några emigrantbrev," *Hyltén-Cavallius-föreningens årsbok 1941* (Växjö, 1941), 188.

*In 1858 young Jöns Wiklund agreed to enlist in the army but at the last moment thought better of it and ran off to Bergen, Norway, where he signed onto a ship. Thereafter his family heard nothing from him for many years. In 1889 the following letter—written in a curious mixture of Swedish, Norwegian, and English—arrived at the old home in Värmland:*

Kukuihale, Hawaii, 29 September 1889

Dearly beloved Father,

I wrote to my brother Oluf a while back in the hope that my letter would find one of my brothers or sisters still living and to my indescribably great joy yesterday I got an answer to my letter from my brother Ole and one from my sister Elin, and they both say that all my brothers and sisters are living and have pretty good health, and that father is still alive, but at present is doing poorly. My mother she has been dead now for eight years and God bless my old mother who I have treated so badly in my day, but I wish from my innermost heart that you who are still in life will forgive me.

Dear Father, it may well be that I have no right to call you that, but you can't believe how deeply I long for a friendly greeting from you. Elin she writes that you had written to me with your own hand but I did not get any letter from you. It could be that the letter has been mislaid.

I know I have been a wild one all my days like almost all seamen are, who don't think about anything but sailing from one end of the world to the other. Just to see new cities and landscapes they have not seen. For time also flies one year after the other until the first thing you know you are an old man. That's how it has been with me. Now for the first time I have stopped to look back at the path I can never go back over; if only I had had the understanding thirty years ago that I have now I would surely have done a lot better for myself and others. As they say, God does everything for the best, but I just can't get it into my square head that everything I have done in my days has really been so much for the best.

But now let that be as it may. I must try to do better in the future. Just at present I have it quite good.

In the year 1877, in the month of October, I sailed on a ship that was called the *Martha Davis*, Capt. Benson, and was to go to Chile in South America, to a city that is called Walparaiso, and from there to Honolulu in the Sandviks Islands.[32] The ship sailed from the city of Boston in America. We came to Honolulu in the year 1878 and there I left the ship and signed onto another that was to go up to the Ice Sea and back to Honolulu, and in the fall of the same year we came back and I gave up the sailor's life. And so I thought, now I will try living on land.

In January 1879 I came for the first time onto a plantation and from that time until two years ago I was first at one place and then another, until in 1887 in July I came to Mr. Purvis at Kukuihaile on the island of Hawaii, and by that time I understood sugar planting as well as any man on the islands. Now I must try to say what a plantation is. A plantation is a piece of land that is larger or smaller, we will say six or eight or ten thousand acres; now an acre of land contains 43,000 square feet or 209 feet to each corner of a square. And of this land around two thousand acres is plowed and planted with sugarcane every year and it takes sugar cane from twelve to eighteen months to grow before the cane is ripe, and when it is ripe the cane is cut down and transported to the factory and is made there into sugar. Here from the Kukuihaile Factory there go out four thousand tons of sugar a year; a ton is two thousand English pounds and costs about 27 *öre* a pound or 504 *kronor* a ton. My job is overseer or boss. I ride around every day and see how many people are working and if they are doing the work right, and hand in my report to the head office every afternoon at five when the work is over. My salary is fifty American dollars a month or 180 *kronor* in Swedish money and everything free, also a free horse. I for my own part have my own horse; I can have a free horse there if I want to, but I think it is better to have my own horse. I have a free stable and wagon.

Here it is summer at all times and there is no winter, here there is green grass and roses the whole year through. Climate very good, the best in the world. Here there grow good fruits like bananas and oranges and grapes. These islands are small. Hawaii is the largest and is about fourteen Swedish miles long and nearly as wide; when I say a Swedish mile I mean 18,000 yards. These islands lie at 158 degrees west longitude and 20 degrees north latitude, or two thousand English miles west-southwest of San Francisco, California. The steamships that come to Honolulu take about six or seven days for the journey. The mail comes from San Francisco and goes every twenty days to England, America, and Australia. Third-class fare from San Francisco to Honolulu costs twenty-five dollars or ninety *kronor*.

The inhabitants here are called Kanakas and are almost like Indians in America, red or brownish. A hundred years ago they were wild and wore no clothes. The people who work here are generally Chinamen, Japanese, and Portugees; otherwise there are Americans, English, German, Danish, Swedish, and Norwegian folk here, but not so many. When these workers first come here they have all signed a contract for three years at a wage of fifteen American dollars a month, or 54 *kronor*; they provide their own food. A white man who is a good worker gets one dollar a day, 3 *kronor* 60 *öre*, and free room and board. Food and clothes are expensive here. Food and laundry for a man costs 72 *kronor* a month, a bottle of liquor costs 8 or 10 *kronor*, a bottle of beer 1 *krona* 80 *öre*, a drink of whisky 90 *öre*, etc.

Like almost all sailors I have never been married and therefore have no children. I have always had good health and I wish that you may have the same for many years yet.

I end my letter now for this time with a friendly greeting to you all, from your son,

Jöns

J. P. Jonsson, ed., "Ett utvandraröde," *Sunnebygden 4* (Sunne, 1959), 22–24.

PART THREE: Farm, Forest, and Factory,
1890–1914

# Background

Although set in its main outlines by 1890, the great migration from Sweden became more varied and complex during its final phase, down to the outbreak of World War I, in response to changing circumstances on both sides of the Atlantic.

Industrialization in Sweden now entered into a period of dynamic growth, accelerating internal migration into towns and industrial areas. From 1870 to 1910 the agricultural part of the population sank from 72.4 per cent to 48.8 per cent of the total, and has since continued to decline. Although there was an overall rise in real wages, especially after 1896, developing Swedish industry was sensitive to fluctuations in the world economy. Periodic crises, such as that of 1907–1909, brought reduced wages and hours, labor unrest, strikes, and lockouts, followed by new waves of emigration. A rising proportion of the Swedish emigrants—more than half after 1911—were now urban, industrial workers, many of them originally migrants from the countryside. Increasingly, therefore, stage migration took place in Sweden, in many cases leading ultimately across the ocean, corresponding to the successive relocation of Swedes in America, from older to newer areas of settlement. In the 1890s, moreover, Sweden abandoned free trade and established tariffs which protected farmers and manufacturers but raised living costs for the poorer, consuming classes in both town and country, thereby adding further impetus to emigration.

A new and important factor in this period was military conscription, adopted in principle as early as 1812 but now applied with increasing rigor. Thirty days' military training was introduced in 1857 and made universal three years later. This was increased to forty-two days in 1887 and to ninety days in 1892. In connection with wide-ranging military reforms in 1901, the period of compulsory service was radically raised to between eight and twelve months, depending upon the branch of service. These mounting requirements were strongly resented by the poorer classes, upon whom they imposed a considerable burden through interrupted employment and lost income. After the long peace they could see little threat to Sweden's security and they tended to suspect the selfish influences of aristocratic officers and wealthy armaments manufacturers. It is hard to tell how great a role conscription played in the emigration. The figures show a notable increase in the emigration of young men reaching the age of induction, and Swedish immigrants in America frequently complained of conscription as a major grievance against the old country. Yet in many if not most cases these young men may well have already decided to leave and therefore seen no good reason to do military service first. Many were later to serve willingly enough in the American forces during World War I.

Meanwhile the lure of America remained strong. In many of the old emigration districts in Sweden the "America fever" was more or less endemic and by this time largely self-generating: to emigrate was the normal expectation for large numbers of Swedes who had no very compelling reason to stay and for whom Chicago or Omaha seemed closer than Stockholm or Norrköping. The novelist Vilhelm Moberg recollected from his childhood in Småland how, as his brothers and sisters one by one left the poor cottage for the Great Land in the West, he early came to the realization that, "Here, in Sweden, one was born and grew up. One went to America after one was grown."[1]

Transportation remained cheap and, with rising wages, within the reach of increasing numbers, while the publicity of the shipping companies now attained its peak. Circumstances in America were meanwhile changing. The census of 1890 revealed that the frontier had ceased to exist: though there were still empty spaces, there was no longer a continuous north-south line beyond which population averaged less than two persons per square mile. The best homestead and railroad land was now taken; most of what was left was remote and unproductive. The last important farming region to be settled lay in the northern tier of states: the Dakotas, Montana, and Idaho. New Swedish settlements here, as well as on the West Coast, continued to be mainly the products of stage migration from the Midwest. The last and farthest of the Swedish outposts thus established were at such places as Warren and Colton, Oregon, and Turlock, California, between 1903 and 1906. There remained, however, one last frontier: in Canada.

Although many Swedes had earlier entered the United States via the St. Lawrence River and the Great Lakes, few had remained in Canada. By 1885, however, the Canadian Pacific Railroad was completed, opening up the vast potential of Manitoba, Saskatchewan, Alberta, and British Columbia, where the first small Swedish settlements now began to appear. By the turn of the century the Canadian West entered its boom period. Large numbers of settlers from the American Midwest crossed the border to take up homestead land on generous terms; among the foreign-born immigrants from the United States, Swedes and Norwegians from Minnesota and North Dakota were particularly numerous. The Dominion government conducted vigorous propaganda in both the United States and Europe, attracting a growing share of the emigration from the Old World. Increasing numbers of Swedes made their way directly to the Canadian prairies. Accounts from there describe a hardy pioneer life like that on the American Midwest frontier a half century earlier. During the Klondike gold rush, from 1896 to around 1900, a number of Swedes made their way to Alaska and the Yukon Territory.

Among the newer immigrants to both the United States and Canada, Swedish lumberjacks, largely from the forests of Norrland, the thinly populated northern two-thirds of Sweden where the timber industry had developed rapidly in the later nineteenth century, assumed a new prominence. Migration, both by stages and direct, was meanwhile directed increasingly toward the cities and into urban employment in the United States, as good land became harder to get and greater numbers of industrial workers immigrated. Thus the flight from the Swedish countryside led progressively to American as well as to Swedish cities; whereas in 1890 only about one-third of America's Swedish-born population was urban, by 1910 about three-fifths had become so. Yet the reverse phenomenon is not to be overlooked: Swedes from Chicago who eventually turned to farming in the Dakotas, the group from Worcester, Massachusetts, which in 1893 founded the Malmo settlement in the Alberta wheatlands, or the factory workers from Youngstown, Ohio, who in 1903 took to raising melons and alfalfa around Turlock in California's San Joaquin Valley. Among the more educated immigrants from Sweden, a considerable number of well-qualified engineers who worked for longer or shorter periods in North America formed a distinctive group.

Migration showed increased sensitivity to economic trends on both sides of the Atlantic. Emigration from Sweden remained high from the late 1880s into the early 1890s (40,990 in 1892). In 1894 it fell off drastically and remained low until the end of the decade in response to the serious depression of 1893 in America and the corresponding hard times in Sweden. After 1900 emigration rose again, reaching new peaks in 1903 (35,439 persons) and in 1910 (23,529), following new economic crises and accompanying labor troubles in Sweden. It will be seen that the peaks were now becoming successively lower than at the high noon of the emigration in the 1880s. At the same time, remigration to Sweden added an increasingly important dimension to the total picture. In 1890 it exceeded 3,000 for the first time and thereafter, down to 1914, it could rise to a high of more than 7,000 a year when times were hard in the United States. In 1894 and 1908 the number of those returning came close to the number of those leaving Sweden. Remigration shows the greater mobility of the newer emigrants. More of them now crossed the Atlantic to achieve limited objectives, usually to earn a stake to improve their conditions at home. Those who suffered failure and disillusionment in America were more often prepared to cut their losses and return to the old country. Yet many who intended to settle down for good in Sweden found they could not get America out of their blood and in time went back. There was much crossing and recrossing of the Atlantic. For the period from 1875 (when Sweden began to keep statistics on remigration) down to 1925, it is estimated that about 18 per cent of the emigrants—roughly one in five—returned permanently to Sweden, a proportion certainly increased by the high remigration ratios of the 1930s. What the statistics can only remotely intimate are the human dilemmas of thousands of individual persons caught between two worlds.

In their letters the immigrants continue to reflect the rising level of public education in Sweden, greater familiarity with American conditions, and more sober and realistic expectations in the New World. With the vanishing of the old frontier more of them express disillusionment, especially during the periodic hard times in America. The majority, however, remain on the whole well pleased with the new land and optimistic for its and for their children's future.

The later immigration period witnessed a luxuriant development of Swedish-American religious and cultural institutions. New denominations included Swedish branches of the Seventh-day Adventists and the Salvation Army. Upsala College was founded in East Orange, New Jersey, in 1893 and North Park College was established by the Mission Covenant Church in Chicago in 1894. There were other less successful attempts to start colleges and academies in a number of other places. Swedish hospitals, orphanages, and old people's homes were opened in Chicago, Minneapolis, and a number of other cities. Swedish theaters were·now in their heyday, and Swedish vaudeville artists like the popular Olle i Skratthult made the rounds to neighborhood halls and small-town "opera" houses. For the entire period from 1851 down to the present, it has been estimated that some 1,200 Swedish newspapers have been published in the United States; the largest number to appear at any given time came out during the first years of this century, in almost all sections of the United States except the Deep South, as well as in Canada. Periodical and book publishing likewise reached their greatest volume. Clubs and societies flourished. Characteristic of this period was the extensive development of national Swedish-American lodges, such as the Order of Svithiod, founded in 1880, the Viking Order (1890), the Vasa Order (1896), and Swedish branches of the Foresters and the temperance Order of Good Templars. In Swedish neighborhoods grocery stores were well stocked with *knäckebröd* in round cakes, kegs of pickled herring, jars of lingonberry preserves, and cured *lutfisk* in hard, dry slabs.

Cultural Swedish America reached its high-water mark by about 1910, when the Swedish-born population was at its greatest, and it continued to thrive down to World War I. Coming from less narrowly provincial backgrounds than their predecessors, the newer immigrants felt greater cultural needs. Yet two disturbing developments threatened this imposing edifice. The first of these was the political and labor radicalism of a growing number of immigrants, the product of hard and often ruthless industrialization in both Sweden and the United States. In both countries socialist parties arose: in Sweden the Social Democratic Party, founded in 1889; in the United States a variety of competing factions around the turn of the century, in particular Eugene Debs's Socialist Party of America and Daniel De Leon's Socialist Labor Party. The same period saw the rapid growth of labor movements in both countries. As Social Democrats were harassed by the Swedish police and labor organizers were purged by their employers, especially following strikes, increasing numbers of them found their way to America, where many became active in socialist politics and labor unions. Swedes were well represented in the radical International Workers of the World (I.W.W.), founded in 1904; the best known of the "Wobblies" was the legendary agitator and balladeer, Joe Hill, born Joel Hägglund in Gävle, who came to America in 1902 and was executed in Utah in 1915 on what is widely believed to have been a trumped-up conviction for murder. These radicals regarded America as "capitalism's promised land." They bitterly criticized conditions and despaired at the American workingman's lack of proletarian consciousness. Holding themselves aloof from the main stream of Swedish America, they channeled their crusading zeal into their own clubs and newspapers.

Despite the groundswell of native populism, Americans on the whole considered socialism as foreign, distasteful, and alarming. The great majority of Swedish Americans were convinced believers in the American dream of individual success through hard work and determination, remained traditionally loyal to the Republican party—the "party of Lincoln"—and regarded their radical countrymen with embarrassment and indignation. As it turned out, radicalism proved only a passing disturbance to Swedish America; it was hurt by its internationalism and pacifism during World War I and what was left was largely eradicated during the Red scare of the postwar years. Its memory has been gratefully consigned to oblivion by most Swedish Americans. Yet it remains a distinct and colorful episode in their history.

The other development was a more insidious but inexorable threat: the widening cultural gap, especially after 1900, between the Swedish-born immigrants and their children, both those who had arrived at an early age and those born in America. Immigrants of mature years could seldom feel fully acculturated in their new homeland and thus naturally found identity and solidarity in a Swedish America composed of people of like background. Their children, meanwhile, acutely sensitive to being looked down upon as "Squareheads," were often embarrassed by their parents' broken English and Old World ways, and sought, at times desperately, to become as "American" as possible, especially in the cities. Many refused to use the old language even when it was spoken to them, with the result that older persons of the second generation today often understand Swedish but cannot speak it. Increasingly after 1900 Swedish congregations faced crises over language and bit by bit a number of the older ones went over to English. Many Swedish Americans anglicized their names to a greater or lesser degree. Nils, Anders, and Karl might become Nels, Andrew, and Charles. Svensson often turned into Swanson, Persson into Pearson, and Jonsson, Jönsson, Jonasson, and Johansson into Johnson; Sjöstrand could change into Shostrand or even Seashore. Some adopted new names altogether. The sons of Sven Svensson from Djursdala, Småland, who came over in the 1860s, adopted respectively the names West, Westerdal, Barton, and Swainson, as well as Swenson. Increasing geographic and social mobility took members of the second generation away from their old communities and thus out of the Swedish-American cultural orbit, as did intermarriage with growing numbers of non-Swedes. Thus at the very zenith of Swedish America signs were not lacking that its days were numbered, not least because of the very success of the Swedish Americans themselves, economically and socially.

From the beginning warning voices were heard in Sweden against the dangers of emigration from the fatherland, both from conservatives anxious to preserve the old order and from liberals who sought to use the outflow of population to demonstrate the need for far-reaching reforms. By the 1890s growing friction with Norway, Sweden's sister kingdom under the union of 1814, leading ultimately to Norway's secession in 1905, as well as the increasingly bellicose atmosphere in Europe, stimulated a patriotic awakening in Sweden, strongly reflected by national romanticism in literature and the arts. The constant drain of youth and vigor to the New World appeared to concerned patriots a symptom of serious flaws within Swedish society, the very survival of which it seemed to threaten through the loss of labor and military manpower. Periodic proposals to restrict emigration through legislation stranded, however, on the basically libertarian principles of Swedish government.

Following ever-mounting private efforts to warn of the perils of emigration, a National Society Against Emigration (*Nationalföreningen mot emigrationen*) was founded in 1907, with influential backing from aristocratic landowners, industrialists, members of the *Riksdag* and even of the royal family, and with considerable financial resources, provided in part by the government. The Society at first concentrated upon propaganda aimed at discouraging would-be emigrants and persuading Swedish Americans to return home. Such efforts met with scant success and indeed aroused much indignation among those they were intended to impress, for the Society was widely mistrusted as an upper-class clique bent on holding down wages in Sweden by keeping labor plentiful. "They forget," wrote one irate Swedish American, "that the average Swede knows just as much about American conditions as authors and journalists."[2] The Society meanwhile embarked upon a more successful "Own-Home" policy, establishing or supporting local loan agencies to help the poor finance small farms and homes of their own, frequently on lands bought up by the Society for that purpose. Its publications now sought to instill pride in the soil of the homeland and in venerable provincial traditions, while providing practical advice to small farmers and homeowners.

In the same year the Society was founded (1907) the *Riksdag* at last appointed a commission to investigate the causes of emigration. This body carried out its work with exemplary thoroughness, publishing its findings in the twenty-one volumes of the *Report of the Commission on Emigration (Emigrationsutredningen)* between 1908 and 1913. The report provided a unique and exhaustive socioeconomic survey of Sweden at that time and has been the indispensable statistical base for research into Swedish emigration ever since. It made unmistakably clear the grievances of the poorer classes against existing society and government, and pointed the way to needful remedies. Among other things, it included anonymous letters solicited from Swedes in the United States and Canada, who were not backward in condemning abuses at home. Many reflected the sentiments of one "A. G." who wrote: "Create an America in Sweden, then I believe your sons and daughters will stay home, otherwise they will not."[3] Reforms followed quickly, inspired in large part by the Commission's *Report*. By 1914, through the combined efforts of people of many diverse views, united only in their determination to make the fatherland a true home for all its inhabitants, Sweden was on its way toward the creation of a new "America."

# Letters and Documents

*The tide of emigration was running strong in 1890 when Gustaf Eriks-son, a shoemaker from Dalarna, came to America. In a letter in diary form, sent from New York, he describes his ocean crossing. We join him and his friend Gustaf L. in Liverpool.*

21 November 1890

Wednesday. In the morning we were woken up early to have time to get ourselves ready. We now got breakfast like before, then started off for the station, the things were again brought by horse and wagon. When we got there we were again stuffed onto a train, to ride about five miles said those who had traveled before. We got off at some place. I don't know if there was any station, I didn't see any. We had to find our way down to the *Majestic* ourselves. We got lost though. Now some began to swear at the agent who couldn't show us where we ought to go. It was swinish to do like that, let us go without guidance. After hav-ing had to go back a long way we nevertheless found our way. God it was filthy along the road, you practically had to wade in it. It must be a necessary evil in England.

The *Majestic* is a large, fine-looking vessel. The vessel itself is painted black, the railing and upper deck white. On both sides around the first and second class cabins run passageways like streets. Up above are the first and second class promenade decks. When we came to the dock we had to stand in a shed from which the cargo was being winched up into the ship, they were busy loading when we came. After we had waited a while we were able to go on board. We were shown to the foredeck, the womenfolk to the stern, we had our quarters two

212

flights down. There all the Swedes were packed in, farther forward on the same level came the Finns. One flight down the English and Germans had their quarters. When we had found where we were to stay, we had to see to our mattresses. We went back ashore and began to look, but we could not get hold of our numbers. When we had gone and looked for a while we each took a mattress and left. We thought, last come, last served. After that was taken care of we went up to watch the activity on land and in the harbor. There are ships' masts wherever you look and the docks crowded closely together. Everywhere there is life and movement. There are many large ships, such large ones as there are here never come up into Stockholm's harbor. There was one of these, an emigrant ship, the *City of Chester*, belonging to the Inman Line, which put to sea at the same time as the *Majestic*.

The ship left the dock but anchored out in the roadstead. The first and second class passengers came on board from stern-wheel boats that came alongside, there was a whole mass of those things. When we went and walked around the deck to find our way around as best we could, a man came and said go forward. They herded us from forward aft, there we went from the one side to the other like a flock of sheep. We were really packed in there, I think we could well have been around 6,700 (on the North Sea we were around 4,500). After a while we had to start moving forward, now the tickets were to be shown, you had to show them to a whole crowd of official types. When that was done we went down below decks where the stewards began setting up the tables, laying a kind of cloths on them, then serving. First they came with a kind of soup strongly seasoned with pepper, then tough meat with potatoes, that was how the first meal on the *Majestic* was. After the food was tucked away and we thought things would quiet down, a man came and yelled in some kind of language to go up on deck. When we got up there we had to go through the same promenade once again that we had just gone through. The first time they had taken the smaller part of the ticket (it was namely in two parts to be torn apart). Now they took the other half, and then we were free. In the evening they set out butter, then there was someone who said bread, does anyone want bread. After we had gotten bread, which was quite good (it was wheat bread) we got tea, as the man said who served it. But it was certainly some kind of dishwater, it was black and bad tasting.

Thursday. Last night we left Liverpool harbor and are now steaming at full speed for Ireland, where people will also be picked up. It is storming, but not so bad. There aren't such big waves as on the North Sea, we have a head wind. You could feel this morning when I woke up that the ship was rolling and the waves striking hard against the sides. There are openings with windows in them on the sides, and when the water comes up against them it sounds so unpleasant, it splashes and sloshes. The bunks shake like hell when you sleep up on top, we got places in the upper bunks down here. We got as traveling companions a bunch of farmers. They sometimes sit below our bunks and play cards, and as is their custom fart like locomotives, clouds of foul vapors. They have their hats on, swear and enjoy themselves. On the North Sea we were only Scandinavians, here it is really cosmic, several nations are represented. The Englishmen are generally skinny and puny, and look as if they would fall to pieces if a real Swede gave them a box on the ear. Now the anchor has been dropped in Kingston's harbor or road-stead. A wheelboat which had a crowd of Irishmen on it laid alongside here too. A whole flotilla of small rowboats also come alongside, they are peddlers, they have apples, milk, herring, and a whole lot of small articles to sell. They go around everywhere and cry their wares.

We lay here in Kingston until around one, then the anchor was raised and the journey over the Atlantic began. A stiff head wind was blowing so that when we came out a bit there were high seas. The ship rolled and shook, it began to feel uncomfortable. I got tired of this eternal rolling, as it seemed. Storms and waves don't interest me any longer. I hate them. If only we were there. But it will go on for a long while, six whole days, so one just has to go and feel uncomfortable.

Sunday. I have not written anything before. All of Friday, Saturday, and half of Sunday have been uncomfortable days. The storm increased on Friday night so that when we woke up in the morning we felt heavy in the head. We still went up on deck. Gustaf L. was in worse shape than I was though. He didn't want anything in the way of food, but I ate a little. In the mornings it was worst, for they (the crew) were busy then, cleaning up there on our promenade area. It was therefore closed off so we had to stay on the foredeck, and there one sea after the other came over the side. There was a smoking salon there for the third class. We sat in there sometimes when there was room, otherwise we had to go below again for the decks were really awash with water by the hour. On Friday morning a number were sick, ourselves included, but no one has thrown up, someone announced. No, the Irishman said one had. Oh hell, one piped up, couldn't he have swallowed it? A burst of laughter rewarded the joke. The Irishmen had to take places wherever there were any to be found, therefore we got one in our quarters. Of the others, most had been home and visited where they came from. They didn't get sick because they had traveled at sea before and were more used to it. Well, Friday, Saturday, and half of Sunday we went around and looked stupid. At Sunday dinner I wanted us to go down and get some food but G. didn't want to. He could not get himself to go down, it was too dirty down there. He couldn't eat anything because he immediately threw it up again. He thought it affected his spirits so that he had so little desire for it. Still, I went down and ate and felt good from it. I then heard that we were to be examined so that if we could not show a vaccination mark we would be vaccinated. Around two-thirty it began. We had to go down below decks, after a while the doctor came. We now had to show our arms and then we got a card on which there was the ship's name, the doctor's name, date, month, and year when it took place. On the other side in five languages it said to keep this card so as not to have to be kept in quarantine and to be able to travel freely on the American railroads. On Sunday afternoon there was good weather, the sun came out too, but the ship kept on rolling. In the evening I also ate. They had a kind of tea, I couldn't drink it, but their bread with margarine was eatable. There were a kind of biscuits in a barrel which we tasted, but we soon became tired of their food. Besides there was a rotten smell from the clothing, that was from the sea water.

Monday. On Monday it was pretty fair but not really good. Sometimes we sat and then got up and walked around. In this way we passed the day.

Tuesday. On Tuesday morning we were wakened by the thundering of the seas as they beat against the sides. It was icy cold and the storm was a stiff one. Today was the worst day of the journey for the wind. Still, it wasn't so bad, for partly one was more accustomed, and the hope of going ashore tomorrow helped keep one's courage up.

Wednesday. Wednesday morning it had quieted down again. We were up early to wash and fix ourselves up, we turned our collars which had gotten dirty in order to look really fine. Thus decked out, we crowded up onto the deck. The ship steamed steadily on, the sea had become peaceful, and we were also cheered by a foretaste of life ashore. Soon forgot all the hardships we had withstood, it is funny how one quickly forgets such things. Immediately it seemed to us, to be sure it had been hard, but it didn't really do us any harm. Now we must go to the railing to look for land. Around nine the ship slowed down, there was a small sailboat which came up to us, it was the pilot boat. Soon he was aboard, now we were going at full speed again. That was a land-mark, but it was around eleven when we first saw the land itself. On the other side of the ship they had spotted land before us.

Hallerdt, "Breven berättar om dalfolk i Amerika," 28–33.

~~~~~~~~~~~~~~~~~~~~~~~~~~~~~~~~~~~~~~~~~~~~~~~~~~~~~~

*Spring was the emigration season. From a rural parish in Dalsland, Gustaf Swenson writes to his brother Jakob in America.*

25 April 1891, Åsen

. . . Now it is spring and the emigrants are streaming out again in great crowds to America. Among those who have left this year I will mention Johan from Hagen and his brothers Tyr and Sköld, Hagberg, Janne Löf, Britta from Ed, Kristina from Olsanre and her man Johan from Åker, they were married. Otto Karlsson and Karl Jakobsson from Frestersbyn and others, all these left on the same day. Also our soldier has resigned in order to emigrate and his brother Blom, and the man from Västergötland is living on the soldier croft and working it this year. . . . Smed Maja and Gustaf Svensson at Forsebol and Albert Hagberg have also gone to America this spring. Now please write and say how you really find it in America, for I have thought much about going there too. . . .

Gustaf

Harnell, et al., *Dalsländska emigrantbrev,* 156–57.

~~~~~~~~~~~~~~~~~~~~~~~~~~~~~~~~~~~~~~~~~~~~~~~~~~~~~~

*Karl-Johan Ellington's background is obscure. (One wonders, for in-
stance, when and under what circumstances he acquired his name.)
There is nothing obscure, however, about his outspoken socialism and
his condemnation of America as the "proletarian hell," based on his
own bitter experience with "rugged individualism."*

At first I slaved for a time on a farm. After that got a job at an organ
factory in Mendota, Illinois. A Swede of the sort that had "come up in
the world" was the foreman over some of the workers there and over me
as well. He had "started out with two empty hands," had had part of
the work on contract for some years; already owned two farms and his
own house in town. No other testimony need be given as to how he
paid and treated the workers in his employ. I soon bade farewell to that
bloodsucker, went to Chicago, and soon after to Moline. There I was
to work in an organ factory, which for the time being, however, was
closed down. It was in the middle of winter and there was little work
to be had in the factories. I went out to a Swedish farmer and there
helped out with all kinds of work for my meals and a roof over
my head.

That boss too was just that kind of model Christian moneygrubber,
who had "gotten ahead through his own enterprise." "Enterprise" in
this case consisted for the most part of bestial labor, bad food, bare,
dirty walls, miserable and insufficient bedding and clothing, and a great
wealth of dirt in those wretched, cold rooms. When I had been there
for a few weeks, my body began to feel strange one day. I was sick. I still
had to go out in the bitter cold to a hay barn some distance away and
load hay. When that was done, Christian Enterprise drove his load of
hay into town and I had to wade home through the snow and cold after
sweating. I had to go up to my attic room and crawl into bed. And
there I stayed. In a few days I was wildly delirious. They finally sent for
a doctor. I then found out that I had typhoid fever. How I lay and
fought with death there I shall not attempt to describe. Will only mention that according to what I later learned, two farmhands had lain sick
with typhoid fever in the same attic room and the same bedclothes
before I had come, and the latter of them had died! But Christian
Enterprise there in that house did not need to go to any extra trouble
over such things. Disinfection and housecleaning mean inconvenience

and some little expense. The old man himself died in his Christian dirt and enterprise a couple of years later. When I had recovered enough to use my legs again, I went in to Moline and got a ride to the Rock Island County Poor Farm, eight miles from Moline. This effort laid me out on a sickbed there in the poorhouse, and only my strength of will and the devoted care of a poor nurse saved me from death. Summer came and I was at last able to limp away from yet another proletarian hell I had gone through, but it was a year before I was quite well again and had new hair in place of that which had fallen out after the illness. Such is the proletarian's lot.

As soon as I could manage, I began work at the organ factory. This was owned by a couple of Swedes who had "gotten ahead" and was to be sure no health resort. The first winter was unbearable. My small, private workroom was supposed to be warmed by a little stove. There were cracks in the floor and under it was some kind of storeroom where it was just as cold as it was outside. The following winters were even more unbearable, for the whole floor was converted into a single large room, and, so that the representatives of Christian enterprise there might save storage space around the walls, they committed the unheard-of stupidity of placing the long-awaited pipes for the steam heating up on the ceiling! Here one had to stand with the steam heat overhead and the icy draft from the cracks in the floor and from a gaping elevator shaft. The whole thing was a special experimental laboratory for investigating just how much an organ builder can physically take. To be afflicted with colds was naturally one's "normal" condition, but in addition, I picked up such a thorough dose of rheumatism that to this day my body is filled with the company's Christian enterprise and consideration of that sort. But a company need hardly give thought to how it goes with a worker's health. Besides, the steam heat was not there for the workers' sake but for the sake of the material. Ugh! And what was more, I was forced to stay where I was, whether they piled up ice or steam pipes around me, for they knew very well that I had my sick sister to take care of and pay living and medical expenses for. He who is thus caught fast so that the company need not even raise his wages when it promotes him to foreman, one need not be concerned about if he kicks about some steam pipes! What the hell would then become of Christian enterprise and the art of "getting ahead"! Keep your mouth shut, proletarians, and when you get stiff from rheumatism, go to hell and cook your back legs in the sulphur cauldrons! . . .

Karl-Johan Ellington, "I proletärhelvetet," *Forskaren* (Minneapolis), March 1905, 95–97.

*Another socialist critic, Fredrik Karlsson, writes back to the newspaper* Social-Demokraten *in Stockholm:*

Chicago, February 1892

To the Editor:

A letter in *Social-Demokraten* from my old friend "Erik" has made me hasten to take pen in hand, not to write any so-called "correspondence"; no, my communication, if it is given space, should be quite modestly entitled a *warning*. It is apparent that the stream of immigration, because of the World Exposition,[1] will be drawn in large part to Chicago in the near future. It would therefore perhaps not be inappropriate to devote a few words to conditions here in this place.

It appears to me as though most of the Swedes here should be very satisfied with their new homeland, which is easily explained since they generally, at least up to the present, have had the needs of their stomachs fulfilled. And sadly enough, the majority of our countrymen still have, strictly speaking, no other needs. This warning is thus not general, something which it otherwise easily could be.

Since there are presently, according to the police, thirty thousand unemployed in Chicago, and according to the newspapers fifty thousand, the mindless throng will simply come here to failure. Insecurity, which under normal conditions is considerable because of arson in collusion with the city administration, is now frightful, especially for working people who appear to have a few dollars. The upper class risks nothing to speak of since it alone has the right to carry revolvers. My warning is directed principally to those who despite all class restrictions have still managed to raise themselves above the level of the common herd.

In America there is no enjoyment for the spirit of those who wish to go beyond the level of prayer meetings and saloon politics. The theater, the only thing here which is supposed to represent art, is more miserable than the coarsest variety shows and does not even give the slightest sign of art or aesthetic value.

It would indeed be tempting to give a full picture of Chicago but as I am no accomplished writer, I must limit myself to a few details. What most strikes a stranger who sees Chicago for the first time is the mass of sooty coal smoke and the dirt which fills the streets, and one would be astounded by this if one did not know that America is—a very free land. As far as the smoke is concerned, it is a very sensitive side of free enterprise and is understandable in an extremely capitalistic society.

But what cannot be considered so understandable is the communal unrest in a society in which all positions of trust are filled through universal suffrage.

But it is just this that is the main cause of the mess. When a professional politician (any other kind can now no longer take part) runs for a fat office, for example mayor of Chicago, he right away has to fork out a couple of hundred thousand dollars to buy up a campaign mob. Once he has been elected, as he must be as long as someone else has not bid higher, the first thing he must do is to get back his money. And so he will make a pile, at least a half million for certain. Why should he otherwise risk his money? One can well understand from this that not very much can be left for the public welfare. . . .

I am pleased that Sweden intends to take part in the Chicago Exposition. The place is suitable. Chicago tends more and more to become the pole star itself of the whole American civilization. Although they will most likely try to gild over various things it will still give the visitors the opportunity to study a capitalistic state such as it can develop freely without any outer, and above all without any preventive, restraints, just as it must necessarily proceed out of its economic development.

It would be desirable for some of those to come here who maintain that socialism is inimical to culture. They could here see what kind of culture their own ideal society is capable of producing. Where masses of children are brought up on the streets just to satisfy the bourgeoisie's lust for making money. Where art and science are ignored since they do not produce enough profit. Where one can with justice speak of hostility toward culture.

I close these lines with the wish that the Chicago Exposition may be not only the most typical, but also the last of the bourgeoisie's great triumphal festivals.

With brotherly greetings,

F. K.

"Bref från Chicago," *Social-Demokraten* (Stockholm), 2 March 1892.

∾∾∾∾∾∾∾∾∾∾∾∾∾∾∾∾∾∾∾∾∾∾∾∾∾∾∾∾∾∾∾∾∾∾∾∾∾∾∾

*From British Columbia a man wrote home:*

19 December 1892

. . . When I came here, I had only two dollars, I did not understand a word. I can now tell you I thought I'd go crazy. For six weeks I cried every night until around four in the morning, then I fell asleep for a couple of hours. I lay on the bare floor in a poor attic, that was my night lodgings. I would not go through such a course again for any price. . . .

Widén, *Amerikaemigrationen i dokument,* 90.

∾∾∾∾∾∾∾∾∾∾∾∾∾∾∾∾∾∾∾∾∾∾∾∾∾∾∾∾∾∾∾∾∾∾∾∾∾∾∾

*The area around Gowrie, Iowa, was settled from the late 1860s by Swedes coming largely from northwestern Illinois. Within a generation it was sending its own offshoots farther west. The freight car had now replaced the prairie schooner.*

Stockholm, Kansas, December 30, 1892

Dear Brother-in-law John and Family,

Peace in the blood of the Lord! Thank you for being so good about writing. Keep it up as you have started. Write often and tell about everything in Gowrie and don't pay attention to my laziness.

Our journey went remarkably well. We all arrived in good order with all our things. I worried a good deal when I was in Iowa about how to get what we had with us from the station here, but that was needless worry, and I have had to go through such experiences many times in my lifetime. We got there on Sunday afternoon and on Monday they came with twelve teams of horses from Stockholm and took all our things at once. The freight cars were weighed in Omaha and all were too heavy except one of mine, which was found to be 2,000 pounds too light. But the other was 4,500 pounds too heavy, so I had to pay $14.63 in overweight charges. If my things had been distributed properly and I didn't have some of Jonson's, I wouldn't have had to pay any overweight. Sandstedt had to pay $30 in overweight for one of his cars.

We have all of us been sick or feeling more or less poorly since we came here, but are better now. There was a little snow here when we came but it soon disappeared. . . .

We are now putting up a corncrib, or kitchen, for we are putting in both windows and doors so that we can use it until we have some wheat to put into it. Later on we will put up a small stable and use the old one for a chicken coop. It is not as imposing as your chicken coop. Come here and you'll see.

The other day I was out and looked over my land, and I was almost tired out by the time I had gone from one end to the other. And the reason for the tiredness was surely that I began thinking of all the work it takes to plow and sow such a piece of land. The men who came to drive our things from the station began talking about how much wheat they had sowed this fall. And among them was one who said he had sowed six hundred acres this fall. Isn't that a lot for a farmer? It is now late at night and all have gone to bed. Must therefore end my letter in the hope of hearing something from you soon. I can't say that I have gotten tired of anything here yet but I think a lot about old Gowrie.

Give our best to all those many people who helped with our move. But first and foremost greetings to you from us all.

Your brother-in-law
C. A. Liljegren

Unpublished letter to John T. Svenson. Provided by Clifford Swenson, Gowrie, Iowa.

*Times were hard in America in the middle 1890s and newly arrived immigrants, being generally the last hired and the first fired, suffered in particular. The Swedes, however, did not usually give open vent to anger, frustration, or despair in their letters home. If hard pressed, they might not write at all, or if they did they most often continued to express a dogged cheerfulness.*

27 August 1893, Graceville

Dear Sister,

I must send some word so that you will know we are alive. I and John Wretabacken are at present out in the country, around two hundred miles from Minneapolis. We are working for a farmer and get $1.75 a day and food. Now we are with an Irishman, a real right believer, you know. There are so many prayers morning and evening and when we eat. John is all right now, he can make the sign of the cross and say "Ave Maria" etc. as good as St. Stephen in Weldon. He does this because he is head over heels in love with one of the unbelievably beautiful daughters of the house. It doesn't take on me. I read my "Gamla Gud med en nödtorftig spis" and sing "Den korta stund jag vandrar här," and so forth. Yes, the days are long enough out here. We have to work from sunup right to sundown and then crawl up onto some haystack and contemplate the lovely August moonlight (until one falls into the arms of Morpheus). It is still a good thing to have work. For as you maybe have heard times are unusually bad here now. Thousands upon thousands are going without work, most of them without money. A terrible lot of tramps go around here and get food for themselves by stealing pigs, chickens, potatoes, and the like. We hope the times will soon be good again so that milk and honey will once again flow in Uncle Sam's land. . . .

Widén, *Amerikaemigrationen i dokument*, 87.

*For the young, when times were hard, there was always tomorrow. For those who were old and alone, far from the place of their birth, there remained only Christian humility and resignation.*

Springfield, 10 May 1894

Dear Niece,

The peace of God be with you. I wish to write to you and tell you that my beloved husband Gustaf Jonsson has by God in his all-seeing wisdom been taken from me. He died the eleventh of April 1894 after some months' illness with dropsy. Now I am alone in a foreign land, but I take comfort in God and hope for His help. He is the same good God here as at home. In Him we find comfort in time of grief. I am living at Anna Maja from Grava's son-in-law's place. Here there are only a few Swedes who are widely scattered around and far between. That is also one of the reasons why it has taken so long with this letter.[2] The property we lived on was not our own. We had it for life. What effects we had were auctioned off. If you could send me a little money it would be good, for I am now too old to do any work. I leave everything in God's hand. Farewell, my beloved ones. Forget not one who is alone in a strange land. God bless you.

Your aunt Maja Johnsson

G. E. Lindgren, "Amerikabreven," *Tibrobygden 13* (1963), 59.

*Remittances from America helped many families in Sweden to improve their circumstances. In this regard an emigrant from Dalsland writes home:*

30 May 1894, Gracewill

Dear Parents, Brothers, and Sisters,

A little letter I would like to write but I'm no good at it. So first I can tell you that I am well and have health to this date.

And I see that you are all well and have health, which is the best thing we have here in this world, and I see in your letter that they are going to auction off the property down at the lake. And you are thinking about buying it and you want for me to help you to pay him. To pay him, that would go all right, but I thought the buildings were in bad shape when I was home, but now they must be much worse. So there is nothing left but hills to go up and down, and then the long way out to the summer pasture with the cattle. But do what you want as far as I am concerned. I'll tell you that I don't think much about going back to Sweden. It would be for your sake if I ever come to Sweden sometime. They say it is bad in America but it is certainly better than in poor Sweden. I think I can understand this from the letters.

Here there is free land for nothing for whoever wants it. It is like it says in the song: America is a free land where there is no king and no meddlesome priests.[3] It is not long since I got a letter from sister Hilma. I have not seen her since I came here to this country. She says she is well and strong. I am thinking of seeing her at Christmas. Now I must end for this time with my poor writing.

Signed, your son Adolf Davidsson

Harnell, et al., *Dalsländska emigrantbrev*, 140.

∞∞∞∞∞∞∞∞∞∞∞∞∞∞∞∞∞∞∞∞∞∞∞∞∞∞∞∞∞∞∞∞∞∞∞∞∞∞

*There were times when news from home could cause much soul-searching.*

1 April 1895, Wolverton, Minnesota

Beloved Mother and Brothers and Sisters,

May you always be well, that is my wish. I have just now gotten through Charlie the sorrowful news that our old father is dead, which was very sad to hear. I wrote a letter when I was in Chicago, to you, Augusta.' I wrote it in February but it maybe didn't get there. Dear Augusta, for that matter all of you brothers and sisters, you must be good to Mamma and comfort her as good as you can in this great sorrow. For Mamma is closest to me. When I heard that Papa was dead it was like I was hit with a stroke. I didn't know what I ought to believe myself. And then it came home to me that if you have been good to your father you will get your reward with God for it, but I know that I have been disobedient toward my father and that I hurt him when I went to America. That hurts me most of all, but I hope he forgave me for it, for I can say that Papa was always good to me. I cannot hold back the tears when I think that Papa is gone, for the home breaks up right away when one of the parents dies. But dear Mother you must not take the sorrow too hard, for if Papa died in God's grace we can see him again in a better land than this one here. I have been quite hardened but this hit me hard, and when I think of Mamma I cannot keep back the tears, for she took everything so hard. And when you go out as I have often done, then you get to thinking about your old home. Charlie was very sad, and he has been very sad that he hadn't gone home and seen Papa sometime when he was living. But he says he will go home in the fall and if not I will go, so you can be sure that we will come home sometime if Mamma may live that long. Both Charlie and Anton want for me to go home now, but that won't happen. Charlie sends best greetings and says you shouldn't be sad and you can look forward to one of us coming home in the fall. . . .

Widén, *Amerikaemigrationen i dokument*, 44–45.

*Atterdag Wermelin was one of the group around Hjalmar Branting which organized the socialist movement in Sweden during the 1880s. For a time he wrote for the newspaper* Social-Demokraten *but, unable to make a living at it, disappeared to America in 1887. A few years later he surprised his friend Branting with the following letter from Denver, Colorado.*

[Late 1895]

Brother Branting!

I presume or rather I hope you will not get a stroke when you receive this letter from one who has long been regarded as dead. It meanwhile does not come from the world of the spirits at all. On the contrary. I am still living in the flesh, although that flesh which dissipation alternating with hard work and privation has still not consumed on me—weighs rather few pounds. My friends maintain (I am still only thirty-four years old) that my hair is beginning to turn gray at the temples; as for myself I have never looked to see as I don't give a damn.

My story is soon told. If this should be the last you hear from me, remember, "He complained not over the number of his days. Fast but good was their passing."

Now you must not imagine that *I am dog gone to hell* since I begin in this way. The world has dealt rather roughly with me to be sure, but it takes a whole lot more *"to take the fight out of Atterdag Wermelin."*[4] I am the same as always. . . .

Now we come to the story of my vicissitudes. As I said, I have slaved at many different places. The most devilish job I have had was at a steel or rolling mill in Pueblo, Colorado. I worked from seven in the morning to six in the evening and three days a week I was forced to come back at seven in the evening and work until twelve midnight; indeed it happened at least a couple of times that I worked until three at night, and then came back and began again at seven in the morning. What do you say about that? What do you say about the fact that my foreman could come to me on such occasions and say—as though it were a great favor—that now I could go home and go to bed? I have worked at that damned hellhole, the steel mill in Pueblo—four different times. The last time it was worse than ever before—worse than anyone can imagine, who has not experienced it. The business did have one bright side to it. I made good money, as much as 100 dollars a month. When I came here I had 140 dollars in debts, when I left I had 150 dollars in savings pretty nearly.

But I had gotten an idea. That was to become free from the necessity of having to work in dungeons of that sort in the future. Here in this country you can take up United States government land under the so-called Homestead Law, 160 acres is the most you can take. When you have had it for five years it becomes yours. The best land has long since been taken. I went up into the Rocky Mountains and settled down on a homestead site. It lies 9,400 or 9,500 feet above sea level. Wheat, rye, and oats do not ripen there, but it is quite a fine place for raising pota-toes and for livestock. I have now had that homestead for two years. There is an old woodcutter's cabin on the place. I live in it when I am up there. I am building a log cabin. The walls are now up to a height of five feet. I do not yet have any livestock, nor any horses, but I now intend to buy some. There is forest for cutting firewood on my land. If I had a team of horses and a strong wagon I could cut firewood and drive it down to a mining town, Black Hawk, which lies nine English miles from my place. The earnings are quite small, but one can live on them. So much for my plans for the immediate future. They would not be complete unless I mentioned that several of my friends intend to go out next summer and take up homesteads beside me, and that we intend to manage everything in common on the principles of socialism or cooperation. Nothing, however, is decided yet, but if you should hear in a couple of years about the Progress Cooperative Association in Spring Gulch, Colorado—then you will know that there is the place where you can find your old friend. So much, as I say, for my future plans. Now for the present.

I now have the best job I have ever had in my life. I am working as a draftsman for the city of Denver. I was recommended by Judge Frost, who was a police magistrate here in town. Judge Frost is a radical socialist and he recommended me because I was so goddamned radical. Tell the governor of Stockholm and Police Chief Rubensson, when you meet them. But the working men here in this country do not have sense enough to vote for their friends. In the last election the so-called Populist party was beaten. Judge Frost was on their ticket for district judge— that is to say, like a *häradsdomare*. He was also beaten. The so-called Republican party triumphed along the line.

You who are agitating for universal suffrage—if you could only see how the workers use their votes here in this country!!!!

Another who has also been beaten is D. H. Waite, former governor of Colorado. He is now publishing a newspaper which is at least as radical as *Social-Demokraten* in Stockholm. You see here what the workers do when they have the vote. But this is not what I was talking about.

I am now working for a kind of authority which is called the Board of Public Works, which carries out all works projects for the city of Denver. The Board is composed of three members, whose time in office runs out on 1 June. As soon as their successors, who will be appointed by the new governor, McIntire, come in, I will get kicked in the tail. It is then (1 June) that I will go out to my homestead and start cutting firewood. I will have enough money to buy a team of horses and a wagon, as I said before. During the time I have worked for the Board of Public Works I have been earning 125 dollars a month. It is this good pay that has put me in a position to clear up all my debts in this country and to begin sending money home.

The People's party movement in America is, as far as I can see, the most hopeful movement in politics that has developed here. Their leaders, like Governor Waite and Judge Frost, have not directly called themselves socialists, not publicly, but if you get right down to it, they admit that they are socialists. Their basic idea is to start cooperation between the farmers in the country and the city workers, so that both of these classes could without the medium of money exchange their products; and as the workers gradually come to understand their own power (if they begin with cooperation) to establish stores owned by workers, workshops owned by workers, all of which establishments should exchange their wares for certificates of labor, set at a value of so and so many hours of work, and so on. What more could a socialist want, especially when he learns that the idea is to boycott all other businesses except those owned by workers and which are run without interest, without rent, without profit, and only to patronize those which recognize that reward for labor is the only just claim to income. The idea is furthermore in this way to bankrupt all private businesses, force them *"to go out of business and sell for a song."* To *"sell for a song"* means that one is in such bad shape that he has to sell everything he has for little or nothing. *And the idea is to thus "swallow the whole country." The question is not about the difficulty in doing it, the question is only to get the laboring people "up to snuff"*[5] (get the workers to understand anything).

Now for the future. It does not look so goddamned dark just now for me personally, although conditions here are otherwise frightful. At least half the population is without work—and I presume it is our Lord in heaven who is feeding them, for they cannot do it themselves. . . .

[John Persson, ed.], "Ett svenskt emigrantöde," *Notiser från Arbetarnas kulturhistoriska sällskap,* 34 (1960):72, 75–77.

*Times had still not improved much by 1897, which held back many prospective emigrants in Sweden.*

26 February 1897, Minneapolis

Dear Brother,

Hearty thanks for your welcome letter. I am glad that you are all getting along well. Regarding your eagerness to come out into the world, it is not so strange. I can understand quite well just how much success you can have as long as you stay at home. But believe me. I know also how the prospects would be if you were to come here. If I were to explain the whole thing clearly I would have to write a whole book. Therefore I will give the well-meant and, so far as I can tell, good advice that you should stay home until we can see how times become in the future. While you are waiting for this you can devote yourself to the joys of youth (long live the *Svear*,[6] you know), for when you come here, if you are like the undersigned, you will only be able to *remember* that you *have been* young. Well, when you have been here long enough you become "tough" and then you are all right, you understand. Then you see things from another angle. And if you have as I have the rare advantage of being able to work as much as you could wish, have no debts outstanding at 6 per cent interest from such and such a date, or do not suffer from unhappiness in love, corns, or ill humor and poor digestion, and have the necessary three meals a day for the so-called fleshly abode, paid a week in advance, you can see the future in the rosiest possible light.

I am not out much for entertainment but if there is some good Swedish affair I am there in a corner. We have Swedish theater sometimes and parties of different kinds which are quite nice. The other day we had a rousing surprise party in honor of Mr. and Mrs. Nils Ringlund. There was a great feed and Ringlund got from us one hundred fifty or so friends a remembrance worth around one hundred dollars, which says incidentally, "He is honored who deserves to be honored." Ringlund and wife are among the best people you could hope to meet. . . .

Widén, *Amerikaemigrationen i dokument*, 63.

*It is, as we all know, easy enough to fall behind in our correspondence!*

Christmas 1898, Wally Springs

I must take up the pen and break our long silence, since a good ten years have passed already and I think it is only a little while that we have been in this strange land, and it is soon twenty years since we left our old homeland and friends who are on the other side of the world ocean. When I look back at the time we have been here, I feel it is just a few months since we left you. It may be that these few lines will come too late to reach our relatives and friends. We don't know whether they are living or if they have gone to their last resting place. I must tell you that we are all living and have good health to this date of writing, and I hope that these lines find you in the same good condition. Yes, health is the best thing we have in this passing life. I have no news to tell you about that is anything interesting to put on paper, but I will write more. I can say that the crops are fine like they have not been for many years. I have written a letter to Uncle at Arnö to find out if he is living and to tell him that Joseph from Bagenäs is dead, and ask him to let his mother and brothers and sisters know. For he has land here that can be sold or any of his brothers can come here and take possession of it, for he had it as a homestead.

I must end this my writing for this time with a warm greeting from us to you all. Our parents send greetings to all their relatives and friends, but first and foremost greetings to you and your old mother from all of us. Signed your cousin

Caspar Nilson

My address is C Nilson, Wally Spring, Minnesota Dakota S. North America

Harnell, et al., *Dalsländska emigrantbrev*, 39–40.

*Swedish communities in America frequently included persons from the Swedish-speaking. minority in Finland. There were also a few Swedes from the far northern border region whose mother tongue was Finnish. Among them were Johan Huhtasaari from Kuivakangas, Norbotten, who emigrated in 1892, and his sister Emma, who followed him in 1903.*

27 July 1892, Atlantic, Michigan

I come to you with a few lines. Let you know that I am well in body and the same gift of the good Lord I wish for you.

I came here to America on the fifteenth of June. I am now living at Jakob Hietala's. Have been working three and a half days at the hay-making at Juntikka's. Now I am working for English-speaking people. Here you don't have to work gratis; here they pay two dollars a day. That lasts for at least a week. Don't have to start before seven, and a lunch hour we have too. In the evening, when the whistle blows at the mine, we can lay down our tools.

It's not so bad here as far as work goes. People can start out quite often at the mine, new ones are taken on all the time. There is always someone who gets hurt too. When I came here a Finn died in the mine. They were blasting and a rock hit him in the head and he died. Day before yesterday three Finns and an Italian were hurt.

When we came to Hancock there were fellows who were looking for two hundred and fifty men to work on building a railroad, two dollars a day. Here they also serve workingmen like gentlemen. Don't have to eat sour milk like back home. There is milk but it is not eaten, is used as a drink.

Clothing is very good and fine, especially for ladies. They are much better dressed than back home. Women have very easy work here. They only cook food and wash underclothes, which are all made of wool. Men don't have to work around the clock like back home either.

Don't know yet if I am going to go to work on the railroad-building when I have finished with the haymaking. Don't grieve, for working-men have it much better here than back home. If only you stay well and keep a cool head. But the money sure goes fast here even if you get one hundred dollars a month. Greet Rova's family and Johan Moskajärvi and his wife, and all the relatives and friends. Hilda and Jakob Hietala send greetings. Isak Hietala too.

Your fond son

Johan Huhtasaari

Harald Hvarfner, "Amerikabreven berättar," Swedish translation from Finnish by Helena Rautio, *Norrbotten* (1962), 123–24.

The Atlantic Mine, 23 September 1895

Dear and Always-remembered Parents, Brothers, and Sisters,

Here I come to you again with a few meaningless lines and let you know that I am feeling quite well in body. This same precious gift of the Lord I wish also for you. Also let you know at the same time that I have just come here to the Atlantic mine from the South to look for work.

It doesn't look like there is work here either. You can't just go and get work like many people think. And I have traveled around in this country from one place to another. When you can't get work you have to travel around and look until you find something that will give you enough to live on. There are such bad times here that you don't have anything left over to save up. You get to feeling so low that you don't feel like writing home either. When you can't send home the money you have borrowed either, then people think that you drink and live a wild life. But I can tell you that these days you have to look ahead and hope that you can keep yourself with clothes and food. It's that way with me too. I haven't been able to send what I have borrowed and can't do so now either, since I have to move on to look for work. But it looks as though times are going to get better. They say that new mines have been opened. Now please be patient and I will send money as soon as possible.

I think I'll end for this time and send best greetings to all the relatives and friends. But first and foremost greetings to yourselves from your son

Johan Huhtasaari

*Ibid.,* 127.

22 July 1896, Hancock, Michigan

Dear Sister Emma,

. . . People live a healthy life and deaths are less frequent and the bonds of love are formed quite often. On the Saturday evening after Midsummer Day, Oskar Strömbäck from Skogskärr and Josefina Taroniemi from Finnish Övertorneå were married. I was at their wedding and was an usher, which is the custom here that three or four pairs of boys and girls go with the bridal couple to the church where the wedding takes place. Two couples go ahead of the bridal couple and one couple comes after. The women expect that soon several couples will get married and I agree with the women about that.

I was at the Atlantic Mine last Sunday to call on the boys from Kuivakangas and hear how it has gone for them since they came here to earn their daily bread.

I must add too that I have other thoughts now than I did before. I have decided to take a helpmeet to wander together with through the joys and sorrows of the world. It means that I will be getting married, although I had always thought of wandering alone in this land. But there has been longing for someone dear to the heart. He who wanders in a strange land closes a door behind him and opens a new one. The strange land is of course not to be preferred above one's homeland, Sweden. But I think we will be able to live together like others do. Here a workingman gets along well, if he is healthy and has work and is a good worker. My wedding will be in the month of March. I wish for my parents' consent and that they wish for God's blessing upon us.

My intended was born in Vitsaniemi village, she is called Hilda Antti, is the daughter of Johan Antti. I believe that Petter knows her. I will let you know later about the time and day. It is still too early to say. One could be resting in the bosom of the earth by that time, who knows. It is not because my household needs a mistress, but love doesn't consider such things. It is the same for poor people as for rich.

End now for this time, another time more.

Your brother, Johan Huhtasaari

*Ibid.,* 128, 130.

13 December 1896, Hancock, Michigan

Dear Brother Petter,

While time and opportunity permit, I will write you a few lines and let you know that my bodily health is fortunately the best nowadays, the same gift of the Lord I wish for you.

And so I must tell a little about my work. I am in the mine nowadays. The pay is usually fifty dollars a month. You can get along well on this if you keep well and are able to keep on the job. You can save up a bit too if you want to and everything goes well. You could also earn for two and spend it all if you wanted to. For me it hasn't been possible to save up for a wife yet either. Don't think there will be a wife so soon with this fellow's name! A bachelor's life is carefree.

Will mention that I have heard over here that you are thinking of taking a helpmeet. One takes a wife, but let me tell you, look out before you enter into that business. It's not just an everyday matter. Don't know either for that matter if it is true, what has been written to me here, that you are thinking of getting married. Don't get mad at me if I tell you it would be best if you came here to America and earned money. Since you are also a healthy young man you would have great possibilities here later on, you who are so economical. If you should consider coming, it would be best to come here in the winter and go by way of Hangö or the Luleå coast road.[7] Next summer will perhaps be a good time. But I am not pushing you to leave the homeland, for your own land is strawberries, foreign lands are blueberries, as the saying goes. Do as you wish, but of course I would send the ticket and travel money, when you answer. Then I will know what you want and I certainly promise you work. Don't know of anything else but best greetings to you all, relatives and friends, but above all to yourself

wishes your brother, Johan Huhtasaari

*Ibid.,* 131–32.

1 May 1905, Hancock, Michigan

Dear and Ever-remembered Mother,

. . . When it gets to be summer one's thoughts go like this to the lovely summers of the North. Nothing can be compared with that beauty. There is never a birdsong in America's dark nights. If you go out you can hear only the mournful croaking of the frogs, where it is marshy.

Here the hills are so jagged and you don't see such pretty little islands and meadows filled with flowers. There is only coal smoke and dusty streets. Coal smoke from many factories so that the air gets heavy. It feels so bad when you have grown up in Norrland's fresh air. I am now in Houghton, a town on the lakeshore. Often in the evenings I hear the crashing of the waves. I don't know of anything more to write about this time. . . .

Emma Huhtasaari

*Ibid.*, 136.


14 August 1907, Hancock, Michigan

Ever-beloved Mother,

. . . If one forgets all else one does not forget the dear home of one's birth, the bright days of childhood. Grieve not over me, dear Mother, I am getting along well here, am well and am earning by work in a home.

Yes, now it is the glorious summer season here too. But it is more glorious to celebrate summer there in the land of a thousand lakes. There, where the hearts and thoughts of many remain always. There it is lovely in the light summer evenings, when one needs no evening lamp.

Write to me who is making hay with you, that would be fun to know. Have not heard news from home for a long time. . . .

*Ibid.*, 138.

5 April 1909, Hancock, Michigan

Ever-beloved Mother, far away in the dear homeland,

I always think of Mother and tears come to my eyes when I think that the seventh year has begun since I left the dear home of my birth. I am not so attached to America that I should forget the homeland. One always feels such a strange longing. Though now I have it very good. I have a good husband. He is no drinker like some of them are here. They drink so there's not enough to live on. My husband is called Valter Gustafsson from Juhonpieti, Pajala. Recently several people from Kuivakangas have been married here. . . .

Here we have beautiful summer weather already. The snow has melted, they are driving with wagons. Last week we had Good Friday off. The miners also had Sunday free then, didn't have to go to the mine.

Mother has not had a photograph taken of herself, since I have not gotten any photograph like I asked. I have no picture of Mother except that inside of me. I believe that I shall never be able to see Mother again in this life.

Valter is getting tired of digging in the mine the whole time, and emigrants keep arriving in crowds and there are also people without work. Last month ten thousand emigrants landed from the old country.

Don't have so much this time, but greetings to all, but first and foremost to dear Mother.

Signed your daughter<br>Emma Huhtasaari

*Ibid.*, 138.

*From Texas, the brothers Carl and Fred Bergman—who as we saw came there from the East in 1884—continue their correspondence with their sisters in Östergötland.*

7 January 1890, New Sweden, Texas

Dear Sister Sofie,

Have thanks for your dear letter with the enclosed calendars. We have waited to write, for we thought you had written. Therefore we wanted to wait for your letter, which we received in the days before Christmas. We hope you have had a good Christmas. It was very sad to hear that good Herr Wigander is sick. May he soon get well, that is our sincere wish. We wish you, the Wiganders, and all our other friends, a good continuation to the new year. With us, Christmas was as usual, nothing out of the ordinary.

We have now moved onto our own land, so now we are our own masters again. I had a little bad luck right after we moved out. I was to town or rather to our nearest railroad station after some lumber for our house. I also had three lengths of pipe for our iron stove. As it happened, the horses shied on me so that the wagon turned over with me and the load. I got my right leg dislocated at the hip, which is quite a difficult spot. The doctor who was called meanwhile pulled it back into place, but I am still unable to walk on it. That happened on 2 December. It is thus almost six weeks since then. The last two weeks I have been able to sit up a bit and with the help of crutches have been able to walk around the floor, but the doctor told me to keep still, for which reason bed is still the place where I stay most of the time. I am otherwise as well as if nothing had happened.

Aside from this misfortune everything seems to be going fine for us. We have built our house and have begun to clear the ground. The land we have bought is far from what you could call beautiful because there is so much brush on it, but when it is once in shape then it will be pretty enough. There were prettier places to be had but they were so expensive that we did not dare buy them. We have paid twelve and a half dollars per acre. We bought 230 acres altogether, but we may give up half of them because I got hurt and that set us back a bit; besides there was more brush than we thought, in any case we have enough with half of it. We also got an untold number of rattlesnakes in the bargain, but we will try to free ourselves from them. The harvest for 1889 was good, beyond what was expected, besides cotton brought a good price. In Texas no oranges are raised, so far as I know. It might be possible because the winters are mostly mild, but sometimes it can get so cold that sensitive trees like oranges would freeze. Peaches, however, grow in abundance here. California and Florida are the actual places in North America where orange-raising is carried on.

Greet Ekströms from us. I have often thought of writing to them, but I always think I have nothing to write about, besides they find out from you about our letters. We are just as fond of them as if we wrote to them. I thought I was going to be able to fill the paper but I am beginning to doubt that I can. To fill out the blank space I will have to do the best I can. First, I must beg your pardon for writing this letter with a pencil, but since I am lying down it was easiest for me. Dear Sister, don't be sad that I have injured my leg, for it must have been God's will and in that case there is nothing to complain about. Maybe it was a punishment for me, or maybe only a warning to others. The horses were frightened by the rattling of the stovepipes. That happened right in town. I had no acquaintances there, but the Americans always show great sympathy in an hour of need. I hardly knew what happened before the doctor was there, the horses caught, and everything in order. A place was even prepared for me in the home of an American nearby, who gave me the best of care for twelve days. I was in too great pain to be moved home to our place, and besides we had no one to look after me except Fred. And the doctor's bill was less, he came to me six times. From the Swedes I had many invitations to be taken care of by families. Our pastor came as quickly as he found out about my condition and invited me into his home, but the doctor would not allow me to be moved until I could do so without difficulty. I longed to get home to our little place. I was glad it was not Fred who was hurt, for I am more used to pain. *Our address is as usual.* Farewell for this time.

A hearty greeting from us.

Carl and Fred

Landelius, ed., *Amerikabreven*, 134–36.

12 November 1890, Elgin, Bastrop Co., Texas

Dear Sister,

Thanks for your last letter. It is always such fun to get letters from our dear sisters and the homeland. Still, we are getting along fine and do not long to return, though our thoughts are often in our former home. I said that we do not long to return; certainly it would be fun to be able to see the dear old family home, and maybe to stay for good. It is hard to say for sure, but I believe that I, or we, would not get along so well. We are now so used to freedom in just about everything, so it would certainly be hard to change. No one ought to find fault with either America or Sweden though, for both are good in their own way and cannot be put to any comparison. . . .

*Ibid.*, 139–40.

24 September 1893, Elgin, Texas

Dear Sister Sofie,

Thanks for your latest letter. It is now quite a while since we got it, although we have not answered it before now. It is fun to hear that everyone is in good health. We are well as usual. Summer will soon be over and fall will soon be here. It has been very dry besides and continues to be, we are hoping and waiting for rain. The harvest this year is below average as far as cotton is concerned. The corn gave a good harvest though. The business situation has been very bad for the last month throughout the whole country, but has now started to get better. We therefore look cheerfully to the future. We have still not finished picking the cotton, but will probably be finished within a couple of days. We have six Negroes and Negresses who pick for us. You should hear them laughing and shrieking. I really don't think you would believe they were people, the way they carry on. They don't like it when you call them Negroes but would rather be called colored men. Among themselves they call each other niggers, blacks, crows, in fact all the worst nicknames they can find, but always take it in a good-natured way. They have a carefree nature. I have never seen a sad Negro. When he has eaten his fill he is always happy; the day after and the future he gives little thought to, therefore they are in most cases poor. As usual

I am very poor in news, so I must now end. Many warm greetings to you and to the rest of the relatives and acquaintances.

Carl and Fred

*Ibid.*, 154.


27 September 1895, Elgin, Texas

Dear Sister Sofie,

Thanks for your letter of 25 May. As we see, all of you are in health. A long time has passed without our writing to you, for which we must as usual beg your pardon for our negligence. I have many times thought of writing, but then something else has come up, so nothing came of it then. Besides we are very poor in news. Everything goes on as usual year after year. The cotton crop was small this year, about half of what it was last year, but prices are almost twice as high as last year's; we will get as much for this year's small crop as for last year's big one, besides we have only half as much work. Times look quite promising. We have gotten a fine crop of corn, the best we have ever had.

You mention in your letter that you heard from someone who had been in America that the Gospel is so little preached in Texas; whoever said that did not know much about Texas. If he had said certain parts of Texas he might have been right, but to take that for the whole situation is highly unjust, for here there is no lack of proclaimers of the Gospel. Here we have Lutherans, Methodists, and Baptists. Each of them maintains that he is right and that those that think or believe otherwise (than themselves) are lost. The question is, which of them is right. What do you think, Sister? We have the Bible to read, if we so wish, but what's the use of reading what you have read many times already? The Bible is a fine book; he who follows the way it stakes out for us need have no fear but rather a peaceful conscience.

I will not hold up America as a pattern, for here as elsewhere there is both good and evil, virtues and vices. Many who come here imagine that America is the land where you can live a pleasant life without working, but when they find that reality is the opposite to what they dreamed of in their imagination, they then try in every way to ridicule and put down America. I end with greetings to you as well as to others who may receive them.

Carl and Fred

*Ibid.*, 159–60.

23 January 1896, Elgin, Texas

Dear Sister,

Thanks for your letter and thanks for the calendars. You don't forget us with the customary gift, though we have nothing to send you in return. I have often thought that we ought to send our photographs, but we never seem to get around to getting ourselves photographed, which can only be considered pure negligence or carelessness. Fred had photographs taken a couple of years back, but they were far from good. As I mentioned before, we have a music band; he had some pictures taken in his uniform, but the pants were worn out so he put on a pair of striped ones instead. He thought they would not show, but they show clearly. Besides, the picture is quite faded. We are sending it so that you can get some idea of how he looks. We have had a happy Christmas and a Christmas-tree party for the children, I mean the schoolchildren. Here it is beginning to get like Sweden, at least at Christmastime, for there is both *lutfisk* and Christmas porridge,[8] besides a lot of other good things, but the latter are more everyday things.

Many Swedes are settled here and more come each year, so there will soon be a little Sweden here, especially around the Swedish church. There is a post office and three stores as well as a Swedish doctor, Carl-berg. The name of the place is *Nya-Sverige*, in English New Sweden. We live about eight miles from there, so we don't consider ourselves to belong to their community. We have also gotten a post office with the name of Lund and a store. Next time you write you may address the letter to our new post office. West of us there live nothing but Swedes for a distance of about sixteen miles. East and south and north of us there lives a mixed population of Americans, Germans and Bohemians, Negroes, and Mexicans, so it is certainly a strange mixture.

You wonder why we write so seldom, if it is because you urge us to turn to the Lord? Don't think that we take it badly, since you wish for our spiritual good. There is no particular reason, just carelessness on our part in not writing more often, so you must excuse us for it. We have not written to Ekströms for a long time but intend to do so. We hope you have had a merry Christmas and wish you a good continuation to the new year. A hearty greeting from us, your brothers,

Carl and Fred

*Ibid.,* 161–62.

15 February 1903, Lund, Texas

Dear Sister Sofia,

Have gotten your letter, many thanks. This is the first time I have written to you in so many years, but as circumstances are I must fulfill my duty. I·have the sorrowful news that our dear brother Carl is dead. He died the thirteenth of February, namely two days ago. Oh, my Sisters, how empty and desolate it is. We were both sick at the same time with typhus, a very common sickness here in Texas. I am, praise God, well, but have to be careful, for Carl was well too, but was careless enough to go out and catch cold so that he had to take to the sickbed which was his last here on earth. Oh, how lonesome I am. I wish I were back in my homeland.

We have had a Swedish doctor, he is called Nordlander, he was a schoolmate in Linköping seminary.[9] He is an excellent doctor, he is my best friend. He was at the funeral, it was so moving I can hardly talk about it. Oh, what a crowd of friends. He is missed a lot in the congregation he belonged to, he was the treasurer. There was not a dry eye in all that big crowd. I am so deeply grateful that he was well taken care of, nothing was wanting. Also I have bought a grave plot, and a monument will be put up to the memory of my dear little brother. I thank God that I am well, for now I have to take care of everything, both the postmaster's job and the store. Yes, there is a lot to do here.

Carl willed his share to me, but I have not opened it yet. He told me that after his death I should give each of you two hundred dollars. I think that Brother-in-law can very well use them. I don't think I can send any before next fall, for then I mean to sell out, for I am so tired of business. I wish for peace and quiet, for there is enough for the rest of my life without working. I have slaved enough. Thank God, we have always had health and luck. I can make out just how much there is; around ten thousand dollars from the store, that is to say from the general store, as well as around four thousand dollars from my farm, so you see we have worked hard but in an honest way. I am so very glad that we did not deny ourselves necessities, we have always been well. Now I think this is enough for this time, will tell more next time. It is raining just about all the time this winter. We haven't had any cold yet. Greet Sister and Brother-in-law. If I come home they will not have to suffer any need, for it would be a lot of money in Sweden. Farewell for this time.

Signed your devoted brother<br>Fred Bergman

*Ibid.*, 180–81.

13  April 1903, Lund, Texas

Dear Brother-in-law and Sister,

Got your letter a few days ago. I have had so much work since Carl died that I could not answer before now. It is too bad that Brother-in-law is ill. Oh, how good it is to have one's health. I am glad and thank God, for I am well again. So sad it was when we both lay ill. I was near death myself, but got well. Oh, how much I miss Carl. I am so sad, so often I wish myself back to the motherland to see you. That would be something new, for it is so many years since I was home, it is surely not the same as when I was young. Old age is beginning to show, for my hair is starting to turn gray. I imagine to myself that I see your children, how they would look at me when I came home, it would be fun to be called uncle. Yes, if everything goes well I will try to go home. I doubt if I can really get along well in Sweden, for there are such great differences in rank with you. Here just about everyone is as good as anyone else, as long as they are honest. I will send you my picture, the way I am now, it is a long time since you saw me.

Brother Carl he wanted me to give you two hundred dollars as a little gift. My situation is quite good, but you can't have them before fall, for then I am thinking of selling the store, which will bring in quite a good price if there is a good crop of cotton. I have a lot of money loaned out since last year, around seven thousand dollars, a large amount in Swedish money. My little farm I will keep as long as it goes up in price. It is so warm today that the sweat is running off me, imagine if you had it so warm at this time of year.

Now the telephone is ringing. Now I'll have a chat with my best friend, the little doctor who took care of us when we were sick. He is Swedish, he has sat on the same school bench as brother Carl. An excellent man, he is called Nordlander. There is so much I ought to write, but can't manage more for I am so tired. There will be more next time. May God keep all of you, wishes your devoted brother-in-law

Fred Bergman

*Ibid.,* 182–83.

26 February 1905, Lund, Texas

Dear Sisters,

Must wish you a happy new year, and answer both of your letters. I ar̩ ɡlad that you got the money for your birthday, but I sent it in time to ɡet there by Christmas. It was a small amount, but more another time. Must thank you for the gift I got, it was a reminder of old Sweden.

Now I must first tell you that we have us a sweet little girl, so now I have something in place of Carl. You asked what my little woman is called. She is called Olga Nygren. She is Swedish. Although she was born here in Texas, she talks Swedish as well as I do, though she prefers English, it goes much easier.

I must tell you that we have had much cold for three weeks' time, we even had snow for two days, something strange for the people of the South. The oats got killed by frost, so tomorrow I will have to sow my oats over again. Also we will have to plant the corn, for it is so warm, so warm that we have to have both the windows and doors open. It is hard on an old businessman to work. For that matter I don't do so much, feed the horses and cattle. They go outside the whole year so there is not so much bother. Milking is a man's job here in the South.[10] Must tell you how many horses and cows I have, four mules, two horses and ten cows, a lot of pigs. I have Negroes working for me this year. You can drive them like animals, for they can take anything except the cold, they freeze so easily, besides they don't have clothes.

We will send you pictures of our house, the little lady, me, the dog and cat, the whole Bergman family. Also we will send our Swedish church in Lund and the parsonage, all Swedish. I don't need to greet for the little woman, for she has written her own letter. . . . Must bring this to a close for now. My pen is so poor, and my fingers hurt so much. Greetings from us both to all of you, from your brother

Frederick and Olga Bergman

*Olga adds:*

26 February 1905, Lund, Texas

Dear Sisters,

Although we are unknown to each other, I will nonetheless try to make your acquaintance through letter writing, for we will surely not get acquainted in any other way since the great wide ocean lies between us.

My dear little old man, he often wishes he could travel to Sweden, but I don't dare to let him go, for perhaps we might never meet again. What would become of me without him? I have no happier times than when we can be together with each other, for he is truly a lovable person, to me a dear husband, indeed happier than I am, who have such a mate, I truly don't know if anyone can be.

Well, I must go on to something else.

We have a little daughter, she will be named *Hildegard*. We will send her picture sometime when we have had a photograph taken of her.

I beg your pardon for this poor letter of mine, for I must say that my Swedish, when it comes to writing to Sweden, is very bad.

Well, there might be something more to write, but my little old man he takes everything to fill up his letter with so that I don't get much to write about.

My letter ends with warm greetings to you both from myself and Frederick and little daughter Hildegard

Olga

*Ibid.,* 188–89.

3 December 1906, Lund, Texas

Dear Sisters,

Must thank you so much for your dear letter which we got a long time ago. I have delayed answering on purpose so that we would have the opportunity to send a little Christmas money, so you can have some fun too. We are blessed with a good cotton crop here in Texas, also we have had a fine fall so it was harvested well, also a good price. I can say that we are well and spry as can be, but time goes so quickly that we can hardly keep up, for as far as I am concerned I have my hands full of work. I am a farmer one day, the other day a gentleman. The thing is, I am part owner in quite a large general store, also I am a shareholder in a bank that belongs just to Swedes. I have been elected one of the directors, but would rather not have to be, for I like the country best. I am healthiest when I can milk my cows morning and evening. I can tell you it is an honor to be able to do everything that comes up in the world, nothing is too good here in Texas. With you at home that won't do. There the poor man has to go with his hat in his hand, here there is no difference as long as they are honest, that is the main thing. Yes, if God blesses our undertakings, all goes well; the Swedes are getting ahead in great strides. . . . Can tell you that we have gotten us a new pastor in our little congregation. Here too I have had something to do, I am treasurer, vestryman, and secretary, so I am never without something to do. Now Sofie will get 200 *kronor* and Hanna the rest, 548 *kronor*, for she needs it more than you, Sofie. Now I must end with many, many greetings from the little woman and the daughter. Yours in haste.

Brother Fredrick

*Ibid.,* 193–94.

3 December 1924, Austin, Texas

. . . It seems strange that Ruth[11] can't write to her cousins, but shame to say, she doesn't know Swedish. She talks quite well, but can not write Swedish. Olga she writes Swedish fairly well, but it goes so slow, so slow. It is slow even for me. . . .

*Ibid.*, 210.

*The Klondike gold rush, beginning in 1896, brought a number of Swedes to Alaska and the Yukon Territory, among them O. A. Classell, who later reminisced:*

On 29 September 1897 we were forced to go into winter quarters because of the ice floes on the Yukon River, which prevented us from continuing on to Dawson. We were three hundred persons in all, and we built ourselves log cabins to live in. The coldest we had that winter was sixty-nine degrees below zero (minus fifty-one degrees Celsius), but it lasted only a few hours. In such cold one stayed inside if possible, kept the stove red-hot, satisfied one's ravenous appetite with pork and beans, etc., read novels, if one had any, and slept fifteen hours a day. The time passed quickly, and there was little sickness in the camp. Occasionally we arranged little festivities, which greatly reminded us of such things in Sweden in the old days, in that we ourselves brought with us food, knives, and forks. I had a little organ which could easily be carried around, and several others had violins, mandolins, cornets, and guitars. We often played together.

In the spring, when the ice broke up in the river, the water rose twenty feet, and the little island, on which we had settled, lay under water for a week. In some places it rose four feet over the island, so that we had to move up onto our roofs and stay there the whole week. On 20 May 1898 we left our winter quarters and sailed off toward Dawson. In one place we stranded on a sandbank, and it took us sixteen days to get loose. On Midsummer Day we arrived in Dawson and there found

18. Swedish housemaids, around 1890. (Folkminnessamlingen,
Nordiska muséet, Stockholm.)

19. A gentleman in full fig, 1899. (Folkminnessamlingen, Nordiska muséet, Stockholm.)

22. A peasant interior from Linnabacken, 1904. (Nordiska muséet, Stockholm.)

23. An America-visitor (center, in white dress) helps with the haying
in Hälsingland. (From the author's collection.)

24. A flower-bedecked girl on her way from Öland to America.
(Courtesy of Kalmar länsmuséet, Kalmar.)

25. Fred Bergman's drygoods and grocery store in Elgin, Texas, around 1906.
(Folkminnessamlingen, Nordiska muséet, Stockholm.)

26. The first plowing on Joseph Hansson's land in South Dakota, around 1910. (Photograph by Joseph Hansson, courtesy of Berton Hansson, Nässjö.)

27. "Here is a little picture of our home . . . " The August Cederlund family in South Dakota, 1910. (J. Hansson, courtesy of B. Hansson, Nässjö.)

28. Swedes at 675 Sheffield Avenue, Chicago, around 1910–1912.
(By J. Hansson, courtesy of B. Hansson, Nässjö.)

29. Swedish carpenters and painters on the job in Chicago.
(By J. Hansson, courtesy of B. Hansson, Nässjö.)

30. Railroad workers on their day off, Aurora, Minnesota, 1913. (Courtesy
of Folklivsarkivet, Etnologiska institutionen, Lund University.)

31. A schoolhouse in South Dakota, around 1910. (By J. Hansson, courtesy of B. Hansson, Nässjö.)

32. Mother reads a letter from America. (Courtesy of Höganäs museum, Höganäs.)

around thirty-five thousand fortune-seekers ahead of us. As soon as I came ashore and had gotten up a tent and provisions, I made a journey on foot of one hundred miles, together with three comrades. With packs on our backs and shovels in our hands, we made our way over mountains and through marshes, dug holes here and there, examined the different types of rock, and managed to eat up our provisions before we returned. We shot a caribou with our revolvers and divided up the meat like brothers.

If we had come to Dawson in 1897 we could have made money by working for others. There they were then paying one to one and a half dollars per hour. Together with others I leased mines, but did not find enough gold to pay for the labor. At times I dug holes on contract and could then earn on the average ten dollars (thirty-seven *kronor*) a day at the rate of six dollars per foot. The ground is frozen the year around, and you have to set large fires to thaw it out. I also worked at floating timber on the river. The best firewood contract I made brought me thirty-five dollars per cord, cut into stove-lengths, but at times fifty dollars had been paid. Within a radius of seventy-five miles around Dawson all the land was taken up by gold diggers when I came there. Foodstuffs were incredibly expensive. During the summer cows were imported, and then you could buy a glass of milk for fifty cents. Butter cost one to two dollars a pound, eggs two and a half dollars a dozen, a meal one to two and a half dollars, and so on.

Ernst Skarstedt, *Svensk-amerikanska folket i helg och söcken* (Stockholm, 1917), 380–81.

*Another Swedish sourdough was Emil Granfelt from Småland, who left an account from the years 1900 and 1901:*

. . . The gold-washing began in May, but we didn't have enough water, for everyone who had mines wanted to wash gold at the same time. There was a whole lot of trouble over that. On the eighteenth of June I quit work at the mine. . . .

That evening I left Bushill and went that night into Dawson. Here I had to stay for two days before I could get ready to go up to my own gold camp. I paid two Germans thirty-five dollars for the trip up to Cape Marine. The trip went well, without any great misfortune. . . .

On the evening of 23 June I left Eagle City with an eighty- or ninety-pound pack to go up to my own mine.

After a long night's march I arrived early in the morning at my cabin. But what a sight, half the cabin was filled with old ice so I had to lie down and rest after the night's march outside the log cabin. But when I had rested a while I was forced to get busy and get rid of the ice. After an hour's hard work I found my old bed.

My cabin is ten feet long and eight feet wide. The window is a little hole in the log wall. The door opening faces the east and measures four and a half by three feet. When the wind blows the door is closed, for a piece of sailcloth has to serve in place of a walnut panel. The roof consists of poles caulked with moss and bark. Half the cabin is my bedroom, but when it rains I must rig up an awning over my bed to keep from getting soaked through. So in rainy weather I sleep by a waterfall. Through the window and the cracks I have not filled with moss the flies have entry. The floor in that part of the cabin not taken up by my bed consists of the same material Adam had in paradise. (Since it was good enough for him it ought to be good enough for me.)

My kitchen I have outside, an iron barrel serves as my stove. My table is a large log and I have a smaller log for a chair. I am very proud of my bake-oven. When I bake, I dig a hole in a pile of earth, the hole is one and a half feet deep. Then I build a large fire so that the earth gets well warmed up and a large heap of coals is formed. When that is done I take, if I have them, two gold-washing pans (these are similar to ordinary frying pans) and put the dough between them. (If I don't have any gold-washing pan at home I lay the dough directly on the fire.) Then I put the two pans together on the fire and pile up the warm earth and coals over them. After an hour I can take out my gold pans and between them I have the best bread you could wish for.

My greatest enemies are the mosquitoes and a bird called the Alaska bluebird. The former swarm around me day and night, and the bird begins shrieking and carrying on every morning at half past three. But my revolver has sent many of them back to their maker.

At first when I came to the mine I could see to read the whole night through if I so wished. But now at the end of July the nights become a bit darker.

On 4 July I was in Eagle City. It was Independence Day and it was celebrated as usual in town with a salute. Fifty cannon shots were fired by Uncle Sam's soldiers.[12]

Later there were all kinds of sports. The Indians took part in a competition that was very funny to watch. Some ten or fifteen Indians competed to see who could get across the river first, with some small, light birch-bark canoes. They paddled with such speed that their black hair stood straight out behind them. A competition which only Indians took part in was to jump on a hide stretched out by many other Indians. Whoever was able to jump highest won the competition. A hunchbacked Indian boy took first prize. Later there were many competitions which only the whites took part in.

A whole lot of Indians with women and children had come into town. They belonged to a tribe with three or four hundred members which lived two English miles from Eagle City. Many of them spoke good English. . . .

Next day I went up to my mine. I then had along with me a large load of provisions. Then I worked in the mine until 23 July, then I left my work to go down to Dawson. . . .

## 1901

New Year's Eve I celebrated at the Grand Hotel in Dawson together with my friend Roy. The dance halls were in full swing as usual and the "sons of the green isle" (the poker players) had gathered around the green table. The money they had earned they let roll. It was either double or nothing for them. The saloon was full of gold miners. Scandinavia was well represented. Dark-haired, talkative Frenchmen and Italy's dark-skinned sons too, were to be seen in the saloon. Everything went peacefully and quietly, no commotion or fights took place. One could go wherever one wished without risking either life or property. Every man knew that if anything happened it would be his loss and the police's gain.

During the evening I met many of my old acquaintances, all of whom were gold miners. I came back to the hotel just in time for the

end of the old year and welcomed the new with twelve shots from my
forty-four revolver.

Karl-Erik Håkansson, "Guldgrävaren från Hjortsberga. Några utdrag från de
anteckningar som fördes av Emil Granfelt under hans vistelse i Amerika
åren 1892–1902," *Värendsbygden* (1961) , 41–43, 45.

*For some of the immigrants, tragedy awaited already at their entry into
the new land. A woman in California later recalled her arrival around
1900.*

At last we were there. Some hours before landing we were told to
assemble up on deck for examination. It was windy and cold, and since
we had to stand there for several hours, we all caught cold. Mother
fainted and was taken to the infirmary on board. Father took us
children to a hotel but we were turned out the following day, for we
had all taken ill during the night. We had fevers and were sent back to
Ellis Island[13] and put into the hospital there. I was separated from
father, brothers, and sisters, and put in a room where there were
already fifteen little girls. Some hours after I came in, the door opened
and a big, dark man with a black beard came in carrying a board under
his arm. I shall never forget how frightened I was of him. He went to
one of the beds and took a little girl who had died and laid the little
body on the board and tied a strap around the dead body and the
board. Then he took it under his arm and went out. I was to see all
fifteen, who were there when I came, carried out in that way. An indescribable terror passed through me every time I saw the black beard in
the doorway.

One day I thought I heard someone calling my name. "Olga, Olga,"
I heard. I tried to get up but just then a nurse came in and helped me
up to the window. Down there I saw Father going back and forth
and calling. He caught sight of me and cried, "Dear child, you are
still alive!"

A week later I heard him call my name again. By then I had
recovered enough that I could go to the window and talk with him. He

had been in quarantine for a week and then he had worked shoveling coal and digging graves on the island. He did not dare tell me that Mother was dead. His clothes were ruined and his fur coat smelled as if it had been burned. When he got out of the hospital his clothes were so dirty that he put them in a tub of rainwater which was under a roof gutter. He washed them as well as he could and laid them out on the grass to dry while he sat on the steps and watched them.

One day, Father met a Swede and asked him to help him to find out about Mother, who he knew should be in one of the many buildings. They went through a long hall and there by a door he saw a bundle of clothes which he recognized as Mother's. He also heard Mother coughing inside but could not go in because the door was locked. He called out as loud as he could, "How is it with you, Johanna?" She answered that she was sick but also hungry. Father then went down to where he had his knapsack and packed up a little of what was left of the food for the journey. When he came back he met a nurse. She let him in after he had gesticulated for a while. He tucked the little package under her pillow and told Mother that all of us children were still alive. Then he was taken by the arm and led out of the room. That was the last time he saw Mother. A couple of days later when he slipped up there the door was open and the room empty. He met a nurse who with the help of a clock tried to explain the time when Mother had died. The next morning he was told to dig a new grave. When he was ready, a black horse came pulling a cart with five unpainted wooden coffins. Father knew that in one of them lay Mother. They piled them up, one on top of another until the grave was filled. About a week later, I heard Father call again. I then saw Father standing down there, black as a chimney sweep from all the coal shoveling, but in any case it was wonderful to see Father again.

Then the time came when I was well again. They brought Father and my sisters so that we then met for the first time since we had become sick. It was a Catholic hospital and next to it was a school which my sisters had been in. They all spoke fairly good English for the short time, not quite four months, they had been there. They talked about Mary and the saints and made the sign of the cross and tried to tell about many other things that we could not understand. The nuns wanted us to stay there but Father would not permit it and we took the boat to New York. Upon landing, we were met by a distinguished-looking lady who had read about our illness in the newspapers and wanted to adopt my sister Anna. But Father did not want to be separated from any of us. We eventually came to Minneapolis, to Sofia, one of our former working girls, who was married and living there. We stayed there for a while until Father found work. He then rented a house for us. Two months later, sister Anna died, twelve years old. The others, except for myself, were taken to a Swedish farmer, where they were well looked after. Father worked for three years as a carpenter and stonemason, after which he went up to Elk River, where he took up land. I had to stay with Father to look after the household. About eighteen years later, Father sold his 160 acres and moved to Minneapolis, where he lived until his death. . . .

Widén, *Amerikaemigrationen i dokument*, 70–72.

*A Swedish maid writes home to her friend:*

[no date]

Dear Augusta Larson,

Forgive me for writing again but I can never wait for a letter from you. I think it is so strange to never hear anything from my friend Augusta. I just wonder if you are mad at me or what it is, you could certainly take a little while to write a few lines to me. It would be such fun to get a letter from you and hear something from Torup and find out how things are with you. I for my part am very well and so far am having fun. We are of course not so many Swedes but enough to have a jolly time, and the American is just as good as the Swede once you can talk with him, and fairly well, though I can't talk so much. But if I could meet you, my friend, then I would teach you to talk English. It is much more fun to talk English than Swedish, and it will go all right to learn now that it doesn't sound so funny. I couldn't wish for anything more than to have you nearby so that I could see you sometimes. But that will surely never be, for to go home to Sweden, I surely won't do that. I seldom think about it, that it would be fun, maybe, if I live for a long time. I would like to know if you are going to get married soon or who your boyfriend is. I think you will tell me. I wonder if Mari is married yet or what? Let me know everything new that you know about and I think there would be a lot if you said everything. Write soon, please. I don't have anything new to tell about, Augusta. I can say that we had a *Swid parti last Sandi nait and de must fun we was nott mor and two girls but latse boys o wi just meck fam for erve day.* I must end with many dear greetings to you. Greet Mamma and Papa and all the acquaintances.

Signed, Emma Anderson

*Ibid.,* 78.

*From his student days at Gustavus Adolphus College in Minnesota around 1900, Amandus Johnson recalled the inspiration that led him to become a distinguished historian of Swedish America. With some friends he organized the Svea Society, which arranged a lecture by the well-known editor of* Hemlandet, *J. A. Enander.*

The hall was full when the affair was to begin, every seat was taken and people stood crowded in the aisles. We had sold three hundred tickets, but then seven members of the Svea Society, half of its membership, had free entry, as well as the professors and other teachers. We took in thirty dollars and had something over five dollars in pure profit. Moreover this caused the Svea Society to become known and talked about, and we received more applications for membership than we could take in because of our requirement for a knowledge of Swedish. Later this was changed so that even those who did not know the language could take part, but to hold office in the Society a person was still required to speak fluent Swedish.

At the stroke of seven, Rector Wahlström opened the meeting with a short prayer and announced that the first number on the program would be a Swedish song performed by a quartet. He then introduced the main speaker for the evening. Dr. Enander had just gotten on his feet again after a serious illness and looked tired and pale as he mounted the platform, but he warmed up when he began to speak about the New Sweden colony and recounted the history of the Swedish Americans. He related, among other things, that Betsy Ross, who sewed the first American flag with thirteen stars, was really Swedish and was called Ros, and that Daniel Boone was also Swedish and his original name was Bonde. He held his listeners spellbound for an hour and a half; he was really a brilliant speaker. When I later began collecting materials on Swedish-American history, I was able to confirm that only half of the information he gave was historical fact, but his speech was in any case captivating and when he had finished all rose to their feet and applauded mightily. He seemed moved and bowed several times before he left the platform. To our surprise, he now no longer appeared tired and worn. After the lecture, Dr. Enander and the professors, as well as Carl and I as representatives of the Svea Society, were invited to Wahlströms' for a late supper. Here Enander made a little speech in which he expressed the hope that his lecture might have inspired someone among the students present to take up the study of Swedish-American history and collect material and write on that subject, for it was a fascinating field for research.

Albin Widén, *Amandus Johnson, svenskamerikan. En levnadsteckning* (Stockholm, 1970), 54–55.

*Karl Gösta Gilstring of Linköping has for many years corresponded with old Swedish Americans about their experiences. Here Mrs. Jennie Monson of Chicago writes about her emigration from Småland in 1904.*

Pastor Gilstring wonders why we came here. For us from Krogstorp croft under Hornsberg manor, it can be said in two words. Poverty and inferiority. We could never dress like others and we were almost afraid to look at people. As soon as I was big enough, there was hard work, and I had to go to the manor every day from six in the morning to seven-thirty in the evening. The lease for the little croft was paid for with three men's workdays and three women's or children's workdays a week. The former was worth one *krona* in the summer and seventy-five *öre* in the winter. Now the croft is uninhabited and the pieces of land attached to it incorporated back into the estate. They will probably plant forest there now. When we were in Sweden in 1950 we went out and walked around and took pictures. Everything was as it had been, but it looked as though a lot of big rocks had crept up out of the ground that had not been there before. Last summer I did not want to go out there at all. There Mamma had to work herself to death and we who were children had a sad childhood.

I worked as a housemaid at Hornsberg from March to November 1903, and I got so tired of that place that I decided to come over here. One had to work from six in the morning to nine in the evening, and during a couple of free hours in the afternoon the chambermaid and I had to sit up on the third floor and sew quilts or sheets.

It was terribly sad when I left home on 10 May 1904. Papa drove me with a team of oxen to Fågelvik, and I went by boat to Norrköping. . . .

Karl Gösta Gilstring, "Amerikabrev," *Linköpings stiftsbok, 1959–60* (Linköping, 1959), 155–56.

*After knocking about on the East Coast, Carl Oscar Borg from Dalsland worked his way out to California on a freighter in 1903. There Borg, who later became a distinguished painter of the American West, had a memorable first encounter.*

. . . The steward let me take a day off and I decided to go into Los Angeles and look around. I do not remember how long the wooden pier was; it had tracks and freight cars on which the cargo was taken ashore. I trudged that long way to land, toward the yellowish, inhospitable shore. No trees were to be seen, but beyond, the purplish bluish mountains. Finally I was on terra firma and followed the road up a narrow valley, Santa Monica Canyon, so as to get up one side onto the clay bluffs. Once I was up there I found large trees and great palms, such as I had only read about or seen in illustrations, but I had not gone far before I met something still more interesting. It was a man on horseback, who came riding toward me. He was of middle age, somewhat graying, but straight-backed and lithe as he sat in his silver-mounted saddle on his horse. He wore a great, broad-brimmed hat, which shaded his sun-tanned face. He wore no coat, only a gray and black checked shirt, and around his throat a red neckerchief, around his waist a belt with a revolver holster, and on his legs wide leather breeches with large silver discs along the sides. On his feet he had gracefully sewn boots and large spurs. In short, he looked like that later film hero, William S. Hart. I did not understand that this was an ordinary rancher or cowboy, to me he seemed a knight from a time long past and even now I can still feel the breath of adventure he conveyed.

Albin Widén, *Carl Oscar Borg. Ett konstnärsöde* (Stockholm, 1953), 48.

~~~~~~~~~~~~~~~~~~~~~~~~~~~~~~~~~~~~~~~~~~~~~~~~~~~~~~

*An encounter of another kind was recalled by Amandus Johnson, who was born in Småland in 1877 and brought to Minnesota at the age of two. In 1906 he returned to the land of his birth to gather materials for his doctoral dissertation at the University of Pennsylvania on the seventeenth-century Swedish Delaware colony, the basis for his classic work on the subject.*

People in Stockholm were friendly and helpful. The waiters in the restaurants were not at all as importunate as at home in America and much more polite. After a week or so I began to like conditions and people in Sweden. When I first arrived I had actually been disappointed. The thing was that my grandfather in Minnesota had always described Sweden to me as a paradise. His heart was back in Sweden and as the years passed he increasingly idealized conditions back home, which in all ways seemed to him much better than in America, even when it was a question of such things as fruit and fish. Apples in America tasted like nothing compared with the juicy apples in Småland, strawberries in Sweden tasted much better than our American ones, and the pike in Långasjö were so marvellous that it was a shame to compare them with the fish in Minnesota. I listened to Grandfather's descriptions and as a child thought about them a great deal, and in my

mind told myself, "Some day . . . some day . . . I will travel to Sweden . . . I will taste the apples and strawberries in paradise and the
good fish that can be caught in Långasjö and which is better than any
other fish." Sometimes Grandfather told old tales and stories about the
most remarkable happenings and then it might happen that Grand-
mother interrupted him and said, "You know that all that was just
talk . . . it never happened." "You cannot prove that it didn't happen," my grandfather would then say, and I got the impression that
they both believed it was true.

I had expected that everything in Sweden would be large and magnificent, in accordance with Grandfather's descriptions. This turned
out not to be so. The little red cottages along the road were picturesque
but not imposing. The trees were small in comparison with the giant
trees I had seen in various places in America, the locomotives were
much smaller than our American engines, the same with the streetcars.
But everything was clean and proper and there were flower beds
around the railroad stations. A little railroad station in America in
those days looked like a junk heap in comparison with a Swedish one—
here trash lay in piles and there were no flowers. The villages in Sweden were not so different from small communities in America, but
everything was cleaner and neater, and there were flowers everywhere.
As far as the larger cities were concerned, they were also as clean and
freshly swept as though they had just been put in order to receive some
distinguished guest.

Widén, *Amandus Johnson*, 90.

*Mrs. Mandus Swenson, who left Östergötland for America in 1907, later
wrote to K. G. Gilstring from East Grand Forks, Minnesota:*

. . . In clear weather we could see the church steeples at Hov,
Högby, Skänninge, Bjälbo, Varv, I think it was, Apuna, Väderstad,
and our own, of course. Omberg Mountain lay like a blue thunder-
cloud to the west. I was born on 15 April 1892. Confirmed on 18 May
1907, on Whitsunday, by my dear Pastor Tyllman, and received my

Bible in the older translation. Although I often was sick then it was a golden time. In the fall, on 14 September, my attest was made out and on the seventeenth I stood, a lonely fifteen-year-old at Mjölby railroad station, never to see my dear home and land of my birth, Mother and Father again. My sister had sent the ticket without asking whether I wanted to come over here. I was the last one. Two brothers were here already. I didn't want to go.

God alone knows how homesick I was. . . .

Gilstring, "Amerikabrev," 160.

*After a couple of years in America, Arvid Pearson from Dalarna claimed a homestead of his own in North Dakota. In 1907 he moved out to his land, as he recounted in the recollections he wrote two years later for his relatives in Sweden.*

I had now worked on the railroad for nearly six months so now it was time to make the trip up to my farm and build my cabin. I requested and received a month's leave from the railroad. Since I had no horses, I had to hire them with Morris Burns as driver; he had two quite good horses, which were needed for the heavy load we had and the long distance to cover. The first day, 11 May, was a fine day so we drove thirty-seven English miles, but toward evening it began to blow cold and snow. It began to get dark when we arrived at Fred White's cattle ranch, where we intended to ask for lodgings for the night, which we did. But we received the answer that they did not put up any settlers, no matter how late and cold it got. Now the thing is that all those cattle ranchers who live out on the uninhabited prairies have great herds of livestock amounting to five or six thousand head, which have grazed freely on the high grass on land belonging to the state. Now when we farmers come and plow up the land for crops, their cattle have to be watched over or fenced in, so they thought that by making it as hard as possible for us they could frighten us away. But this attempt failed for now as this is written hardly any of these big cattlemen are left. I said that we would be glad to sleep out in the barn or in one of his outbuildings, but he answered that if we did not get out right away, he would use his rifle, which was hanging on the wall. I informed him that we had two rifles on the wagon, which we had especially brought along in case of need, but since we had no wish to use them on any human being, we drove on. I later heard that he had burned down the cabins of a couple of neighboring settlers, but they took the law into their own hands and shot twenty-two of his horses right before his eyes in return. He has now left his place there and sold everything.

Meanwhile there was another place six miles from there we intended to drive to, but sadly enough our horses were tired out and there we were out on the cold, dark prairie without any place for shelter. There was an abandoned sod house that was used for sheep, the west and north sides had already fallen down. We tethered our horses out of the wind, we ourselves tramped back and forth to keep warm, waiting for morning to come. That was one of the longest and loneliest nights I have ever spent. The only thing that disturbed the stillness of the night was the whistling of the cold wind and the howling of hungry wolves. I carried my loaded rifle on my shoulder, ready for the least attack from their side. Finally at four o'clock the first light of day began so that we could continue our long journey. We now drove twelve miles. There we let our horses rest out the day and got some much-needed rest and sleep ourselves, for the people at that place were settlers themselves and had their hearts in the right place.

The third day came. We were now rested; it was quite cold the whole day. We drove twenty-five or twenty-six miles that day. Neither of us knew the way, all we had to go by was the sun and the map. We now intended to make it to Bullhead's cattle ranch that evening, from which place I had only six miles to my land. Before we arrived there we met two men who came driving a wagon. We asked for directions. They were on their way to the post office, told us to drive down to their place, which was only ten minutes out of our way, and stay over night. We thanked them for the invitation and drove on. When we had gone a bit farther we saw the house they had described in the distance, but as I had some doubts about their generous offer I decided that while the horses rested, I would go ahead on foot and see that we were not duped. And right enough, it was an old cattle shed; they naturally thought we would be dumb enough to drive down there with our heavy load and then be stuck there with our tired-out horses, but that time they deceived themselves. We cursed up and down those who had no pity on the worn-out horses. It would not have been wise for them to be present at that moment; they would have had their hides beaten black-and-blue for sure, for my driver was so angry that he was practically hopping with rage.

We arrived at the Bullhead ranch in the evening. We got room for our horses, a bed to sleep in and food in the evening and in the morning before we left, it cost us nothing, so we said that we had met white folks once again. Next morning a little way from there we got stuck with our load so that we had to carry everything across a creek in order to get across. But that was nothing new. It was not the first time we unloaded, we had done it many times before on this journey. The six miles from this cattle ranch to my land wasn't any distance now; we had to drive right over the prairie with our heavy load. It went very slowly. Finally around dinner time we began to get close, but now the question was to find the right place. There were stones set at each corner so that you could know where you were, but it was almost impossible to make them out, I was almost sure we were on my land but to be sure it was best to ask someone. There was a cabin a good distance away so I decided to go there and inquire. No sooner said than done. When I got there the owner himself was not home, his name is Stettner, but his wife and two small children were home in the newly built cabin, where you could see out through every crack between the planks. I explained my business and asked where I now was, but unfortunately she was German, could not speak a word of English. I can speak and understand a little High German but she talked Low German, so I got nowhere. I tried in every possible way to make myself understood. I got the idea of making a little sketch, I made a little drawing and she then understood what I wanted to find out. She went after their homestead papers, and here it did not take me long to find out where I was. I was on the middle of the south line of Section 14; I now had to go one and a half miles west and one mile south to get to my land, and by looking at my watch, I knew how many minutes it took to go one mile. I thus came to my own land. My driver had believed the whole time that the land was poor here, but when he could see how high the grass was and how thick it was, he said it was the best he had seen so far.

Well, the eighty-mile-long journey was now over, but I was now alone with my load of lumber, cookstove, household utensils, and provisions, and when the provisions were gone the nearest store was in Dickinson, which was also the nearest post office. What would people in Gustafs parish think if they had to go all the way to Sala to shop and for their mail? . . .

Hallerdt, "Emigrantminnen," 85–89.

*Johan Albert Waldenkrantz, who had worked in mines and foundries at home, emigrated in 1907. He first took a job in an iron mine in Minnesota but soon moved out to the new frontier on the Saskatchewan prairies. During a visit to his native Dalarna in 1960–1961, he wrote the following account.*

My first work in America was on a steam shovel which scooped off the earth down to the ore. The ore was then loaded directly into railroad cars. I worked at that for a year and then began working on a diamond-toothed drill. The pay was then $2.50 per day. The country was a lot like Sweden, so we got along well, but many things were unlike what we were used to from Sweden. I had belonged to the Order of Good Templars in Sweden and had my transfer card with me so that I became a member of the lodge in Eveleth.

We had originally thought that when we had earned a little money we would go back to Sweden, but in September 1909 we decided to go up to Canada and take free land. We had acquaintances there already, which would make things easier for us with the language, etc. The trip to Canada was cheap, for homesteaders could ride on the Canadian railroads for one cent a mile. We came to Bircks Hills, the nearest railroad station, and were able to ride from there with a Norwegian farmer with oxen. The land there was already taken, but the Canadian government had opened a new district a little farther south, so it was just a matter of picking out a quarter section of land (around 130 *tunnland*), but the land was overgrown with forest, so it was hard work to bring it under cultivation. We went into a town called Prince Albert, where the land office was located, and there we had to pay ten dollars to get the land claim registered in our name. But before we became owners of the land, we had to live on the claim for at least six months a year for three years, and during that time break thirty acres of plowland. But the land was difficult to work so it required six years before we became owners of the claim. The first winter we had to live in a house that stood empty, the owner had gone down to the States. The house was located two kilometers from our homestead, so we had to build a house on our land as soon as possible. I began cutting timber in the forest on the homestead, it was aspen, for there was no needle forest, and then I did some clearing where the fields were to be.

I first built a house that was intended as a chicken coop, but that had to do as a dwelling house while the farmhouse itself was being put up. In the spring of 1910 we moved out to our own property. We bought two cows and some chickens so that we had milk and eggs, besides which there were plenty of wild rabbits and grouse. That was our good fortune, for we had three Swedish miles to the nearest store, and our visits to it could not be so often. I bought a team of oxen and plowed up two and a half acres of land which I planted corn on. After that I started building our dwelling house, which took up most of the summer before it was ready to live in. At the end of the summer that year I began working on railroad construction in the province of Alberta, which for my part continued for some months. In the spring of 1911 the clearing and breaking of ground was continued. I and my brother-in-law had bought a stump breaker which we used to pull out the biggest stumps with, the smaller ones we chopped off close to the ground. When I plowed I borrowed a team of oxen from a neighbor so that I had four oxen on the plow, and since there were almost no rocks and the biggest stumps were gone, the plowing went very well. The mosquitoes were a nuisance, but had the advantage that the oxen kept a livelier pace. In that way the work continued for some years and the plowland increased. There was hay to be harvested, the grazing for the livestock was good, and all the calves that were born lived; in that way we got quite a large herd of stock. In 1912 our second child was born, so now we also had a son. In the year 1913 a railroad was built in the vicinity of our settlement, which meant that we now had only ten English miles to the nearest railroad station. We now started sending cream to the dairy and in this way had a source of income. We were several neighbors who took turns driving to the station. After a time some of us decided we would build a community center. We began cutting timber which we hauled to a saw to be cut into lumber and went on with the building of the house. All the work was done free. We got help from some, but a number were so fanatically religious that they were opposed to a meeting place for the settlement. We had earlier formed a discussion club and before the community center was completed we had our meetings sometimes here sometimes there among the members. We had also formed a lodge of the Order of Good Templars. . . .

*Ibid.*, 92–95.

*The following letter found its way to a rural parsonage in Sweden.*

14th of November 1907

Honored Pastor,

The undersigned wishes herewith to ask whether the Pastor knows if there is any woman by the name of Anna Katarina Bergstedt. That was her maiden name about twenty-four years ago. I would like to know where she is. If the Pastor would be so kind and inform me where she is I am sending herewith a letter to her in case it should reach her. She lived at Vedlösa at the above-named time and her father was a miller. I am sending the Pastor an America-dollar for the trouble. My address is . . .

Einar M.

*Enclosed was this letter:*

Dear Anna,

I wonder how you have it and if you are living. I have it very good here. It is a long time since we saw each other. Are you married or unmarried? If you are unmarried, you can have a good home with me. I have my own house in town and I make over ten *kronor* a day. My wife died last year in the fall and I want another wife. I only have one girl, eleven years old. If you can come to me I will send you a ticket and travel money for the spring when it will be good weather. We live very good here in America. I have been here for fourteen years. I can send greetings from your uncle. He is in the same town where I am. It is around twenty-four years since we saw each other. You must wonder who I am. My name is Einar, who worked over at Vensta for Adolf Johanson when you were at Andersons', and you were my first girl-friend. If you can't come maybe you know somebody else who wants to become a good housewife. If these lines should reach you please write right away and let me know how things are with you. Signed, your old friend Einar. . . .

I will write a few words in English, *I am Loved joy of all my Hart j hav bin driming af bort joy y hoppes dat joy vill bi my vife*

*Respechtifulli*
*Godd Bye*

*j am sand joy one worm kiss.*

Sweden, *Emigrationsutredningen* (Stockholm, 1908–1913), *II: Utvandringsväsendet i Sverige* (1909), 154.

*Naturally, in the course of things, letters like this one—probably from Massachusetts—could reach the old home:*

12 January 1908, Winchester

Dear Parents-in-law,

I must write a few lines and tell you that it is I who have stolen your son, whom you will never get back again, for I want to have him always. We are getting along wonderfully here. We only wish you could come and see us. That would be the greatest joy we could have. We have a nice little home with four rooms, and it is very pretty here in the summer, it is almost like at home in Dalsland. Well, I must end, for I do not know how welcome my lines may be. Many warm greetings to you all from your

devoted

Christina

Harnell, et al., *Dalsländska emigrantbrev*, 147.

*From her journey to Canada in 1908, Mrs. Hulda Belin of Rockford, Illinois, born in Småland, later recalled:*

So the train continued on and we were in Michigan, U.S.A., and then into Minnesota's snowy wastes. The train made a stop and off of the train climbed a youth; he was tall and gangly, eighteen or nineteen years old, and you could see he was Swedish. Not a person was to be seen at the stop, that little square wooden house. He stood there alone and as though lost. He had no overcoat and it was cold. No one was in sight to meet him and no dwelling houses were to be seen. Then the train went on and he stood there alone. I have often wondered what his fate was.

Gilstring, "Amerikabrev," 161.

*Young George F. Erickson arrived in the iron-mining country on Michigan's northern peninsula in 1909 and remained there until his death in 1950. For more than forty years he corresponded faithfully with his boyhood friend Linus Paulin at home in Västmanland.*

10 January 1910, Stambaugh, Michigan

Best Friend and Comrade Linus,

First of all, I thank you most heartily for the long letter I got today. . . . You talk about much news from Järnboås, but it is bad with work as usual. I consider myself lucky to get away from there, for there was nothing else to do but stay at home and have nothing to do if I had stayed there. Here in America you don't have to go without work if you want to do something. I never had to look for any work. I got it anyway, so there is certainly a difference here and in Sweden, where you have to go and bow and scrape and ask everywhere and still not get anything. I have it quite good here. . . .

Now I will write a little about how I spent Christmas. On Christmas morning I was to the Swedish Mission Church here, then I was at Uncle's daughter's and son-in-law's and spent Christmas Day. I can also tell you to show about the Americans' lust for work that we worked on Christmas Eve, but we got to quit at three-thirty, so that was liberal still. . . . Much can change in a year. We certainly didn't think the day before Christmas Eve in the evening in 1908, when I went to see Gunnar, Ivar, and Forsberg, that we would be in America, all of us, by the next Christmas, but that's how it can go. I don't regret it at all. I have not had any homesickness, for when I think of them there at home I can't help thinking of the bad times and how hard it is to make a living. . . .

Unpublished letters of George F. Erickson, 1909–1949.


20 February 1910

. . . Yes, here in America everything goes quickly. You can't understand where so much ore goes, so many thousands of tons that are brought up every day around here, and that's nothing compared with what is brought up in other places. You ask if it is hard to learn English. It's not so good. You can learn to understand a little here and there when you hear a couple of people talking but if you try to say something yourself then it comes out half English and half Swedish. I haven't been here long yet but I know more or less what the names are for things like, for example, *hus* haus, *häst* horse, *ko* kau, *höns* kicken, *kalkoner* turkey, *svin* piggs, *hund* dogs, *näsduk* hänkerkif, *stol* sit, *pappren* peprer, *skor* shus, *kläder* sut, *mössa* caps, *handskor* mittens, *skorta* skirt, *flicka* görl. Well that is enough now. Now I can say *"I dont know"* (*aj dont nå*). I don't know any more. But if you could be on a shift with people who speak English the whole time then you could learn quickly. When you are young you learn fast. Also it makes a big difference if you have someone to teach you what this word and that means, so if there is some word which I have heard during the day I go up to Uncle and ask him what this and that means, then he tells about it and then I know next time. But to try and read English is like putting Latin in front of the cat, for it is not pronounced anything like it is spelled and there are many words with letters that are never heard when they say the word. A *knif* is spelled *knife*, pronounced *najf*. Well, Linus, you know more English than I do, I believe, so it is not worth it for me to boast about my learning. . . .

*Ibid.*

[June?] 1910

Now I have gotten the Nora newspapers so now there will be some reading and I will see if there is any news from the old neighborhood at home. That is what I look for first when I get them. . . . You ask if I have seen any airships yet but I have not, to tell the truth, but there are so many automobiles. They drive with them wherever you go, soon you won't be able to walk on the roads because of those things. . . . Well, by now you must have the Americans[14] in Järnboås again, I wonder how they are going to find it there. When you write tell me how they seem to get along under Swedish conditions. Old Americans like that always find a great difference in conditions between Sweden and America. I heard a good story the other day, there was a man who told it to me in English. There was a Swede and an American who stood and talked, and the American told the Swede about everything in this country, but to everything he told about the Swede said, "We have exactly the same thing in Sweden." Finally the American got mad and said, "I know one thing which you still don't have in Sweden, you don't have any Indians." But the Swede was not without an answer and replied immediately, "We have Indians in Sweden too, but we call them *Nor-*

*wegians."* So now you see what we have in old Sweden, it is not behind any country on earth. . . .

*Ibid.*


26 December 1910


. . . Today is the day after Christmas and a very nice day, but yesterday, Christmas Day, there was a regular blizzard. I was up at four in the morning and was to *Julotta*,[15] so you see I have not forgotten the old ways and customs so far. I also got Christmas presents, so I have had quite a pleasant Christmas. I wonder how it has been back home, whether you have had any fun, but I'm sure you did, for Christmas in Sweden is generally celebrated much more than what they do here. Here everything is going along as usual, you work hard as always to manage in the U.S.A., to improve your finances so you can travel home to Sweden some time and see your friends and relatives, if you live and have your health. It would sure be fun to come home and visit some time, and we could talk like before and discuss with each other like we used to do. But aside from that, I am glad that I am not home but here where I am, for as far as economy and working conditions are concerned America is far ahead of Sweden for a poor workingman. So it is better to make your way here than in Sweden, but at the same time you have to be clever, a good worker, and reliable. A man who drinks a lot has no future here. There are so many people that they have demands on a man; but otherwise the Swedes are highly valued as workers, so highly even that if you go and ask for work the boss may ask if you are Swedish, in that case you get work right away. Now I have written a little about conditions here, such as I have found them at this place, but as you know they are different in different places. There are not many pleasures here and you understand that this is because one was not born here and so you don't get in with people the way you would wish. You know that those who are born here they believe they are rather finer than those who come from another land. . . .

*Ibid.*

[Fragment, Winter 1911]

. . . You ask if there is anything to do in your free time on the long winter evenings and to that I can answer that regarding both amusements and evenings things are not so good. There is a so-called Electric Theater here where they have shows on Saturday and Sunday evenings, but that is all. I have been into a couple of the saloons but I have never taken a glass of beer or liquor, so I am an absolutist so far. In this little town with maybe forty-five hundred inhabitants there are twelve saloons, and all of them do good business. Five minutes from here is another town which I have written you about before, with two thousand inhabitants, and there they have thirty saloons. From this you can understand that there must be a lot of drinking when there are so many saloons and that there are good profits in it. . . . There are a great many Hjulsjö people around here. Among them there are two big fellows who are brothers. One of them came here last summer the other was here before and has the nickname "The Baby." Sunday a week ago they made a disturbance at that theater I told you about, so they were arrested by the police and both fined twenty dollars. So you can't just behave any way you want here either. . . .

*Ibid.*

2 April 1911

. . . I was out of work for two weeks, but then I got it back again and now I am working good and proper, for in May I did thirty-two shifts, so that is one more shift than there are days in the month. . . . I have an Italian for a partner now, so I am not with the Finns any more. He is a wild one, this fellow. Sometimes we are real good friends and sometimes we fight. He thinks he ought to be able to scare me but I have shown him the opposite. He is quite a good worker but so stubborn and selfish, and he doesn't understand a bit of English, so when I say anything he thinks I am scolding him because then he gets mad and starts swearing in Italian. But when he is at his worst I just take the wagon and the fellow and everything and do as I want anyway. You know I am stubborn too and no Italian is going to come and be a boss over me. I have had many different sorts of partners since I came here and I have gotten along well with all of them, but this one here he is the worst. But I will be able to take care of the rascal all right. . . .

Today they are having elections here in Stambaugh, so you can be sure things are lively. New city councilmen are going to be elected, if I may call them that. Here they have another name, "township board," but I think it is practically the same thing. Yes, there is a terrific hubbub over politics here in America and no ways are considered too low to make use of. Here above[16] are the names of those who are running against each other for chairman. One is a man of the people and the other a company man. It will be a hard fight. You know the big mining companies do everything they can to get in their candidate. They give people free beer and liquor and cigars just to get people on their side. There is no country on earth with so much graft as America. When they work so hard in a little place like this, what would it be like in bigger places? . . .

*Ibid.*

11 June 1911

. . . I see from your letter that you have not gotten America out of your thoughts yet, but are thinking about it still. From what I understand times are better in Canada than they are here at present. . . . you know that Gunnar is out in Canada, and he writes that there is plenty of work of all kinds and he wants me to come out. . . . What are you doing for fun in the evenings now? You must be riding your bicycle wherever you go now.[17] I can imagine you ride back and forth from the hired hands' cabin at Hägerud and Finnhyttan. That used to be the usual way to walk before and must be still. Now Gustav and Erick are there too, so in that old hired hands' cabin you must still be having fun I expect. I imagine I see you sitting there shooting the breeze and playing whist now and then, and maybe you say a word or two about me, how I am getting along. Yes, it is fun to correspond like this with each other, it is as if we had a conversation together sometimes and we understand each other so well, maybe better than we did when we saw each other every day almost. You see better afterward, after you have become separated. When we were together we didn't think about it so much as now. I can never be as close to anyone here as I was with you, and it is not hard to understand why. You and I, we can almost say we have become blood brothers, and although we are far apart the bonds will surely never break between us.

I see that you too have thought about America, certainly because of the military service, and that is not surprising. But one thing I ask before you make up your mind, to reason carefully and think everything over. You know you have a good home and I don't think your parents would like for you to leave, and you don't have to go for economic reasons but would go just because of the military service. I am not afraid to say that you would get ahead just as well or better than many others who have come over, and you would soon learn the language well enough to manage. You are used to working so everything would go well, it wouldn't be any problem. But as long as one has a home in Sweden and parents one ought to think of them first of all. I say just as my uncle said to me, "Do just what you yourself want." Now, if he had painted a tempting picture of America and then when I came here I felt disappointed, I would naturally have put the blame on him. Since I acted in accordance with my own best judgment I have no one but myself to blame, no matter how badly things go. For my part, it was the same whether I came to America or some other place, for I would not have stayed at home in any case. I had to make my living, and Järnboås is doubtless one of the worst places for a workingman to make a living. But one thing I can almost guarantee you is that you would be able to get ahead here too with ability and hard work, and one can go farther here than in Sweden. This is all I have to say and I hope you understand me. . . .

*Ibid.*

20 August 1911, Iron River, Michigan

. . . Now we will soon have fall again. I will never forget two years ago at this time, when I went and dug sod and was so anxious to earn the money to travel to America. Now it is already two years since then, think how time flies. I am still working at my old job, have now changed partners again so that I now have a half-crazy Italian as a partner again. You can be sure I keep him going all day, we fight and finger wrestle but I always come out best. He is real big and rough but he can't manage anything anyway. They are strange comrades one has in this country, but it makes no difference as long as you can get along. I am working in a shaft five hundred feet deep and twelve feet square, that's really some hole. . . .

You ask if there is any trade union movement around here. That there is, but it moves ahead very carefully because it is not strong enough yet. It is called the "Mineworkers' Union" and consists mainly of Finns and Italians. They built a meeting hall this summer and in fact they intend to dedicate it today. There is a mine which has shut down because of the labor union activity. The workers went on strike and the employers answered with a lockout, so now the work has stopped. The workers can never win in this case because the employers lose nothing in any event. They have so much ore up unsold that they don't care if the mine is closed down for a year or so. The workers there were almost all Italians and they have money enough to go back to Italy again, every one of them. . . .

I wonder if there is going to be an exposition in Stockholm next summer?[18] I understand that if you take a trip home they will grab you and off you go to Hyggängen Barracks in Vesterås, and I don't think I have much desire for that. So I think it is best to stay where I am for the time being. I certainly think you ought to be able to make a trip home and be home for a month or so and then go back again without them being able to hinder you. But I have not been here long enough yet. And so one more thing before I end, when you write letters to me from now on, send them unfranked, for it costs me only ten cents to pay the postage here and I'd be so glad to do that if only you keep on writing. . . .

*Ibid.*

4 November 1911

. . . I wonder if Ture Lindblad didn't travel home a week ago. He left here last Sunday and said he was going to go to Sweden, but if he did or not is more than I know. But if he went there, he must be home when you get this letter. If he is now bragging and talking big about America, don't believe any more than you think is true, for you know the Lindblads and how they are. . . . I can tell you I keep my partner, the Italian, worked up these days, I talk about the war between Italy and Turkey[19] and I say that the Turk is going to do away with all the Italians there are in Italy, and then when they are finished with them they are going to come after those who are in America. But then he gets mad, you can be sure. He said that if Italy would go to war with Sweden they would give the Swedes a real licking, but I tell him that all the Italians would freeze to death long before they got a glimpse of Sweden. I think it is fun to tease him because he gets so mad. . . .

*Ibid.*

1 July 1914

Will now write and let you know that I am here again at my old place and have started working for my daily bread again. The trip went fine. I went with the Scandinavian America Line, *Frederik VIII*, a fine boat, completely new. I got to see both Copenhagen and Christiania. . . . It took seventeen days from Järnboås to here, but I am satisfied with my trip. . . . You may be sure it was hard to leave again but I also thought it was good to get away from everything that was oppressive and all I would have had to do if I was going to stay in Sweden. Here you are in any event a free man in a free land. . . .

*Ibid.*

[September 1914]

. . . I have a girl I like a lot, but she has gone to Chicago where she is going to stay till next summer, so it is a bit sad, of course, but it can't be helped. Now you probably think I am head over heels in love, but that is certainly not the case. You said to me one time at home that I had too high thoughts about girls in general. But here in this country I don't have such high thoughts about the girls as I had at home, for the girls here in this country have another kind of upbringing, demand an awful lot of fuss and attention, and I don't respect that. So if I find a girl here who is different from the others I respect her, for there are not many of them. Now you understand that I am not so dumb but that I see quite clearly in this case. There are girls here who doll themselves up enough to frighten you. They would be better as scarecrows than anything else, so if you need any of those I can send you a boatload. . . .

It is strange to see so many kinds of people gathered together in a country and still there are no quarrels. Here Germans and Frenchmen work side by side with Russians and Italians,[20] here the one is no better than the other unless one is a better worker than the other. America is a marvellous land, all in all. . . .

*Ibid.*

~~~~~~~~~~~~~~~~~~~~~~~~~~~~~~~~~~~~~~~~~~~~~~~~~~~~~~~~~~~~~

*The Swedish government's Commission on Emigration* (Emigration-sutredningen), *appointed in 1907, among other things solicited from Swedes in the United States and Canada information concerning their backgrounds and experiences, as well as their views on the causes of emigration from the homeland. Many responded, providing a wealth of biographical data. Under cover of anonymity they also felt free to criticize Sweden's shortcomings—and in some cases conditions in North America—with unusual candor.*

E. C. S., Pennsylvania. *Emigrated 1871.* From Östergötlands län.

I was born in October 1850 in Östergötland. My father was a charcoal burner and had nine children. The croft was large enough so that he could keep a cow every other year, if he bought a little straw. For the croft he had to provide a hired man and a hired girl to the manor during the busiest time of the year. And so his lease was revoked and he came to America and is now ninety-two years old. The first thing I remember is that we lived in a little cabin in the greatest poverty. Around the age of seven I had to go out and rock children's cradles, that was my first occupation, and then herd geese, pigs, and sheep. In this way I worked for the manor until my fourteenth year, when I was confirmed. I also had a little schooling, nine months altogether, two days one week and three the other. The children were too many, so that boys and girls had to go every other day. After my confirmation, I hired out to a big crofter. My wages were set at twenty-five *riksdaler*, a pair of boots, two shirts, and a pair of mittens per year. Then I came to another crofter, where I got herring five times a day and had to be at the manor at four o'clock in the mornings and quit at eight-thirty in the evenings, and then go a mile and a half home to get a little oatmeal and milk and four hours' sleep.

In 1871, on the fourth of April, I left the old home and landed in New York on 4 May. Now I was at last in the promised land, without family, without friends, and almost without money. Here I wandered back and forth like a deaf-mute. I had a ticket to Chicago and now set off for there, and then through some mistake of the railroad personnel I was sent the wrong way, so that I had to stay alone over a Sunday at Niagara Falls. There I got locked in the station house from Sunday morning to Monday morning. I showed my ticket to a hackney driver and he took me to another station, from which I got a seat to Chicago. Here there were cries from all sides: Come along to the Emigrant Home, but I had been warned about Chicago's emigrant runners, so I followed no one but took my knapsack and went off alone without knowing where. After wandering around for a while I caught sight of a sign on which there was written: Carl XV's Hotel. I went in there and was well received by a Smålänning.

Here I stayed until the following day, when a gardener, P. from Rosehill, came and wanted to hire people. He offered sixteen dollars a month, room, and board, plus a dollar extra if we provided our own bedclothes, which we promised to do. I together with many others were given places in a hayloft, and since we were all emigrants it didn't matter so much for we could not speak an English word. When we were to get paid at the end of the month, instead of seventeen dollars which we had been promised, we got eight dollars, some ten dollars. I myself got twelve dollars since I did not want to stay on, and that I had no desire for, since Mr. P. used too much of Chicago's garbage to feed his emigrants with, and he was too stingy to let us go to get a drink, and he didn't want to keep a water boy, but we had to stretch out on the ground and drink out of marshy water holes, wherever we could. So. P. became a millionaire, and we who worked for him caught sicknesses of various kinds. I for my part got the ague. And so I wanted to see if I couldn't find America such as I had heard it described before I left home, and so I made my way back to Chicago and Carl XV's Hotel.

Now we were recruited through an employment agency to go to Wisconsin and work on the Wisconsin Central Line. In wages we were to receive $2.50 a day and a free trip, which was to be taken off our first pay. Instead of $2.50 which we were promised in Chicago, we were now offered $1.75 per day, with food and lodging at $20 a month. Our quarters consisted of some logs rolled together with a little straw inside on the bare ground. We arrived there on a Wednesday evening, worked Thursday and Friday; on Saturday morning it rained, and then almost the whole work gang made off for town and we took out tickets for Chicago again. Once back in Chicago we returned again to Carl XV's Hotel.

Now my ague, which I had gotten at Rosehill, had fully developed and we were now at the end of June. One day, when I began to shiver, I went outside the hotel wall and sat down. While I sat there and froze so that the teeth rattled in my mouth, a man came walking up the street outside. Right as he was walking, he fell to the ground. He had gotten a sunstroke just as I was sitting and freezing. Now I was in the worst situation I had ever been in in my whole life, sick and without money or acquaintances, with two hundred *riksdalers'* mortgage on my muscles for my journey over. Like a sleepwalker I wandered up and down the streets of Chicago. Was this really the highly praised America?

I finally left Chicago and made my way to Pennsylvania, where I worked on the railroads for about four years; then I entered into matrimony with a girl from my native place. She had a little money, and I had saved up a little so that we bought a little farm of 20 acres where we settled down, bought three cows, a horse, and a few implements.

This farm we kept for two years, then we sold it; we bought another of 120 acres for $1,000, sold 50 acres of it, and that made me free of debt. Now we worked on this for a couple of years and then there was a saw-mill nearby which was for sale and we bought it for $2,000. Now I sawed timber both for myself and for others so that in two years I had paid for the sawmill, but then it burned down and I had no insurance. I rebuilt it right away and began sawing again.

Now I began buying up larger and smaller pieces of land with timber, and that went fine. My old farm was sold, a larger and better one bought, a general store started, town properties purchased, and then I started building houses in the towns of Youngsville and James-town, New York. So today I have 300 acres of land, a good farm, good sawmill with a planing machine; two stores, eight houses in the towns, and ten leaseholders who pay me an annual income of $900. Meanwhile we have brought up eight children, of which some are married. I pay an annual tax of $175. My assessed value is approximately like this: my farm $3,000, woodland $2,500, sawmill with equipment $3,000, horses and other livestock and farm implements $1,500, lumber on hand $3,000, town property in Youngsville $10,000, in Jamestown, New York, $2,500. If I had stayed behind in Sweden, I would have been a hired hand, at the very best a crofter.

Sweden, *Emigrationsutredningen*, (Stockholm, 1908–1913), *VII: Utvandrarnas egna uppgifter* (1908), 158–60.

L. J. S., Nebraska. *Emigrated 1871.* From Östergötlands län.

I was born on a count's estate in Östergötland in 1828. In 1840 I took service with a farmer, in 1844 with a crofter; the wages were wretched. In 1846 I came to the manor and got twenty-eight *skilling* for eighteen hours a day. Was often insulted. Worked for the count for twenty-five years. He was a friendly man but the countess was very haughty. A lieutenant, who was in charge of the poor-relief box there, one day remarked that the poor could starve as far as he was concerned. This comment gave rise to great bitterness and a large number, among them myself, emigrated to America, which I have never regretted. Here you are treated like a human being, wherever you are. And the military service in Sweden is a curse. Away with it! Wish that all the poor Swedes were here. In my youth we had great poverty, and now I would not want to go back to Mother Svea.

*Ibid.*, 160.


J. M. B., Connecticut. *Emigrated 1887*. From Stockholm.

. . . I ought to be competent to give some thoughts and impressions from my experiences and wish to say that for my own part I have found America better than Sweden and Germany[21] in many respects. First and foremost, I, who have always been a poor workingman, have always been put on the same level with any man whomsoever, out traveling, in company, at political meetings, and other social occasions, and have been respected as a man, despite my being of Swedish birth. I doubt whether a foreigner in Sweden would be as accepted there as I and other foreigners generally are here. Then come working conditions: certainly, one takes the "dog year"[22] into account in America, but I wonder if someone who came to Sweden and could not even say yes or no in Swedish would get paid as well as another who could speak the language of the land? And it is claimed that they are mean to green-horns. Sure, that is what the poor fellow himself believes, because he does not know what is going on. That the American sometimes makes fun of the foreigner's inability to understand things, you can hardly blame him for. And so we have business life. A foreigner, for example, has work, but still under limited economic circumstances, and sets up housekeeping. He may then buy all his furnishings without money if he wishes—yes, but he must pay dearly for it, it is said! But is it not worth a few per cent more to be able to pay as little as you wish per month or week?

Yes, so it is all the way down the line; you are respected (if you behave yourself), you are trusted, you are valued, though everything has its limits. Indeed, some have the idea that when they have become citizens, can speak English fairly well (for farther than that the emigrant can hardly come), and begin to understand a little about politics and so forth, they are fit for one thing and another, and when they are then beaten in the election campaign, they consider themselves badly used.

Sweden has—I hope—changed for the better during the past twenty years, but as far as my memories go back, what part did a poor working-man have in politics? No one should think that I wish to make offensive or harmful remarks about old Sweden. No, certainly not! I understand very well that a people is formed according to its laws, and if the law had been relatively similar to the American from one hundred years back to the present, the ways of thinking of the Swedes in Sweden would have been different. In sum: *You can not blame a man for what he don't know.*[23]

Wages in America and Sweden, as well as how they stand in relation to the prices of goods, ought to have a chapter of their own. I will only mention a few things. In America: daily wages of $2.50 to $2.75, even $3.00. Cost of goods: a good hat $2.50 to $3.00, a pair of good shoes $4.50 to $5.00, a good suit of clothes $18, $20, $22, and $25, and so on. In Sweden: the daily wages the same amount in *kronor*. Cost of goods: a good hat, 6, 8, 10, and up to 12 *kr.*, a pair of shoes 12, 16, 18, 20, and 22 *kr.* A suit of clothes 30, 40, 50 to 60 *kr.* Everything else in proportion. This little table alone seems to me sufficient to understand why people go to America and where the desire to emigrate has its origin. . . .

*Ibid.*, 165.


C. W. H., Canada. *Emigrated 1893*. From Uppsala län.

When we Swedes come together here in America,[24] the conversation often turns to the grievous emigration from Sweden, but at the same time to the endless difficulties an emigrant has to withstand. Each one of us has unfortunately "tasted the bitter chalk." For first to wander around in America seeking land and then right from the first shovelful to bring a farm under cultivation is by no means an enviable lot. Many have gone under faced with these hardships and left the earth to its fate. We all agree with the idea that if the Swede suspected the hardships and deprivations which would meet him here, he would stay where he was. For there are no privations in Sweden that can be compared with all the reverses that can overtake him here. But so long as America can offer the new arrival a gift of 160 acres of good land, so long will he remain quietly at his post, so long will he suffer in silence. The gift is a compensation for his troubles, a comfort for his privations, and the American authorities get empty, worthless land settled by an industrious population; the best working force comes from Scandinavia.

But the best time for emigration is now past; all the valuable land is now taken. If there should possibly be a few thousand farms left, these are only a drop in the bucket, the ever-broadening stream of emigration devours everything in its path. Well-situated land is now only to be found where the climate is too cold for Swedes. Someone should— thus the discussion usually ends—travel to Sweden and tell our countrymen about all this. Without fear, rather with the truth as my foundation, I wish mainly to consider the following:

America has for long periods and up to the present been a fortunate place for emigrants. To get a considerable and fertile piece of land at little cost is certainly a great gain. With this land, many have brought themselves up to independent circumstances here; many have attained prosperity. In Canada an overwhelming flood of land-seekers is expected next year—several hundred thousand, the newspapers say. Canada is where they are coming, for in the States all the land is taken up. But already last year large crowds of disappointed persons had to pass this place by. The province is already inhabited up to one hundred miles north of the northernmost railroad in Canada. The climate is too cold and all agriculture north of the fifty-second parallel must be unprofitable. So it appears at present. All Scandinavians lose their working strength in their early years. The climate and the unsuitable nourishment are the causes of this. The lack of rye bread also plays a part. But the poor water and the altogether too cold winds must be the main reasons. The water causes kidney trouble and the storms bring lung ailments. Both these kinds of illness often consume one's strength to work.

All the necessities that must be bought are extremely expensive, for the trust companies control the whole market. A liter of lamp oil costs four times as much as in Sweden and an ordinary unplaned board, six inches wide and twelve feet long, costs eighty *öre* in Swedish money. No wonder that settlers lack the means to put up large houses with good furnishings. These houses are often so insufficient that the fireplace must be kept going from morning till night. The comfortable Swedish tile stoves are entirely missing here. A single stove must in most cases warm up the whole house, even if it is two stories high. If wages are high for part of the year, expenses rise accordingly. Earnings are by no means great. A workingman here, for example, who has no bad habits and has worked hard for six years, has no money saved up. Nothing more than his clothes.

Everyone must pay dearly for flour, even those who have a thousand sacks of grain on hand, since there are no flour mills. Rye meal is not on the market and wheat flour seems harmful to the health, when it is eaten by people who have not grown up with such flour. Herring, the workingman's healthful fare, is more expensive than pork and for that reason cannot be included in everyday meals. Generally speaking, the foodstuffs here seem to be unhealthy for Swedes, for a newcomer is often sick for the first months before he gets used to them.

Swedes die early, between fifty and fifty-five years of age. Few reach their sixties and by then they have long since become broken down and useless. I myself have lost my excellent health in this country and have no hope of recovering it fully before I have moved back to Sweden again. Water is in many places insufficient during the winter. People have to drive it in or melt snow for the livestock. I myself have experienced this.

Truth and justice are very little respected in America. The newspapers, for instance, often contain great, fabricated untruths. In Sweden the inhabitant has all the protection he could wish. A good government with a universally beloved king and excellent public servants is a guarantee that the letter of the law must be observed. It is often very different in America. The citizen commits a crime and the authorities "turn a blind eye." The public servants also commit crimes without any punishment. Disorder often reaches the point where a raging mob seizes an arrested Negro from the police and turns to lynch law. He is literally burned alive without benefit of either trial or investigation. The terrified police can do nothing about such misdeeds, or rather, they do not want to. To say nothing of other disgraces.

Instruction in religion is entirely absent in American schools. Coming generations will thus eventually become heathens like our forefathers in times out of mind. One seeks in vain for churches and spiritual exercises. Sweden has the advantage of having the state church control the preaching of Christianity and the confirmation of children. I wonder when this will become law in America! There is also a great difference between well-raised and neglected children with respect to behavior between Sweden's and America's youth.

The English language is extremely difficult to learn to spell—it is not so to learn to speak. Extremely few newcomers or immigrants learn to write it.

The climate is not suitable to Swedes. In certain places sunstroke frequently occurs; in other places the winter cold is unbearable. Hailstorms often completely destroy the crops over wide areas. The most frightful, however, are the snowstorms, the so-called blizzards, for they are mortally dangerous. Many a traveler has been buried alive in the snow drifts, others succumb at their homes, getting lost between buildings; some are snowed in in their houses and freeze to death. Sweden's climate and Swedish weather conditions are certainly the most suitable for Swedes.

The taxes are raised here every year. Swedes complain about the high levies, but these levies are always assessed according to their incomes. Here high taxes are imposed without any consideration of the taxpayer's circumstances. Everyone must live and support himself as best he can manage. There is no poor relief here.

But naturally some good things can be said about America. For example the equality that prevails between high and low, rich and poor. Or the great fertility of the soil, etc., etc.

*Ibid.*, 188–89.

Mrs. E. C., West Rulland. *Emigrated 1896.* From Kristianstads län.

I was born in 1879 in Kristianstads *län*. My parents leased a farm there. When I was eight years old, my father died, leaving me and another daughter, four years old, as well as my mother. When the auction was over and the debts paid, there were 120 *kronor* left. My mother had two sons from an earlier marriage, one fourteen and the other sixteen years old at the time of my father's death, but they were out working for others. So some years passed and we moved down to the village. Mother worked out for farmers for forty *öre* a day (when she worked in the rye fields, she got fifty *öre*), and in between she wove cotton material and sold it. Then my brothers went to America and sent her a little money now and then, about twenty *kronor* twice a year, and that helped enough so that she did not have to go to the commune for help.

When I was thirteen years old, I had to go out and work. I was only a child when I came to work for a railway crossing guard and stayed there a year. I got my food and one *krona* when I left. Mother had to provide my clothes. Then I stayed at home while I went and read for confirmation, to the great annoyance of the farmers around there. When I was sixteen, I took service and got thirty *kronor* the first year, the second year thirty-five *kronor*. I had to work like a dog, go out and spread manure and dirt from the ditches during the summer, and on the snowiest days of winter I had to carry water to eleven cows. This besides all the other work. Work every minute from six o'clock in the morning until nine at night, Sundays and weekdays, always the same. No wonder that hired girls do not want to work for farmers. Whoever has done it knows all too well what that means. The hired man often has hard work, but he has his room to go to when he has finished his work, and he has his noon break, but when does the hired girl get to rest? While the others take it easy around noon she has to run out into the woods and fields to milk, and then she has to wash dishes when she is finished with that. By then the others are ready to go out to work again and naturally she has to go along. So it was for me, so it is for all farmers' hired girls. Never a free moment. I took hire for the third year, I was to have forty-five *kronor*, but then my brother's wife died here in America and then he sent tickets for me, my mother, and my sister. It was in 1896 in the fall that we left Sweden. I had long wanted to go but Mother did not want to. I saw that I would never have anything left over no matter how hard I worked at home. Mother had to help me with my clothes, mend my everyday clothing and stockings—it was unthinkable that I should have enough free time for such things.

As I said, we came here. Mother and Sister stayed with my brothers and I took service. At first it was hard and I did not understand what they said to me, but they were kind and after a while I understood more or less what they wanted. I got two dollars a week at first, and then I got three dollars. Every Saturday I got my pay. I was free every evening after six o'clock and every Thursday afternoon to go out or to do my own work. And what work! At first I was ashamed to get paid for what little I did. I had to learn to cook as quickly as I could, then there was the washing and ironing every week, and the housecleaning. There was such a great difference in my eyes, I got time to rest and time to look after my clothes. I served here for four years and then I got married. My husband, who is Swedish, is a machinist at a marble quarry and earns up to $100 a month, or some months $60, $70 or $80. Two years ago we bought a little farm for $1,000 and have built a house. The place is twenty-eight acres in size, and we have three cows and one horse plus smaller house animals. My brothers have bought a farm that feeds forty cows and two teams of horses. They paid $4,500 for it and that is the fruit of their labor. One has been in America fourteen years, the other seventeen years. Whoever wants to work can get ahead in America. It is a good country and has been a support to many poor people, both from Sweden and elsewhere.

*Ibid.,* 205–6.

L. F. L., Minnesota. *Emigrated 1891.* From Norrbottens län.

Born on a medium-sized farm in one of Norrbotten's coastal parishes thirty-odd years ago, with a strong desire to learn, which I early had the chance to satisfy, already as a boy I acquired a strong lust for adventure. I had not, however, thought much about a trip to America, even though I had been in touch with several returned Swedish Americans and though my sister had emigrated to America in my sixteenth year, in the fall of 1889.

But at a book auction at the courthouse in the fall of 1890 I bought a batch of books, and among them I found one with the title *The Truth about America.* I have long since forgotten the author's name, but it was apparently one of your predecessors in the movement to prevent emigration.[25]

This book contained a mass of the most ridiculous lies about America, of the same kind as the stories one reads from time to time in our conservative newspapers back home, with which they think they can frighten the simple Swedes, as when they frighten small children with the boogeyman. They forget that the average Swede knows just as much about American conditions as authors and journalists. The book in question, as I said, painted America in colors as somber as ever any medieval priest could paint the Evil One's abode. This caused me and others who read the book to reflect over what motives could lie behind such a book, and we came to the conclusion that it must be above all to frighten people out of emigrating, and secondly to make the little man satisfied with conditions in Sweden. How successful this was is shown by the fact that all the farm boys in the village to whom I lent the book kept me company over to America the following spring. There were of course many other causes besides, which helped us to decide to leave: the idiotic class differences, lack of the vote, military service, etc. The economic situation was the least important reason, for all of those who went from my home village that spring were from well-to-do farm families.

Although I have now been in this country for sixteen years I still follow the course of events back home and take great interest in the welfare of my homeland. The Swedish American newspapers, of which I read a half dozen, every week include a couple of pages of news from Sweden as well as special correspondence on the events of the day. If the Swedish newspapers would publish half as much about Swedish America, perhaps they would judge us more fairly at home. I have never visited Sweden since I came here, but I feel a deep love for the land where my cradle stood, where my old father lives, and where my mother's remains lie at rest. I have forgotten all that was hard at home and have only the happy memories of childhood left.

But now, through many of my friends who have made visits to Sweden, many of them with the intention of staying there, I have learned that Mother Svea does not receive with much love her children who return from "the great outwandering." As soon as a Swedish American sets foot on his native soil, everyone tries to get his claws into him in some way. They double the prices on everything he needs. "He comes from the land of swindlers, so we'll fleece him," they think. The working class is jealous of him and the upper classes make fun of him because his manners are somewhat different from those of the Swedish nobility. They idolize foreigners but despise their own countrymen who have been away for a time, especially if they have been successful. Those who back home have inherited a fortune or get a large salary for doing nothing and have managed to get through the *gymnasium*, they are naturally immeasurably higher on the Swedish social ladder than someone who has earned his fortune by his own work and who has acquired learning through the school of life and experience that the Swedish upper classes could never acquire. Because I do not want my illusions to be crushed, I have never since visited Sweden.

My life here in America has gone through many changes. My "dog years" were especially hard for a youth who was not used to working for others. I worked at sawmills, in the forest, on farms, at a newspaper press, etc., was a census taker and a policeman, until nearly fifteen years ago I got the position in the postal service which I now have. It is not a high position, but under the same circumstances I could never have gotten anything like it in Sweden. My salary is $900—over 3,300 *kronor* a year. When it is considered that when I took the examination for the position I had not gone a single day to an American school and still made a grade of 97 per cent, that is not so bad. My working time is six or seven hours per day.

It could thus never occur to me to leave this position and return to Sweden, where a person who has not acquired academic degrees has no chance to get a position in public service. That the Swedish postal service should wish to profit from my experience is not to be expected, for if they want to know something about our postal service, they send someone on a study grant, a candidate in philosophy, for instance, who hangs around the big cities for a few months, after which he and those who sent him believe he knows everything about the subject.

The reasons why it would be impossible for Swedish Americans to get along well in Sweden are many: the ridiculous "title sickness" and silly class system, the groveling of the low and the arrogance of the high, the antipathy against Swedish Americans and "self-made men," the bureaucracy and pedantry, the complicated system through which the wealthy seek to keep political power, the forced militarism, and the whole system that makes it impossible to acquire through one's own work as good an income as that mass of good-for-nothings who have managed to obtain certain academic degrees from the state and the commune to do nothing. I consider it fruitless to work against emigration or to try to bring about a remigration of Swedish Americans as long as conditions at home are the way they are. Both Swedes and Swedish Americans have greater demands on life than the ruling class in Sweden is willing to fulfill. Let them therefore go their way. You can surely fill their places with Slavic and other lower kinds of people with smaller requirements and more suitable for your present system, for to expect the ruling class to change the system for the benefit of the little man is expecting too much.

*Ibid.*, 218–20.

F. S., Minnesota. *Emigrated 1902.* From Blekinge län.

I was born in northern Blekinge, did my military service in 1896 and 1897 in the Blekinge Battalion. After finishing my service, I worked here and there, but soon I began to think, how shall I get my own piece of land? I began to look to the future, but I could see no prospects. Although I tried everywhere, it was impossible to get any land for myself. Then I remembered how bravely I was supposed to defend my fatherland, and so the thought arose: I have nothing to defend except the rich man and his property. It is impossible for me to get even a handful of the land I have learned to serve and obey. At the age of twenty-one I was grown-up enough to be used for a target but I was not grown-up enough to have any voice in the burning questions of the day; for that I was too poor.[26] So I thought: my rights as a Swedish citizen have been stolen from me, I must seek somewhere else. Through hard work I had managed to save up fifty *kronor*. I took my fifty-*kronor* bill and went to my father and said: I know you have no money but will you not stand security for me so that I can borrow a little more; I am going to America. I was thus able to borrow a little, seventy-five *kronor*, and went to Uncle Sam's land in 1902. Here there was much to learn and also to forget. The worst thing seemed to me to be the language. I came to a Swedish boss with my hat in my hands and my knees shaking, but quickly learned that even a millionaire need not be addressed in any other way than you yourself are addressed. I then found work here in town for two dollars a day; am now making up to three; have during this time saved up a little capital, which I never could have done in Sweden. Let the democratic spirit prevail more in Sweden, reduce the earnings of those who live in luxury, reduce taxes, let a person get a piece of land at a reasonable price, and Sweden will become a blossoming land.

*Ibid.*, 233.

N. L., Minnesota. *Emigrated 1902*. From Norrland.

. . . Then, regarding the reasons why so few Swedes return, it can be said with assurance that the principal reason is the free and democratic customs in America which make it so that they thrive so remarkably within a few years. But not a single Swede without means thrives here the first two or three years, and many become crazy with homesickness, but they cannot get together enough money for the trip home. Their goal now becomes to get this together, and in the meantime they begin to understand the language a little, and so they want to earn a little more than the trip home. And when they have gotten this small sum together they begin to speak as though they are beginning to get along a little better, and then it is just as though everything they have suffered in this country was Sweden's fault. They begin to speak of how they starved in Sweden, were beaten in the schools in Sweden, and so on, nonsense which they convince themselves and others of. Coming from poor peasant homes, never having had the chance to see what was great and beautiful in Sweden, but here thrown into the big cities, they get the idea that Sweden is nothing and America everything. The strangest thing of all is that they cannot and will not become good friends and comrades with a Swede or Norwegian if they can speak and understand the language a little. This proves, I should think, that the so-called dog years here are so hard and leave such bitter fruits that one's whole character is transformed. It is not to be wondered at if this poor Swede becomes proud to be called an American; he is still too ignorant to find out the dark sides of America. He does not see the hypocrisy, corruption, the rotten political ethics, and he does not see the hidden feet of clay upon which the colossus rests. . . .

*Ibid.*, 252.

M. M., North Dakota. [Year of emigration not indicated.] From Värmlands län.

I am a woman, born in Värmland and belonged to the poor class. I had to go out and earn my bread already at the age of eight. Most of what I did was to look after children. Had to get up at four o'clock in the morning with the others. Seldom got anything to eat or drink before eight o'clock, for the coffee mixed with rye was thought dangerous to the health. I got rotten herring and potatoes, served out in small amounts so that I would not have the chance to eat myself sick. That was my usual fare. In particular a corporal of the crown and his wife, who I was with for two summers, distinguished themselves by their stinginess and cruelty. From the military on land and sea protect us, dear Lord! Poor conscripts who have to serve as slaves under such wretches!

I did not have time to go to school very much. I had to learn the catechism, naturally, and that I had to do during the time I was watching the cows or some child. But I was not allowed to neglect Sunday school, for they wanted to drill into us poor people certain biblical passages, such as "Be godly and let us be contented," and so forth. Meanwhile the rich heard, "If your sins were red as blood, yet would they be white as snow," etc. So passed the days of my childhood and I got far enough along so that I was considered worthy of being admitted to holy communion, which is supposed to be a turning point in a person's life. But whichever way I turned things, the future looked just as dark. Still I had to struggle along five more years before I could be considered a proper hired girl and get any wage. And what a wage! And what work! No hope of saving anything in case of illness, but rather I could see the poorhouse waiting for me in the distance.

Then one day, I was then in my seventeenth year, the hour of freedom struck. I got a ticket from my two brothers, who had managed to get to America, after living through a childhood like mine. I was soon ready to travel, my few possessions were packed in a bundle: my New Testament, which I had gotten from the pastor, a bad report card from school, one *krona* in money which two kind women gave me. Thus prepared, I set off with a light heart for the great land in the West. And I have never regretted that journey. Certainly I have had to work, but I was considered a human being even when I was poor. Have a good home here. Am not burdened with love for the fatherland so I have no wish ever to return to Sweden, and I do not believe many Swedish Americans can stay there for long either. Would be best to get the Chinese to emigrate to Sweden. I remember when I was at missionary meetings in Sweden, how they cried and complained over the poor Chinese and his poor soul, and gave substantial contributions to improve his condition. Best to chase out your poor countrymen and take in the dear Chinese instead. . . .

*Ibid.*, 255–56.

*The government's Commission on Emigration also sent out investigators to areas at home of traditionally heavy emigration to America. Here one of them, G. Gerhard Magnusson, reports on what he found in the Jösse region of Värmland:*

If you go into a home to see how a peasant lives and to find out his opinion on the emigration question, you should not be surprised to hear that he has some or all of his children in America. On the contrary, you soon find that it is hardly worth the trouble to try to find any farm where none of the immediate family are in America. On the bureaus you find the American portraits of those who left most recently; on the walls hang American group photographs of perhaps fifteen or twenty relatives, all of whom are in the U.S.A. You can go from cottage to cottage and constantly find these American portraits and all kinds of American knickknacks. Here you find a lampshade with some English sentence on it; there on the rocking chair hangs a chair tidy with the names of the months in English on it and a Swedish-English dedication from a daughter or son-in-law; there on the sideboard are colored glasses with gold rims and "Fortune favors the brave" in ornate letters; in the stereoscope on the window table there are, among forty-two pictures, only two from Sweden, the old match factory in Jönköping and the Göta Canal, while all the others are from the U.S.A. There you could see how genteel folk live in New York, how they are married in glittering salons filled with guests in formal attire, how they eat delicacies at tables groaning under the weight of glittering champagne glasses and bowls of fruits, how they stroll in enchanting parks with purling fountains and neatly clipped lawns, how they ride in immense streetcars or in elevated trains, how they amuse themselves aboard the stately Atlantic ocean liners, etc., etc.

The little boy or girl grows up in this American milieu. The only pretty things they see and know about are American knickknacks and American pictures; the only news they hear from out in the world comes to them through the letters which father or mother reads aloud when mail has arrived from the older brothers or sisters in Illinois or Massachusetts. There are English turns of phrase in their language and a kind of facetious commiseration with conditions back home in Sweden, such things as readily impress small children and increase their already awakened longing to "go over" to that wonderful land. Never can it be so fine and genteel in Jösse as it is in Chicago or Idaho; one never hears such wonderful things about Sweden as about the U.S.A. And if anyone ever comes to visit, it is an elegant lady or an equally elegant gentleman from America, who used to work out in the fields here at home and was called by some ordinary name, but who now lives on money and has a much prettier and finer name. So it appears to the children in the home. They grow up and are raised to emigrate.

The finest portrait on the wall at home is possibly Grover Cleveland, William McKinley, or Theodore Roosevelt, and after that the German imperial family. The books to be found are picture albums from the U.S.A. or Swedish-English dictionaries and "statistical calendars" of America. The only thing Swedish you find is some finely lettered biblical quotation framed and on the wall.

When you later have the chance to hear old farmers in a reading room or café in Arvika conversing in English, you understand how it all fits together and find it hardly surprising. Many have been in America and have returned—you notice that, when you go along the roads, in the clothes and Panama hats on some of the men working out in their fields as if they were on the farm in Minnesota. Many, both young and old, are learning English so as to get ahead better when some fine day they "go over" to America. Everything seems to be a preparation for emigration. The upbringing is based upon it and it is much easier to borrow money for an America-ticket than for the fare to travel, for instance, to Stockholm. Since all the relatives furthermore are already in America they consider it much more secure to be able to go there than to go to Stockholm or Gothenburg, where they perhaps have no relatives at all. And now and then some Swedish American comes to visit. He need seldom travel back alone to his new homeland;

most often he instead takes back with him a whole colony from his home tract.

Sweden, *Emigrationsutredningen, VIII: Bygdeundersökningar*, Part 2, G. Gerhard Magnusson, "Jösse härad i Värmland" (Stockholm, 1908), 82–84.

*Comrade Erland Blomkvist reports on the progress of the Movement on the West Coast in the New York Swedish socialist newspaper,* Arbetaren:

4 September 1912, Carlton, Oregon

To *Arbetaren*!

The undersigned, who departed the promised land of forest-ravagers and logging-camp slaves[27] in the month of July 1911, landed here in the land of dollars and humbug, and find myself at present in Carlton, a town in north-west Oregon. During the period of three or four months when I worked in San Francisco, I belonged to our organization's club there. The impressions I got about the spread and success of our ideas are unfortunately anything but bright. The comrades there, who are few, have a hard task to carry out and hard ground to break. I got the impression that the majority of the Swedes who arrived here ten to fifteen years ago have. if you consider development and political attitudes, been completely stunted in their growth. They do not know about our movement, socialism, and do not want to know about it. The majority have, while staring themselves blind at the dollar, forgotten that they are workers, slaves under capital. Indeed, some of those who in the old country were links in the great international chain of brotherhood have, since they came here, deserted our cause, have scrambled up onto the backs of their comrades and have been thrown into bourgeois society, are bigwigs in the Patriotic Society,[28] etc., etc., ad infinitum. That these individuals are not better is not so surprising, for they have not for a long time had anything to sustain them but what the San Francisco Swedish newspaper, *Vestkusten*, has served them.

Here is a sample: "Our esteemed comrade and brother Mr. Bergse will this summer undertake a journey to our fatherland, to his native place on Öland. There will be great rejoicing on Öland, indeed all Sweden shall rejoice." It sounds, said the peasant——.[29]

Monday, 2 September, I made a trip by rail to attend a club meeting in Portland. Arriving at my destination, I found my way to the club's headquarters and it did not take long before I was introduced and acquainted with some twenty or thirty pioneers, comrades in ideas. After some hours of edifying debate, we set out to see and hear first-hand how the Socialist party's candidate for president, Debs, could repair his party's platform, from which Roosevelt had stolen the planks.[30] At this meeting there were five to six thousand in attendance and it was hard enough for Mr. Debs to hop around between the remaining planks, but he managed. The undersigned, who is not particularly well acquainted with the language, cannot here report to the readers of *Arbetaren* what this hero of reform had at heart, but I got the idea that the S.P.'s platform must be put together from old and quite rotten timber when a Colonel Roosevelt can make use of it. Here I had the pleasure of helping for the first time with agitation and that consisted of providing, as well as we could, Debs's listeners with announcements about the meeting of the Socialist Labor party's presidential candidate, Arthur E. Reimer,[31] which is to take place on 4 September. After fulfilling this task, we marched off to the club headquarters and there received the happy news that the comrades in Astoria had awakened and that a club had been started there. We rose to our feet to give a cheer for the comrades who tread the "plank-laid streets of Astoria."

On Tuesday the fourth I attended for the first time a meeting of the club and we were some thirty enthusiastic comrades there assembled. Under the chairmanship of Comrade Berg and to the hard blows of his gavel the business was quickly expedited. Reports and memoranda were presented from every possible committee you can think of, here subscription lists for the expansion fund, there reports from local and party committees, here one could not escape from being assigned to sell brochures—yes, there was the work, bustle, and activity that you can only find and see at a socialist club meeting where there is will and strength that shies at no obstacles to advance our ideas. When everything was taken care of and the treasurer had made an appeal for the payment of dues before balancing his books, the undersigned conveyed the greetings of the red youth and comrades in the old country. The chairman thanked me and with a powerful blow laid the gavel on the table as a signal that the meeting was over.

Well, now that meeting is just a memory, but a memory I shall not soon forget. My impressions from Portland encourage me and I believe the comrades there have raised and are fighting for our strongest bastion on the West Coast. All honor to them!

I now wish to end my letter by conveying to the comrades in Portland my thanks for the friendship shown me and I hope that we shall meet again. Until then and in the time ahead we should join our Scandinavian hands together still more strongly and may our first goal be to bring within the framework of the club all the Scandinavians living in and around Portland. We should help each other and we should raise our banner so that our comrades in all lands may see the Scandinavian name. When we have raised the red flag, our standard, so high that it shines as a symbol and brings light into every dark and dreary worker's home, *then* shall we have done something, *then* may we reap the fruit of our labor.

With greetings and handclasps,
Erland Blomkvist

"Några intrvck fran Västkusten," *Arbetaren* (New York). Thursday, 12 September 1912, p. 4.

*With the cold weather began the logging season. Here a Swedish lumberjack tells of the winter of 1913–1914 at his lumber camp on Lake-of-the-Woods in western Ontario:*

One of the company's men met us at the landing and served as a guide, and then we had to trudge over hill and dale with blazes on the tree trunks to show the way. By sundown we had reached the place which was to serve as our home until the end of March and it was with a light heart that we put down our packs and made ready for our evening meal.

Where the boat had dropped anchor our winter supply of provisions lay unloaded and covered with large tarpaulins, waiting for strong ice to be hauled to its final destination by sled. The winter supply of potatoes was stored in an old hunter's cabin nearby, and the first question the company's agent asked when we landed was who would volunteer to tend a fire in the cabin to keep the potatoes from freezing. We had in the group an older man who was to do lighter jobs and he volunteered right away. The following Sunday our potato watcher came to visit and ate dinner with us, and in honor of the day he had made himself fine or, rather, he had shaved. But his face looked like a half-scalded pig for he was completely without shaving things. As a razor he had used a piece of glass and for a mirror a bucket of water which he reflected himself in.

Our lodgings were built onto a large barge, which had been towed out from the sawmill and lay anchored at the lakeshore, but since it was not large enough to put up the whole work force, the first thing on the program was to build new quarters on land, and when they were ready they were exclusively the Swedes' lodgings.

A bosun who had served in the Swedish navy was detailed to supervise the building of our new quarters. To the question as to where the building timber should be gotten from, the reply was, "Take saws and axes and go with Oskar and Verner, they will haul it back." When we had come a little way out into the forest, we were told to cut down some giant trees, ca. two feet in diameter, and when these had been cut into certain lengths, they were dragged to the building site and rolled up to the master builder on timbers. The walls grew in height and our bosun stood like a sea captain on his bridge and gave orders, and with well-aimed blows of his ax got the logs to fit together in the corners, and before we knew it the building had risen to its intended height of seven feet on the sides. After the end walls and roof joists the roof was laid, and this was done in such a way that small cedar poles were laid side by side and covered with a layer of tar paper. On top of this was laid a thick layer of fir branches.

When that was done, preparations were begun for caulking. A couple of fellows were told to dig down to soft clay, others carried water or split small branches and pounded them into the cracks and then this "plaster" was smeared over. In connection with plastering I can't resist the temptation to mention what I heard a newly arrived

Swede tell about some years later. The person in question worked for a company and a cabin of this type was his sleeping quarters. When it got on toward the later part of the winter and the sun got warm in the daytime, some of the caulking came loose, which caused a strong draft around his head, where he lay and slept. Since clay was impossible to get because the ground was frozen four or five feet deep, good ideas were at a premium. As usual in all logging camps, oatmeal was served for breakfast. So he got an idea. He took a newspaper with him to breakfast and when he had taken himself a good serving of oatmeal he let it disappear into the newspaper on his knees to smuggle out later, after breakfast, and use to fill up the cracks in the wall, and a few servings of porridge saved the situation.

The furnishings in our building consisted of floor and bunks, plus a long log, chopped flat on one side, which went across the whole room and lay on the flat side with the ends on the lowest bunks and thus served as a bench or sofa. The floor was made like the ceiling of small cedar logs with the difference that when they were laid, they were evened off with a kind of adz. Bunks and doors were of planks and the window was ready-made. If I remember rightly, it took three days from the time the first tree was felled until that solemn moment when we moved in. After a big fire was lit in the huge stove and all were shown their sleeping places and had made up their improvised beds, those who lay in the upper bunks could contemplate the stars through the opening around the stovepipe in the roof. But it made little difference, for the big stove often made it too warm for them on the upper level.

When the living quarters were ready and everything had settled down, everyone was assigned his job, which he normally stayed with throughout the winter. We were completely isolated from the outside world for six weeks. The day before·Christmas Eve the bookkeeper went in to Norman and came back the day after Christmas Day and had with him a caravan of timber drivers who were to haul the timber down to a protected bay, where it was unloaded to be floated with a tugboat down to the sawmill in the summer.

Topics of conversation in the evenings covered everything possible but as Christmas drew near, they began to concentrate more and more on memories from Sweden. When Christmas Eve came and we had eaten our supper a kind of pious feeling lay in the air. There was not the noise and merriment that were otherwise so typical of our evenings.

Many sat by themselves dreaming. The standing rule, "lights out" at nine o'clock, did not apply that night, and when nine o'clock had passed one of our accordion virtuosos started to play melodies from the homeland and it did not take long before there was a thunder of Swedish singing in our cabin which continued with only short pauses until Christmas morning had come. When it was already a good bit into Christmas morning, our bosun began "Var hälsad sköna morgonstund"[32] with a voice many ministers would have envied him for, and we joined in as best we could, and a little better.

Next day around eight we were up and about again before breakfast and Christmas Day was just like any other day except that the cook added a few extras to the food. The day after, the bookkeeper came with the timber drivers and had with him the company's mail pouch, and I daresay that never was Saint Nicholas more heartily received than our bookkeeper when he came with the mailbag.

The rest of the winter passed without anything noteworthy. One day was like the next. It was often painful to leave the warm cabin and go to work in minus 30 to minus 40 degree weather, but it did not take long before you worked yourself warm and were full of work lust. So much the more wonderful it was when evening came and we marched home to our cabin and food really fit for a feast after the day's work.

If I remember rightly, it was 26 March when our camp broke up and we were driven over the ice to Norman with one night spent along the way. At the company's office our band of foster brothers broke up. Many of the Norrlännings[33] stayed in Kenora to wait for work at the sawmill, and three herring fishermen from Bohuslän headed back to Saskatchewan. . . .

Widén, *Amerikaemigrationen i dokument*, 82–85.

*In reply to a recent inquiry Iris Andersson of Stockholm recalled an episode from her childhood in Uppland.*

. . . You asked in a letter about our relationship to some emigrant. Yes, there was a cousin to our mother, we don't remember the name.

They, her husband was along, came to Ledinge, and they were older retired people then. She was a spectacle for us. She had all kinds of necklaces and bracelets, the fanciest clothes, she swished and jangled around, high bust, great high hairdo, pretty teeth, with *gold* in them. But when evening, or rather morning, came, then all the finery had disappeared. She looked so little and worn. No bust, no hair, and the mouth—well, it just wasn't there! Her husband looked the same both night and day. He was bent, ached in his joints, but good and kind. But she was always on the go. I can't say either how it was that they came to America and how they had it as emigrants. . . .

*From Minnesota, Emma Blom writes home to Jämtland.*

18 May 1915

It has been a hard winter for me as long as the children were going to school. I had five children to have ready, off to school, and two at home, all of them so young and difficult, all under nine years old. But I am glad that they have gotten a good start with reading, although it cannot be so much in one winter. The children began school on 8 September and they went every day until 30 April and will begin again in September. Three of our children will go then, this winter only Mikael and Jenny went, but we had three for other people. You want to know if they are reading English. Yes, I must say in all truth that English is just as usual for us as Swedish is in Frostviken. It comes just as easily for our children to read English as it does for Agda to read Swedish. But we are thinking of teaching them Swedish ourselves. Mikael can read a little Swedish. We are near to the school, only five minutes' walk, it is right beyond our pasture. Here in this country the children never receive any Christian instruction in the public schools. The Bible is strictly forbidden in school, because there are so many kinds of people and so many doctrines. The parents must take care of that themselves. Around here they are mostly Catholics. Our children have gone to Sunday school every Sunday for a long time now, to a pastor, and we are teaching them to read the Bible ourselves. We have books and newspapers of all kinds in both languages and when they have learned everything they are to learn in English, we are thinking of sending them to a Swedish-speaking Lutheran pastor for a winter for confirmation instruction. There are many people in this country who never let their children go to communion school but all our children will go. . . .

Widén. *Amerikaemigrationen i dokument*, 56.

# EPILOGUE

# Epilogue

The coming of World War I in 1914 did not stop Swedish emigration to America but it marked the end of its dynamic phase. The war effectively closed the Atlantic to regular emigrant traffic for nearly five years, reducing it to a trickle. Postwar economic adjustments, in particular the American slump of 1921, thereafter kept Swedish immigration at low levels until 1923 when it sharply rose to 24,984 persons, evidently largely from a backlog of emigrants held up by the war and its aftermath. The following year the number was less than one-third as large and during the remainder of the decade only 6,000 to 9,000 Swedes annually entered the United States. The basic prewar trends continued: a high proportion of the emigrants were industrial and forest workers, and as before many went to Canada. No new Swedish settlements were established; the new arrivals either went to older ones or dispersed throughout the continent.

The dramatic drop in Swedish immigration between 1923 and 1924 can in part be explained by new, restrictive American policies. Since before the turn of the century there had been increasing apprehension in the United States over the growing volume of immigrants, particularly from southern and eastern Europe, a feeling which was intensified by the strong nativist reaction of the war years. In 1921 Congress set immigration quotas for each nationality at 3 per cent of its number in the census of 1910. This intentionally favored the older immigrant groups from northwestern Europe, including Sweden, and made liberal exemptions for near relatives of persons already resident in the country; thus it did not prevent the high Swedish immigration of 1923. In 1924, however, a new immigration law set quotas at 2 per cent of each foreign-born group as of 1890 until 1929; thereafter total immigration was limited to 150,000, with quotas proportioned according to national origins in the census of 1920. This cut the Swedish quota down, first to slightly under 10,000, then in 1929 to around 3,300. At first waiting lists for the quota show that the law of 1924 apparently kept Swedish immigration somewhat lower than it would otherwise have been. But during the later 1920s the Swedish quota was usually undersubscribed, and it has remained unfilled every year since 1930, except for 1948–1949.

The fundamental causes for the end of the great migration must therefore be sought in Sweden itself, above all in a declining birthrate after the 1860s and particularly after 1900, in continued industrialization, and in the series of reforms from 1907 onward by which Swedish government was democratized and the first beginnings of a program of social welfare were undertaken. In meeting problems of supply during World War I, the government established precedents for far-reaching public regulation and strengthening of the economy, which could later be applied to social ends. The war, by impeding emigration, furthermore provided a welcome opportunity for the National Society Against Emigration, which reached its peak in membership and activity during those years, encouraging and aiding thousands of persons in modest circumstances to acquire their own small farms and homes. High wartime prices for their produce meanwhile allowed many small farmers to pay off old debts and mortgages.

The broad extensions of suffrage in 1907 and 1909 (made universal for both sexes in 1921) greatly strengthened the Social Democratic party, which by 1914 emerged as the largest group in the Riksdag's Second Chamber. Social Democrats served in the wartime coalition cabinets and in 1920 they formed their first cabinet under Hjalmar Branting. The advance of social democracy was paralleled by the growing strength of the labor movement. Increasingly, working-class Swedes looked to their unions and to the Social Democratic party—rather than to America—to provide security and a decent standard of living. The cooperative movement during the interwar years played a rapidly growing role in assuring small farmers adequate returns for their produce and small consumers moderate prices for basic necessities.

In 1930 the United States was hit by the Great Depression, from which it emerged only gradually by the end of the decade. In that year remigration for the first time exceeded immigration from Sweden, and it continued to do so uninterruptedly down to 1940. The depression affected Sweden later than the United States, and when it did the Social Democratic government that came to power in 1932—and has remained there to date—was able to cope with it effectively. Sweden's unique blend of private enterprise, producer- and consumer-owned cooperatives, and state regulation was greatly admired throughout the Western world, not least because of Marquis Childs's widely read book, *Sweden: The Middle Way*, first published in 1936.

World War II reduced migration between Sweden and America even more drastically than did World War I. Since 1945 Swedish emigration to the United States has varied between one thousand and three thousand persons a year, with remigration normally from one-third to three-quarters of the annual immigration. The postwar arrivals have been notable for the large proportion of professionals, business people, and skilled technicians among them. Their overall educational level is high and they are fully a part of their national culture in a way that most of the old immigrants never were. Many keep their Swedish nationality, expecting eventually to return home, and consider their presence in America simply a matter of opportunity. A large number can better be characterized as "Swedes in America" than as "Swedish Americans." Meanwhile, as few Swedes have left Sweden since World War II, their own country has itself come to receive considerable immigration from abroad. By the end of 1973 foreign residents amounted to over six hundred thousand persons or about 7.3 per cent of Sweden's population of 8.1 million. Of these nearly half were from other Scandinavian nations, principally Finland, the remainder largely from eastern and southern Europe. Thus the Swedes now see in their midst others undergoing the same kinds of adaptations that their own earlier relatives had to face in America.

After 1914 the immigrants' letters gradually chronicle the passing of cultural Swedish America. Here too World War I marks a turning point, for it produced a strong reaction in America against everything considered foreign, and many Swedish Americans had at first been isolationist, in some cases pro-German, in sympathy. More basic to the decline, however, was the dwindling flow of immigrants fresh from the old country in the postwar years. As the first generation aged and died, it was only to a small and diminishing degree replaced, particularly after 1930. The churches went progressively over to using English, to the point where little more than an occasional early-morning Christmas *julotta* service can now be heard in Swedish. The separate Swedish denominations have thus lost their special role and have merged with the national American churches, the most notable example being the Augustana Synod, which in 1962 was absorbed into the Lutheran Church in America.[1] The membership of most of the clubs and lodges is both aging and declining. They have lost much of their specifically Swedish character and the mother tongue is little used in their activities any more, even by the old-timers. Swedish-language newspapers have gradually gone out of business or merged until currently only seven of them remain in the United States and two in Canada. It is incidentally a sign of the continued westward drift of the Swedish-born population that no less than four of these newspapers are located on the Pacific Coast.[2] Some columns in these papers are now usually in English and the prominence among their advertisers of chiropractors, rest homes, and funeral directors tells its own story. Books and periodicals in Swedish are no longer published in North America.

The new, postwar immigrants feel little need for a Swedish America. Better educated and more cosmopolitan than the older immigrants, they mix more easily with the American population as a whole but are at the same time better prepared individually to preserve their own national heritage. Rapid communication permits them to fill their cultural needs directly from Sweden. There they can order books, magazines, newspapers, kitchen utensils, while any good American supermarket now carries *knäckebröd*, lingonberries, herring—if not always *lutfisk*. To return to the homeland to visit now takes only a few hours by jet plane. The recent arrivals have come from a very different Sweden from that left behind even a few decades earlier, and they thus feel little in common with the older Swedish Americans.

This gap is meanwhile symptomatic of an even deeper cleavage between Swedish America and the old country, with roots extending well back into the last century. Partly because of resentment and envy on the part of those who stayed home, the Swedish American has often been ridiculed in the press and on the stage in Sweden, represented as an ignorant hayseed, gaudily dressed, and boastful in his barbarous Swedish about the "greatest country on earth." Swedish Americans in their turn are often disturbed and indignant about socialism, irreligion, the "new morality," strident anti-Americanism among much of the younger generation, and—paradoxically—the modernization and "Americanization" of their old homeland. Through what still remains of their own Swedish America, they cultivate the memory of a Sweden that they know no longer exists.

While the second generation was largely lost to the old culture, it has been frequently observed that the third generation, secure in its place in American society, has often found a new pride and curiosity concerning its ethnic origins.[3] Many in the third and later generations—including those of only partly Swedish descent—being better educated, have learned more about the Swedish national heritage than their forefathers could ever have known. They have much to be proud of, not only in Sweden but in Swedish America as well.

The Swedish contribution to America has been great. Immigrants from Sweden were a sturdy and vigorous stock. The land they broke equaled at least the entire cultivated area in the old country itself, while the forests they felled, the miles of track they laid, the ore they mined, the city blocks they built can scarcely be estimated. Americans as diverse as the poet Carl Sandburg and movie actress Ann-Margret, Chief Justice Earl Warren, nuclear physicist Glen Seaborg, and astronaut Edwin "Buzz" Aldrin, to mention but a few, have traced their roots to Sweden. But beyond this, the Swedish immigrants brought to the American community values and characteristics that have survived the old language and customs, and that have served America well: uprightness, honesty, pride in work, matter-of-fact pragmatism, good-natured stoicism, self-reliance and self-respect, a strong sense of fairness and justice—all qualities amply illustrated in their letters.

The effects upon the old homeland have been as great, or greater, for the new Sweden is in considerable measure the creation of the great migration. Sweden in the nineteenth century was an underdeveloped country with serious problems of overpopulation and poverty. Without the safety valve of emigration it could have degenerated into a vast rural slum, incapable of accumulating the capital needed to develop its natural resources. Emigration helped to keep wages and living standards up, unemployment and welfare burdens down, while the nation underwent the transformation from an agrarian to an urban and industrial society. The emigrants moreover sent home large amounts of money, to the benefit of countless families and of the economy as a whole; between 1906 and 1930 these remittances averaged about eight million dollars a year, or about one-quarter of Sweden's annual balance of payments.[4] The large class of poor tenant farmers and landless agricultural laborers has almost disappeared. Agriculture and industry have benefited from returned Swedish Americans who brought with them both capital and practical experience. The great reforms of twentieth-century Sweden were, to a large though immeasurable extent, motivated by the need to create a "new America" to compete with the attractions of the great republic across the sea. Thus the emigrants contributed strongly to the changes in Sweden which brought the great migration itself to a close. The rise of various religious denominations and of religious toleration, temperance and other humanitarian movements, clubs and lodges, trends in architecture, literature, and the arts, fashions in dress, popular music, entertainment, slang, and even children's names reflect unmistakable American influences at all levels of Swedish life. Finally it may be suggested that certain traits in the modern Swedish psyche may have derived from or at least been accentuated by long and close contact with North America: a hard-driving business sense, the fast pace of work, reverence for technical ingenuity and effective results, freedom from confining tradition and readiness to experiment, a fierce sense of democracy in government and society, and a growing respect for the self-made man.

# APPENDIX

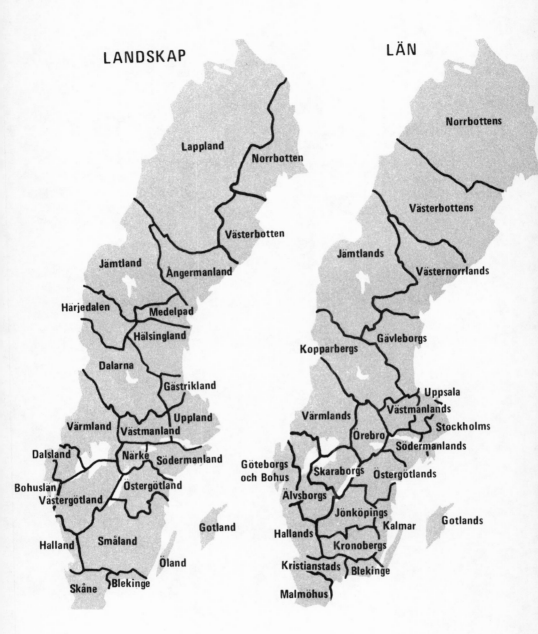

Maps of the Swedish provinces (*landskap*) and districts (*län*). (Adapted from
Nils William Olsson, *Tracing Your Swedish Ancestry*, Stockholm, Royal Swedish
Ministry of Foreign Affairs, 1965. Courtesy of the author.)

# Appendix

## A Word on Swedish Terms

The Swedish terms that appear in this book—and which I have tried to keep to a minimum—are all explained in the footnotes, usually where first introduced. By finding the word in question in the index, the explanatory note can be located. Under the key index entries, *Weights and Measures* and *Currencies,* the terms used from these respective categories are listed.

## Note on Swedish Regions and Their Inhabitants

As the maps will show, Sweden is composed of twenty-five historic provinces or *landskap* (the word is the same in singular and plural). Since the seventeenth century, however, the country has also been divided for administrative purposes into twenty-four districts or *län* (also singular and plural). Some of these districts have the same names and boundaries as old provinces, like Östergötland or Värmland. Others have the same names but different boundaries, like Söderman-land or Jämtland. Yet others have altogether different names and boundaries, like Malmöhus or Kronobergs *län*.

This is complicated, but two considerations help to avoid confusion. First, when an administrative district is referred to, the word *län* invariably follows its name. When a Swede simply speaks of Västerbotten, for instance, he means the province or *landskap* rather than the much larger Västerbottens *län,* which must always be specifically identified in this way.

Secondly, although the old *landskap* no longer have any administrative significance, Swedes traditionally identify with them, rather than with the *län,* except in official connections. The inhabitant of a *landskap* is designated by a name deriving from that of his province, usually with the ending *-ing* (*-ska* for a woman). Thus a *Värmlänning* or *Värmländska* is from Värmland, an *Ölänning* from Öland, and so on. The name Norrland applies collectively to the whole of northern Swe-den—about two-thirds of the country—and its inhabitants may be referred to as *Norrlänningar* as well as by their provincial names.

# NOTES, BIBLIOGRAPHY, AND SOURCES

# Notes

## Introduction

1. John F. Kennedy, *A Nation of Immigrants* (New York, 1964).
2. Census figures do not indicate the numbers of persons of foreign origin after the second generation, but those with some Swedish descent are now estimated to number anywhere from six to twelve million.
3. My editorial practice largely follows that set forth by Theodore C. Blegen in his pioneering anthology of Norwegian immigrant letters, *Land of Their Choice: The Immigrants Write Home* (Minneapolis, 1955). See pp. xii–xiii.
4. What, for instance, were the folks at home to make of Sander Nelson's mention of life in "*junitji stät*" (United States) in 1875, of Jöns Wiklund's reference in 1889 to "*en acer o Lan*" (an acre of land), or of J. S. Olsson's statement the same year that "*I somras flacka jag alrun från von plats til en annan*" (Last summer I knocked all around from one place to another)?
5. Most of the names mentioned in this Introduction and the section commentaries refer to persons represented in the letters and documents. See the Index.
6. Carlo M. Cipolla, in *Literacy and Development in the West* (Harmondsworth, 1969), 115, estimates basic literacy in Sweden by 1850 at 90 percent, the highest rate for any of the major European countries he surveys for that period.

## Part I. The Pioneers, 1840–1864
## Background

1. See John Williams, *The Rise, Progress and Present State of the Northern Governments*, 2 vols. (London, 1777), 1:649–50; Baron Gustaf D'Albedyhll, *Recueil de mémoires et autres pièces authentiques, relatives aux affaires de l'Europe, et particulièrement celles du Nord, pendant la dernière partie du 18e. siècle*, 2 vols. (Stockholm, 1798), I:191–96.
2. A *bonde* (plural *bönder*) owned his own farm (*gård*), most often as freehold property but in many cases as a hereditary copyhold on land under a manor (*herrgård, säteri*) which involved certain fees and obligations. By 1850 *bönder* comprised about one-third of Sweden's population. A *torpare* (singular and plural the same) worked a smaller plot (*torp*) belonging to a farm or manor on a fixed-term or revokable lease, in return for labor service and/or rent in produce or money. In 1850 *torpare* were about half as numerous as *bönder*. The rest of the rural population consisted mainly of various types of landless agricultural laborers.
3. See Summarisk redogörelse för folkmängden i Djursdala annex, församling af Tunaläns och Sevedes prosteri, Calmar län under år 1867, at Statistiska centralbyrån, Stockholm. By 1973 the population of the parish had declined to 488.
4. Vilhelm Moberg's emigrant novels appeared between 1949 and 1959 and were promptly translated into English. (See the Select Bibliography.) Eyvind Johnson's four-part *Romanen om Olof*, which came out in the 1930s, and Per Anders Fogelström's Stockholm series, beginning with *Mina drömmars stad*, from the 1960s, have unfortunately not been translated into English.
5. One *riksdaler riksgälds* at this time equaled about $.25 in American money; thus Cassel was here speaking of about $250.00. It should be remembered that one dollar was a decent day's wage for a laborer in the 1840s.
6. Ernst Skarstedt, *Vagabond och redaktör. Lefnadsöden och tidsbilder* (Seattle,

318     Letters from the Promised Land

1914), 289–90. Sweden. *Emigrationsutredningen,* 21 parts in 9 vols. (Stockholm, 1908–13), *VII: Utvandrarnas egna uppgifter* (1908), 144.

7. The terms *dräng* and *piga* are often translated as "manservant" and "maidservant," in accordance with older English usage. Since these expressions in English now connote domestic service, I prefer "hired man" and "hired girl," for both did outdoor farm labor. In Sweden *drängar* and *pigor* were normally hired on contract by farmers for a year at a time, receiving food and lodging, some articles of clothing, and a small sum of money.

8. See A. L. Klinckowström, *Bref om de Förenta Staterna, författade under en resa till Amerika åren 1818, 1819, 1820,* 2 vols. (Stockholm, 1824) [in English translation by Franklin D. Scott, ed., *Baron Klinckowström's America, 1818–1820,* Evanston, Ill., 1952]; C. U. von Hauswolff, *Teckningar utur sällskapslifvet i Nord-Amerikas Förenta Stater,* 2 vols. (Norrköping, 1835); C. D. Arfwedson, *Förenta Staterna och Canada åren 1832, 1833 och 1834,* 2 vols. (Stockholm, 1835); *Nybyggare i Nordamerika, deras öden och utsikter* (Stockholm, 1818), based on Morris Birkbeck's *Notes on a Journey in America* (Dublin, 1818); Frances Trollope, *Domestic Manners of the Americans,* 2 vols. (London, 1832); Charles Dickens, *American Notes* (London, 1842); Alexis de Tocqueville, *De la Démocratie en Amérique,* 2 vols. (Paris, 1835, 1840; Swedish translation, 1840).

9. Johan Bolin, *Beskrifning öfver Nord-Amerikas Förenta Stater . . . och råd för dem, som vilja dit inflytta* (Wexiö, 1853).

10. *Emigrationsutredningen, VII,* 187.

11. Gustaf Unonius, *A Pioneer in Northwest America, 1841–1858,* trans. J. Oscar Backlund, ed. Nils William Olsson, 2 vols. (Minneapolis, 1950), 1:287–90.

12. [Peter Cassel], *Beskrifning öfver Norra Amerikas Förenta Stater . . .* (Västervik, 1846).

## Letters and Documents, 1840–1864

1. The old English "ell" is here used to translate the old Swedish *aln* which equaled about 2 feet. In 1878 Sweden went over to the metric system.

2. The matter of public education was much debated in Sweden at this time, until in 1842 a school law was finally passed, requiring primary schools in each parish; the example of America in this regard aroused the high hopes of the liberals and the grave misgivings of the conservatives. See C. Emanuel Carlson, "The Best Americanizers," in J. Iverne Dowie and Ernest M. Espelie, eds., *The Swedish Immigrant Community in Transition: Essays in Honor of Dr. Conrad Bergendoff* (Rock Island, Ill., 1963), 31–50.

3. Tocqueville. *De la Démocratie en Amérique (Democracy in America),* vol. 1, chap. 17.

4. Cf. C. U. von Hauswolff, *Teckningar utur sällskapslifvet i Nord-Amerikas Förenta Stater,* 2 vols. (Norrköping, 1835), which on the whole was strongly critical of the United States.

5. The Swedish mile (*mil*) equals approximately 6 English miles.

6. The Swedish *tunnland* equals nearly 1.2 acres.

7. The conditions for purchase of public lands described here refer to the United States preemption law of 1841. The Cassel group did not move to the proposed new location but remained at the place described above, near the present Four Corners in Jefferson County. Later in 1846, a group of new arrivals from Sweden, after vainly seeking the Cassel colony on the Des Moines River, settled at Swede Point (now Madrid) in Boone County. They were doubtless misled by this letter.

8. In 1834–1855 one Swedish *riksdaler banko* equaled about $.40 in American money (not to be confused with the contemporaneous *riksdaler riksgäld* which equaled about $.25). The old *lispund* amounted to 12 pounds, 18 ounces.

9. The old *kvarter* amounted to about half a pint.

10. The old *skålpund* equaled about a pound.

11. The *tunna* came to four bushels; here the reference is to half that amount.

12. By the end of the century, Swedish carpenters played a prominent part in the building of the midwestern cities.

13. About $250.00.

14. These temperatures are doubtless given according to the Centigrade, or as it was called in Sweden after its eighteenth-century Swedish inventor, the Celsius, thermometer. Thus twelve to sixteen degrees below zero Centigrade would be ten degrees below to four degrees above zero Fahrenheit.

15. These comments seem to reveal the writer's preconceptions about America, most likely deriving largely from Unonius's and Cassel's widely publicized accounts.

16. It is unclear what Myrén means here by the "Swedish church" in New York unless it be Olof Hedström's Methodist Bethel Ship or a temporary place of worship for the Janssonists during their stay in the city.

17. The Janssonists.

18. Jonas Olsson from Söderala, Hälsingland (here also referred to inconsistently as Jon and Johan) was the leader of the Janssonists aboard the *Charlotta* and in charge of their pooled funds, a role which led to some dissension upon their arrival in New York. Following Erik Jansson's death in 1850, Olsson became the real leader at Bishop Hill. His brother, Olof, had come to America in 1845 as the sect's advance scout, locating land for its settlement in Henry County, Illinois.

19. Probably 500 *riksdaler riksgälds* or $125.00.

20. The smallest coin up to 1855, equaling about a twelfth of a cent.

21. "Swedish corn" (i.e., *korn*) is barley.

22. From sugar maples, which grow in Illinois.

23. The Janssonists distilled and sold liquor to outsiders but did not use it themselves.

24. "Apostles" refers to Erik Jansson's picked elders in the colony.

25. The reference is to the first Schleswig-Holstein war between Denmark and the Germanic Confederation, 1848–1849. Swedish sympathies were strongly pro-Danish.

26. Helsingör (Elsinore), in Denmark, directly across The Sound at its narrowest point from Swedish Helsingborg.

27. *Brännvin* is spirits distilled from grain or, more commonly, potatoes. Flagrant misuse of alcohol was an old evil in Sweden: during the 1820s, the annual per capita consumption of *brännvin* is estimated at 40 liters (as against 5 to 6 liters in the 1970s), giving rise to the Swedish temperance movement in the 1830s, largely inspired by American examples, which Esbjörn and most of the Swedish-American clergy warmly supported.

28. The old Swedish *kanna* roughly equaled a pottle, or half a gallon.

29. Frantz Hahr, a Swedish drawing and music teacher who had emigrated to America in 1849.

30. Peder Hjalmar Hammarskiöld came to Charleston in 1844, Carl W. and Hedvig Hammarskiöld to North Carolina in 1849. Rosalie had known the family in Sweden.

31. Published in 1852.

32. The newspaper *Skandinaven*, which was published in New York from 1851 to 1853, had been a joint Scandinavian venture.

33. *Torpare* and *torp* are frequently translated with the British terms "crofter" and "croft."

34. The reference may be to the Scottish publicist, Robert Chambers (1802–1871), who traveled in both North America and Scandinavia.

35. Within the next decade and a half, most Swedish immigrants were reaching

their destinations in America by rail and steamship within this length of time.

36. *Brännvin.*

37. George Scott (1804–1874), an English Methodist missionary whose work in Stockholm between 1830 and 1842 strongly influenced the Swedish religious "Awakening" of the mid-nineteenth century.

38. The Swedish Methodist missionary Olof Hedström maintained his Bethel Ship in New York from 1845 to 1875, welcoming and assisting thousands of his arriving countrymen.

39. In Andover, Henry County, Illinois.

40. Johan Teofil Nathorst (1794–1862), Swedish agronomist and expert in sheep raising.

41. This observation reflects the agitation of the strongly anti-foreign and anti-Catholic Know-Nothing Party of the early 1850s.

42. That is, a man from the province of Skåne. See "Note on Swedish Regions and Their Inhabitants."

43. *Den Swenske Republikanen,* published in Galva, 1856–1858.

44. *Corps de logis:* the manor house proper on an estate, as distinct from detached wings and other outbuildings.

45. *Sörmlänning* is a man from Södermanland.

46. *Knäckebröd,* a hard, crisp, unleavened rye bread made in flat, thin cakes.

47. One *riksdaler* and 45 *skilling riksgälds* would be about half a dollar; prior to 1855 the *riksdaler* was divided into 48 *skilling.* The old *lod* corresponded to about half an ounce.

48. The reference to the goldsmith Troil localizes the writer at Bishop Hill.

49. The immigrant depot at Castle Garden, on the Battery in Manhattan, was opened the year before, in 1855, and continued in operation until replaced by Ellis Island in 1892.

50. *Torpare* or small tenant farmers were called *husmän* in Skåne. Rosalie Roos had made similar observations in South Carolina; in 1853 she wrote: "*Torpare* on many estates in Sweden are much worse off than slaves on many plantations and more liable to be mistreated, indeed, more enslaved than the latter." (*Resa till Amerika,* 111.)

51. The Civil War, which began in April 1861.

52. Sweden and Norway (joined in a dynastic union under the Swedish royal house from 1814 to 1905, though under separate constitutions and governments).

53. *Rixdaler* equals *riksdaler.* In 1855 the *riksdaler banko* and the old division into 48 *skilling* were eliminated, and the *riksdaler riksgälds* ($.25 U.S.), now called the *riksdaler riksmynt* (or simply *riksdaler*), divided into 100 *öre,* became the single basic unit of currency.

## Part II. The Great Farmer-Land in the West, 1865–1889
### Background

1. Official statistics from both Sweden and the United States lack precision for the early period of the migration and throughout do not of course show illegal departures and entries. Actual Swedish immigration to America for the entire period from 1840 to 1914 may exceed the official figures by as much as 10 per cent.

2. Though there was much variation from year to year, a recent study shows that of the Swedish emigrants traveling with the ten largest shipping lines in 1883–1885, slightly over half went on prepaid tickets. See Kristian Hvidt, "Informationsspredning og emigration med särlig henblick på det atlantiske transportsystem," in Kristian Hvidt, ed., *Emigrationen fra Norden indtil 1. Verdenskrig. Rapporter til det nordiske historikermøde i København 1971 9–12 august* (Copenhagen, 1971), 132–33.

3. On transatlantic fares, see *ibid.*, 150–51; on wages, see Florence E. Janson, *The Background of Swedish Immigration, 1840–1930* (Chicago, 1931), 425–27.

4. Skarstedt, *Vagabond och redaktör*, 205.

5. Before the establishment of the International Postal Union by the Bern Convention of 1874, international postage comprised the separate sums payable to each country through which a piece of mail passed, based on internal rates and units of weight, resulting in high and variable postage. (Letters between Sweden and the United States generally passed through other countries, usually Great Britain.) In 1874 standard international rates were established; from 1878 to 1920 the first class overseas rate remained at 5 cents for the first ounce and 3 cents for each additional ounce.

6. George M. Stephenson, *The Religious Aspects of Swedish Immigration* (Minneapolis, 1932), title to chap. 21.

## Letters and Documents, 1865–1889

1. "Runners" were sent by hotels, boardinghouses, railroad agencies, etc., to solicit patronage. As they often tended to sharp practice, the term "runner" came to be more or less indiscriminately applied to anyone who sought to victimize immigrants in the cities along their way. All too often they were countrymen of those they preyed on, capitalizing on their natural trust for those who spoke their own language.

2. "Can" is doubtless here a direct translation of the Swedish *kanna*, equalling about half a gallon.

3. Here Swenson's memory played tricks on him after fifty years; if he saw the Statue of Liberty it was not on this occasion, since the statue was erected in 1886.

4. P. T. Barnum's American Museum on Broadway, containing a bizarre collection of curiosities, was a leading attraction in New York and much commented upon by foreign visitors, who generally saw in it a prime example of the much-derided American "humbug." See, for instance, Hultin, *Resa till Amerika 1864*, 132 and facing illustration.

5. *Drängar* and *pigor*: male and female farmhands.

6. Palm Valley, in Davis County, was named after the above-mentioned S. W. Palm and his family, early settlers in the area who came from Småland.

7. *Hallänningar*: people from the province of Halland.

8. *Smålänning*: a man from Småland.

9. In its dealings with the warlike Plains Indians, the United States government often promised economic support to compensate for the loss of hunting grounds; failure to honor such promises frequently led to tribal uprisings. Note that the government interpreter in this case evidently has a Swedish name.

10. In English in the original.

11. In English.

12. In English.

13. Under the old *indelning* system, groups of farmers were responsible for the support of a soldier, providing him with a cottage and a small plot of land. Thus the soldiery lived dispersed throughout the countryside during most of the year when their regiments were not mustered. In the old rural society they generally had low status.

14. The administrative districts or *län* are not to be confused with the historic provinces (*landskap*). Jönköping *län* is one of the three administrative districts into which Småland is divided. See "Note on Swedish Regions and Their Inhabitants."

15. Her geography is a bit fuzzy: Sweden comprises 173,378 square miles, Iowa 56,290.

16. Eric Norelius (1833–1916), who emigrated from Hälsingland in 1850, was one

of the leading pioneer pastors of the Augustana Lutheran Synod and twice its president, as well as its foremost historian. See his *De svenska lutherska församlingarnas och svenskarnes historia i Amerika*, 2 vols. (Rock Island, Ill., 1890, 1914); Emeroy Johnson, trans. and ed., *The Early Life of Eric Norelius (1833–1862): Journal of a Swedish Immigrant in the Middle West*, Augustana Historical Society Publications, vol. 4 (Rock Island, Ill., 1934); and G. Everett Arden, trans. and ed., *The Journals of Eric Norelius, a Swedish Missionary on the American Frontier* (Philadelphia, 1967).

17. Old dialectical form of *Sverige*, Sweden.

18. "Wod hul" and "Ward hult" are intended to mean Woodhull in Henry County, Illinois, in an old area of heavy Swedish settlement; "Iellenogs" for "Illinois" makes better sense phonetically in Swedish than in English.

19. Gustav I Vasa, king of Sweden (1521–1560) and one of the nation's great heroic figures, reestablished Swedish independence following domination by Danish kings under the Kalmar Union established in 1397.

20. She must actually be speaking here of the so-called prairie wolf or coyote.

21. The Lindgren family was at this time living on a leased farm near Manhattan, Kansas; their own property, named "Lindesfrid" after their first farm in Skåne, was located nearby.

22. A temperature of 45 degrees Celsius (Centigrade) is hot—113 degrees Fahrenheit!

23. John Ericson (1803–1889), inventor of the screw propeller and designer of the Union ironclad, *Monitor*, during the Civil War. He was born in Värmland and after some years in England moved in 1839 to the United States, where he spent the rest of his life.

24. *Gymnasium*: higher secondary school, corresponding roughly to the last year or two of high school and the first two years of college in America, emphasizing traditional academic, particularly classical, studies.

25. From Gällinge in northern Halland, a distance of about 21 miles.

26. Reference here seems to be to a Chicago newspaper of this name, not to the *Nordstjernan* of New York, founded in 1872 and still in existence.

27. This was one of the first of the numerous mergers in the history of the present-day *Svenska Amerikanaren-Tribunen*, including the absorption of its old rival, *Hemlandet*, in 1914.

28. In English.

29. Pastor Paul Peter Waldenström (1838–1917) was the leading figure of the Swedish Mission Friends.

30. In 1873 the *krona* of 100 *öre* replaced the *riksdaler* as Sweden's basic unit of currency, with its value fixed on the international gold standard at 3.73 *kronor* to $1.00 U.S. (or 1 *krona* to about $.27), until Sweden abandoned the gold standard in 1931.

31. *Boställe*: dwelling provided for an official by the state or a private employer as part of the conditions of employment, a characteristic arrangement in Sweden. In the countryside, it usually meant a military officer's residence.

32. "Sandviks": Sandwich or Hawaiian Islands.

## Part III. Farm, Forest, and Factory, 1890–1914
### Background

1. Vilhelm Moberg, *When I Was a Child*, trans. Gustaf Lannestock (New York, 1956), 26.

2. *Emigrationsutredningen*, VII, 219.

3. *Ibid.*, 259.

## Letters and Documents, 1890–1914

1. The World's Columbian Exposition, held in Chicago, May–October 1893.

2. The author of this letter evidently could not write herself. In the earlier nineteenth century, the common people in Sweden were expected to be able to read the catechism to qualify for confirmation and therefore full adult rights, but many—especially women—never learned to write.

3. From the emigrant ballad, "Petter Jönsson, eller Resan till Amerika," believed to have been composed by the Swedish-American newspaperman Magnus Elmblad in 1875: "Han wille bort till det stora landet i väster/ där ingen kung finns och inga kittsliga präster."

4. Italicized passages in English in the original.

5. Italicized passages in English.

6. *Svear*: original ancestors of the people of central Sweden; in poetic or rhetorical usage, the Swedish people.

7. Hangö (Hanko) is in southwestern Finland; the Luleå coast road runs down the Swedish side of the Gulf of Bothnia.

8. *Lutfisk*: dried fish, usually cod, cured with lye (*lut*), which must be leached out with water before cooking. Christmas porridge is made from rice cooked in milk.

9. The Linköping *folkskoleseminarium* or teachers' college, which Carl had evidently attended briefly in 1877–1878, but which Nordlander actually had not.

10. Milking was man's work everywhere in America, much to the surprise of Swedish immigrants.

11. Fredrick's daughter Hildegard now used the name Ruth.

12. Eagle City lay on the Yukon River just inside Alaska; Dawson, the center of the Klondike country, was upriver in the Canadian Yukon Territory.

13. Ellis Island became the immigration station for the port of New York in 1892, and the great majority of European immigrants passed through it after that date.

14. Visiting Swedish Americans.

15. *Julotta*: the traditional early morning Christmas church service, so timed that the sun rises just as it is ending.

16. George was writing on the letterhead paper of the Stambaugh Public School Board, on which his uncle served as secretary.

17. For ordinary people, a bicycle was an impressive acquisition at this time.

18. The Stockholm Exhibition of Arts and Crafts had been held in 1909; there was no further exposition there until 1930.

19. The Tripolitan War, 1911–1912.

20. World War I had broken out in August.

21. During the period of the great migration, a certain number of Swedes emigrated to other European countries; some of them eventually came to America, as in this case.

22. "*Hundår*," the "dog year" (or years), meant the hardest period for the immigrant after his arrival, before he could learn English, properly orient himself, and make a decent living.

23. In English.

24. Swedes often used the name "America" loosely. Like many of his countrymen in Canada, C. W. H. had probably come up from the States.

25. The writer of this letter, like many of the respondents, suspected the government's Commission on Emigration of being in league with self-interested opponents of emigration from the upper classes.

26. The franchise was liberalized in 1907 and 1909; in 1921 the last property qualifications on the vote were removed with the final establishment of universal suffrage for both sexes.

27. The reference here is to Norrland, the northern part of Sweden. This area was heavily exploited by lumbering interests in the late nineteenth and early twentieth centuries, and a growing number of emigrants were coming from it at the time this was written.

28. It is not clear to what society the writer is here referring, but as a socialist in this period, he was staunchly internationalist and thus opposed to "bourgeois" national patriotism.

29. Evidently an uncompleted folk saying, the meaning of which may be guessed.

30. For the presidential election of 1912, William Howard Taft, the incumbent, was renominated for the Republican ticket over Theodore Roosevelt, who thereupon ran for the Progressive party. Eugene Debs was the Socialist party candidate. All three were defeated by the Democrat, Woodrow Wilson.

31. The more radical and doctrinaire Socialist Labor party, backed by most immigrant European socialists, was constantly at odds with Debs's Socialist Party of America.

32. The traditional hymn for the *julotta* service early on Christmas morning, with deep emotional associations.

33. *Norrlänning*, a man from Norrland or northern Sweden.

## Epilogue

1. The present Evangelical Covenant Church of America, being of purely Swedish origin, has remained in practice, if not in theory, an essentially ethnic denomination, though it retains few specifically Swedish characteristics.

2. The surviving Swedish-language newspapers in the United States are at present *Nordstjernan-Svea* (Brooklyn), *Svenska Amerikanaren-Tribunen* (Chicago), *Texas-Posten* (Austin), *Vestkusten* (San Francisco), *California Veckoblad* (Los Angeles), and *Svenska Posten* (Seattle). *Norden*, for Swedish-speaking Finns, is published in Brooklyn. In Canada only *Canada-Svensken* (Scarborough, Ontario) and *Svenska Pressen* (Vancouver) are still published in Swedish.

3. See Marcus Lee Hansen, "The Problem of the Third-Generation Immigrant," in Augustana Historical Society, *Publications*, vol. 8, no. 1 (Rock Island, Ill., 1938); also Will Herberg, *Protestant, Catholic, Jew* (Garden City, N.Y., 1956).

4. Franklin D. Scott, *The Peopling of America: Perspectives on Immigration*, American Historical Association Pamphlet 241 (Washington, D.C., 1972), 64.

# Select Bibliography
## (Revised and augmented 1989)

The emigration was long neglected by Swedish historians, who considered it either of little interest or, worse, a humiliating episode in the nation's history. Thus most of the historical work on the subject has until rather recently been done in the United States, mainly by persons of Swedish birth or descent, writing for the most part in English. Only in the past three decades — in part through the stimulus of Vilhelm Moberg's immensely popular emigrant novels (see below) — have Swedish historians turned seriously to what the late Archbishop Nathan Söderblom considered the greatest development in Sweden's modern history. During this time, they have more than made up for lost time. Between them, American and Swedish scholars have to date produced one of the richest historical literatures for any immigrant group in North America. Since the publication of this book in 1975 a surprising number of important works have appeared, as will be seen. Regarding the historiography of Swedish emigration and Swedish America, see Ulf Beijbom, "Clio i Svensk-Amerika," in Lars-Göran Tedebrand, ed., *Historieforskning på nya vägar. Studier tillägnade Sten Carlsson 14.12.1977* (Uppsala, 1977), 17–37, and my own "Clio and Swedish America: Historians, Organization, Publications," in Nils Hasselmo, ed., *Perspectives on Swedish Immigration* (Chicago, 1978), 3–24.

In the vast bibliography of American immigration history, representative collections of the letters and documents of particular nationalities have been surprisingly few; special attention ought, therefore, to be called to Theodore C. Blegen's pioneering collection of Norwegian immigrant letters, *Land of Their Choice* (Minneapolis, 1955). A valuable Swedish collection is Albin Widén, *Amerikaemigrationen i dokument* (Stockholm, 1966), based largely on materials borrowed and later returned to their owners in response to an appeal by the magazine *Jordbrukarnas föreningsblad* in 1963. Hans Norman and Harald Runblom, eds., *Amerikaemigrationen i källornas belysning* (Gävle, 1980) contains much useful documentary material. This book, *Letters from the Promised Land*, has also been published under the title *Brev från löftets land* in Stockholm (1979, 1985), giving the source materials in the original language.

An excellent, brief introduction to the overall study of migration is provided by Franklin D. Scott, *The Peopling of America: Perspectives on Immigration*, American Historical Association Pamphlet 241 (2nd ed., Washington, 1984). For a fuller treatment, Maldwyn Allen Jones, *American Immigration* (Chicago, 1960) and Philip Taylor, *The Distant Magnet* (London, 1971) may in particular be recommended. Popular introductions specifically to the Swedish migration include Albin Widén, *Vår sista folkvandring* (Stockholm, 1962), Nils Hasselmo, *Swedish America* (New York, 1976), Ulf Beijbom, *Amerika, Amerika* (Stockholm, 1977) and Lars Ljungmark, *Swedish Exodus* (Carbondale, Ill., 1979; originally published as *Den stora utvandringen*, Stockholm, 1965). Allan Kastrup, *The Swedish Heritage in America* (Minneapolis, 1975) is a mine of information. Ernst Skarstedt's pioneering survey, *Svensk-*

325

*amerikanska folket i helg och söcken* (Stockholm, 1917), contains a great deal of material that is still of interest. There is, unfortunately, no general work on the Swedes in Canada.

Amandus Johnson, in *The Swedish Settlements on the Delaware*, 2 vols. (New York, 1911), treats Sweden's early North American colony in detail. For the sizable recent literature on this subject, see Raymond Jarvi, "The 350th Anniversary of the New Sweden Colony on the Delaware: Recent Books," *Swedish-American Historical Quarterly*, 40 (1989), 134–39. For the pre-emigration period, see also my article "Sweden and the War of American Independence," *William and Mary Quarterly*, 3rd series, 23 (1966), 408–30. Alf Åberg, *De första utvandrarna* (Stockholm, 1984) deals with individual Swedes who came to the New World before and at the beginning of the great migration. The conditions giving rise to emigration from Sweden are the subject of two American studies, Florence E. Janson, *The Background of Swedish Immigration, 1840–1930* (Chicago, 1931), a classic of its kind, and John S. Lindberg, *The Background of Swedish Emigration to the United States* (Minneapolis, 1930), both of which draw heavily upon *Sweden, Emigrationsutredningen*, 21 parts in 9 vols. (Stockholm, 1908–13), the findings of the Swedish government's official investigation and an indispensable source. The results of important recent Swedish academic research on the emigration are summarized in Ann-Sofi Kälvemark, ed., *Utvandring* (Malmö, 1973) and especially Harald Runblom and Hans Norman, eds., *From Sweden to America* (Uppsala and Minneapolis, 1976). These works will also provide useful references to a number of recent Swedish studies of emigration from particular regions. Ulf Beijbom's essays in *Utvandrarna och Svensk-Amerika* (Stockholm, 1986) provide many valuable insights. In *Transatlantic Connections: Nordic Migration to the New World after 1800* (Oslo, 1988), Hans Norman and Harald Runblom deal with the subject in its broad regional context. The same authors' *Nordisk emigrationsatlas* (Gävle, 1980) provides migration distribution maps for the entire area, some of which also appear in the aforementioned book.

Nils William Olsson, in *Swedish Passenger Arrivals in New York, 1820–1850* (Chicago, 1967) and *Swedish Passenger Arrivals in U.S. Ports, 1820–1850 (Except New York)* (St. Paul, Minn., 1979) gives valuable biographical data for many of the earliest pioneers of the emigration. See also Axel Friman, "Swedish Emigration to North America, 1820–1850," *Swedish Pioneer Historical Quarterly*, 27 (1976), 153–77. The definitive work on settlement patterns and geographical distribution of the Swedish element in the United States and Canada is Helge Nelson, *The Swedes and the Swedish Settlements in North America*, 2 vols. (Lund, 1943), the second volume of which contains useful maps. There is a sizable literature, mostly in Swedish and from the turn of the century, on the history of Swedes in special localities in America. The following in particular may be noted: William Widgery Thomas, Jr., "The Story of New Sweden," *Collections and Proceedings of the Maine Historical Society*, 2nd series, 7 (1896); E. W. Olson, Anders Schön, and Martin J. Engberg, *History of the Swedes of Illinois*, 2 vols. (Chicago, 1908); Emory K. Lindquist, *Smoky Valley People* (Lindsborg, Kan., 1953), on Kansas; J. Iverne Dowie, *Prairie Grass Dividing* (Rock Island, Ill., 1959), on Nebraska; Olav Isaksson and Sören Hallgren, *Bishop Hill: A Utopia on the Prairie* (Stockholm and Chicago, 1969); Phebe Fjellström, *Swedish-American*

*Colonization in the San Joaquin Valley in California* (Uppsala, 1970); and Byron Nordstrom, ed., *The Swedes in Minnesota* (Minneapolis, 1976). In *A Community Transplanted: The Trans-Atlantic Experience of a Swedish Immigrant Settlement in the Upper Midwest, 1835–1915* (Madison, Wisc., 1988), Robert C. Ostergren traces in fascinating detail chain migration and cultural transfer between Rättvik parish in Dalarna and Isanti County, Minnesota. Otto Robert Landelius, *Swedish Place-Names in North America*, trans. Karin Franzén, ed. Raymond Jarvi (Carbondale, Ill., 1985) provides information on many Swedish settlements.

George M. Stephenson's important *The Religious Aspects of Swedish Immigration* (Minneapolis, 1932) deals not only with the churches but with many aspects of Swedish-American cultural life. J. Oscar Backlund gives a brief survey of journalistic activity in *A Century of the Swedish American Press* (Chicago, 1952). Ernst Skarstedt, in *Våra pennfäktare* (San Francisco, 1897) and *Pennfäktare* (Stockholm, 1930), provides biographical details on Swedish-American journalists, authors, and poets. Martin S. Allwood, *Amerika-svensk lyrik genom 100 år 1848–1948* (Stockholm, 1949) is an anthology of Swedish-American poetry. G. N. Swan, *Swedish-American Literary Periodicals* (Rock Island, Ill., 1936) is useful, as is E. Walfrid Erickson, *Swedish-American Periodicals: A Select and Descriptive Bibliography* (New York, 1979). In *The Divided Heart* (Oslo and Lincoln, Nebr., 1974), Dorothy Burton Skårdal analyzes literature in the Scandinavian languages written in America, with emphasis upon its value to the social historian. Henriette C. K. Naeseth has written on *The Swedish Theatre of Chicago, 1868–1950* (Rock Island, Ill., 1951). Note, too, Anne-Charlotte Hanes Harvey, "Swedish-American Theatre," in Maxine Seller, ed., *Ethnic Theatre in the United States* (Westport, Conn., 1984), 491–524. An interesting side of Swedish-American culture is covered by Robert L. Wright in *Swedish Emigrant Ballads* (Lincoln, Nebr., 1965), which gives music and texts in both Swedish and English. The language of the immigrants is discussed by Nils Hasselmo, *Amerikasvenska* (Stockholm, 1974). The visual arts are treated in Mary Em Kirn and Sherry Case Maurer, eds., *Härute — Out Here: Swedish Immigrant Artists in Midwest America* (Rock Island, Ill., 1984). In *Swedish-America, 1914–1932* (Uppsala and Chicago, 1971), Sture Lindmark considers cultural retention versus Americanization during an important transitional period. On this theme, see also Robert S. Salisbury, "Swedish-American Historiography and the Question of Americanization," *Swedish Pioneer Historical Quarterly*, 19 (1978), 117–36.

The evolution of Swedish-American political opinion, particularly regarding foreign affairs, is traced by Finis Herbert Capps in *From Isolationism to Involvement* (Chicago, 1966). Sten Carlsson evaluates aspects of the Swedish role in American politics in *Skandinaviska politiker i Minnesota 1882–1900*, Acta Universitatis Upsaliensis, Folia Historica Upsaliensia No. 1 (Uppsala, 1970). Swedish political and labor radicalism has been relatively neglected; see, however, Henry Bengston's *Skandinaver på vänsterflygeln i USA* (Stockholm, 1955), by a veteran of the events he describes, and Gibbs M. Smith, *Joe Hill* (Salt Lake City, 1969).

The role of America and of emigration in Swedish public opinion is treated by Harald Elovson, *Amerika i svensk litteratur 1750–1820* (Lund, 1930), Nils Runeby, *Den nya världen och den gamla* (Uppsala, 1969), and Ann-Sofi Kälvemark, *Reaktionen mot utvandringen* (Uppsala, 1972). See, too, Franklin D. Scott, "Sweden's Constructive Opposition to Emigration," *Journal of Modern History*, 37 (1965), 307–35, which, like Runeby's study, discusses the spread of information about America. Lars Wendelius, *Bilden av Amerika i svensk prosafiktion 1890–1914* (Uppsala, 1982) and Gunnar Eidevall, *Amerika i svensk 1900-talslitteratur. Från Gustaf Hellström till Lars Gustafsson* (Stockholm, 1983) deal with the treatment of America, including its Swedish immigrants, in modern Swedish literature. Ulf Beijbom and Rolf Johansson in *Drömmen om Amerika* (Växjö, 1971) recreate the popular image of America among the common people of Sweden. American state and commercial propaganda to encourage emigration is studied by Lars Ljungmark in *For Sale: Minnesota* (Gothenburg and Chicago, 1971), while the activities of a Swedish emigrant agency are presented by Berit Brattne in *Bröderna Larsson* (Uppsala, 1973). Kristian Hvidt in *Flugten til Amerika* (Århus, 1971), dealing with Danish emigration, likewise gives much information on the selling of America.

The accomplishments of persons of Swedish background in various areas of American national life are the subject of Adolph B. Benson and Naboth Hedin, *Americans from Sweden* (Philadelphia and New York, 1950), though they tend somewhat uncritically to glorify their group. Franklin D. Scott discusses "American Influences in Norway and Sweden" in *Journal of Modern History*, 18 (1946), 37–47, as does Torvald Höjer in "Swedish Immigration and the Americanization of Sweden: Some Reflections," in *Swedish Pioneer Historical Quarterly*, 10 (1959), 43–51. Nils William Olsson gives a useful introduction to "Tracing Your Swedish Ancestry," in *Swedish Pioneer Historical Quarterly*, 13 (1962), 160–74 (reprinted as a pamphlet by the Royal Swedish Ministry of Foreign Affairs, 1965, 1974). A fuller guide to Swedish-American genealogical research is Carl-Erik Johansson, *Cradled in Sweden* (Logan, Utah, 1972). My own experience in tracing a Småland family in Sweden and America is recounted in my book *The Search for Ancestors* (Carbondale, Ill., 1979).

The most important autobiographical works, by Gustaf Unonius, Eric Norelius, Hans Mattson, Ernst Skarstedt, and others, are either included among the sources for this collection or mentioned in the footnotes. Notable biographies include O. Fritiof Ander, *T. N. Hasselquist* (Rock Island, Ill., 1931), Emory Lindquist, *An Immigrant's American Odyssey: A Biography of Ernst Skarstedt* (Rock Island, Ill., 1974) and *Shepherd of an Immigrant People: The Story of Erland Carlsson* (Rock Island, Ill., 1978), and Paul Elmen, *Wheat Flour Messiah: Eric Jansson of Bishop Hill* (Carbondale, Ill., 1976). Albin Widén presents an interesting collection of immigrant reminiscences which he largely obtained through oral interviews in the 1930s and 1940s in *Nybyggarliv i Svensk-Amerika* (Stockholm, 1972). In *Svensk-Amerika berättar* (Stockholm, 1982), Folke Hedblom recounts similar recollections gathered during the 1960s on visits to the United States to tape-record surviving Swedish dialects.

In a category by themselves are Vilhelm Moberg's writings: the great novels *The Emigrants* (New York, 1951), *Unto a Good Land* (New York, 1954), and *The Last Letter to Sweden* (New York, 1961), as well as the autobiographical novel *When I Was a Child* (New York, 1956), which describes growing up in an old emigration district in Småland, all excellently translated by Gustaf Lannestock. The trilogy —

actually four volumes in the Swedish original—formed the basis for Jan Troell's magnificent films *The Emigrants* and *The New Land*. Moberg's *Den okända släkten* (2nd ed., Stockholm, 1968) gives impressions of the emigration and of Swedish America which he gained through the research and travel underlying his novels; it has been translated and edited by Roger McKnight as *The Unknown Swedes* (Carbondale, Ill., 1988). See also his *Berättelser ur min levnad* (Stockholm, 1968) and Gunnar Eidevall, *Vilhelm Mobergs emigrant-epos* (Stockholm, 1974).

This selective list of books and articles is not intended to be anything like a comprehensive guide to writings on Swedish emigration and Swedes in America. The standard bibliography is still O. Fritiof Ander, *The Cultural Heritage of the Swedish Immigrant: Selected References* (Rock Island, Ill., 1956), which is, however, greatly in need of updating. Extensive bibliographies are also to be found in Stephenson, *Religious Aspects* (1932), in Nelson, *Swedes and Swedish Settlements*, I (1943), in Runeby, *Den nya världen och den gamla* (1969), in Kastrup, *The Swedish Heritage* (1975), and in Runblom and Norman, *From Sweden to America* (1976). A particularly valuable source for the early period is Esther Elisabeth Larson, *Swedish Commentators on America, 1638-1865: An Annotated List of Selected Manuscripts and Printed Materials* (New York, 1963). An invaluable bibliography of Swedish-language works published in North America is *Svenskt tryck i Nordamerika. Katalog över Tell G. Dahllöfs samling*, ed. Gunilla Larsson and Eva Tedenmyr (Stockholm, 1988). *Guide to Swedish-American Archival and Manuscript Sources in the United States* (Chicago, 1983) is an indispensable scholarly resource.

The leading Swedish institutions devoted to the history of the emigration are the Emigrant Institute in Växjö, which opened its doors in 1966 and maintains an archive, library, museum, and publication series, and the Emigrant Register in Karlstad, founded in 1960, which is primarily concerned with tracing emigrants from the province of Värmland and which since 1968 has published a popular magazine in Swedish, *Bryggan*, and in English, *The Bridge*, on Swedish-American topics. In the United States, the Swedish-American Historical Society (originally the Swedish Pioneer Historical Society), established in 1948, has since 1950 brought out the *Swedish-American Historical Quarterly* (prior to 1983 the *Swedish Pioneer Historical Quarterly*). It has also come out with a series of books (including this one), while the Augustana Historical Society in Rock Island, Illinois, has had a book-publishing program since 1930. The American Swedish Historical Foundation in Philadelphia maintains its museum and previously published a *Yearbook* (1944-73), *Bulletin* (1947-52), and *Chronicle* (1954-56). The earlier Swedish Historical Society of America, founded in 1905, went out of existence by 1934, but its *Yearbook* (1907-26) and quarterly *Bulletin* (1928-32) remain particularly valuable sources, containing many documents in the original Swedish as well as in English translation. *The Swedish American Genealogist*, published since 1981, also includes material of historical interest.

# Sources and Credits

Adelswärd, Baron Axel. Unpublished letters from America, 1855–1856. By permission of Baron Gösta Adelswärd, Åtvidaberg, Sweden. Copies provided by Professor Franklin D. Scott, Claremont, California.

Andersson, Eric H., ed. "Några emigrantbrev." *Hyltén-Cavallius-föreningens årsbok 1941* (Växjö, 1941). By permission of *Rektor* Eric H. Anderek, Älmhult, Sweden.

Andersson, Fru Iris. Unpublished letter, Stockholm, 10 April 1972, to Mrs. Aina M. Barton.

Andrén, August. "Som emigrant i USA på 1860- och 1870-talen." [Ed. Albert Sandklef.] *Halland och hallänningar, Årsbok 3.* Halmstad: Föreningen Hallands biblioteks vänner, 1956. By permission of *Fil. dr.* Albert Sandklef, Varberg, Sweden.

Berg, Ruben G. *C. J. L. Almquist i landsflykten 1851–1866.* Stockholm: Bonniers, 1928.

Blomkvist, Erland. "Några intryck från Västkusten." *Arbetaren* (New York), 12 September 1912, p. 12.

Bolin, Sture. *En skånsk prästson i Amerika.* Lund: Gleerups förlag, 1960. By permission of Fru Sture Bolin.

[Bondesson, August]. *August Bondessons visbok.* 2 vols. Stockholm, 1903.

Ekblom, J. E., arkiv, Uppsala landsarkiv. Letters from A. Andersson and Anders Larsson. Photostats provided by Dr. Nils William Olsson, Minneapolis.

Erickson, George F. Unpublished letters, 1909–1950. By permission of Mrs. Martha G. Johnson, Chicago. Copies provided by Professor Franklin D. Scott, Claremont, California.

Gilstring, Karl Gösta. "Amerikabrev." *Linköpings stiftsbok 1959–60.* Linköping, 1959. Pp. 152–65. By permission of *Lektor* K. G. Gilstring, Linköping, Sweden.

[Hallerdt, Björn, ed.] "Breven berättar om dalfolk i Amerika." *Dalarnas hembygdsbok 1966.* Falun: Dalarnas fornminnes- och hembygdsförening, 1968. Pp. 25–62. By permission of *Landsantikvarie* Björn Hallerdt, Luleå, Sweden.

—————. "Emigrantminnen." *Dalarnas hembygdsbok 1966.* Falun: Dalarnas fornminnes- och hembygdsförening, 1968. Pp. 63–96. By permission of *Landsantikvarie* Björn Hallerdt, Luleå, Sweden.

Harnell, Georg, et al., eds. *Dalsländska emigrantbrev.* Mellerud: Logen Mellerud 664 Vasaorden av Amerika, 1963. By permission of Logen Mellerud 664 Vasaorden av Amerika, Mellerud, Sweden.

Hultin, Måns. *Resa till Amerika 1864 med emigrantskeppet Ernst Merck.* Ed. Erik Gamby. Uppsala: Bokgillet, 1958. By permission of Erik Gamby, Uppsala, Sweden.

Hvarfner, Harald. "Amerikabreven berättar." Trans. from Finnish to Swedish by Helena Rautio. *Norbotten* (1962), pp. 121–40. By permission of former *Landsantikvarie* Harald Hvarfner, Luleå, and Fru Helena Rautio, Kuivakangas, Sweden.

Håkansson, Karl-Erik. "Guldgrävaren från Hjortsberga. Några utdrag från de anteckningar som fördes av Emil Granfelt under hans vistelse i Amerika åren 1892–1902." *Värendsbygden* (1961), pp. 30–46. By permission of K.-E. Håkansson, Hjortsberga, Sweden.

Jonsson, J. P. "Ett utvandraröde." *Sunnebygden* (1959), pp. 20–27.

*Jönköpingsbladet,* 26 May 1846. "Korrespondens från Östergötland."

Karlsson, Fredrik ["F. K."]. Letter of February 1892. *Social-Demokraten,* 3 March 1892.

Kronberg, Sven J. *Banbrytaren. Historisk skildring af nybyggarlifvet i Nordvästern under en tid af trettiofem år 1870–1905.* Rock Island, Ill., 1906.

Landelius, Otto Rob., ed. *Amerikabreven.* Stockholm: Natur och Kultur, 1957. By permission of O. R. Landelius, Gråbo, Sweden.

Liljegren, C. A. Unpublished letter to John T. Svenson, 30 December 1892. Provided by Clifford Swenson, Gowrie, Iowa.

Lindgren, G. E. "Amerikabreven." *Tibrobygden 13* (1963), pp. 53–59. By permission of Kyrkefalla Hembygds- och Fornminnesförening.

Lindgren, Ida. *Beskrifning öfver vår resa till Amerika 1870. Dagboksanteckningar.* Ed. Gustaf Lindgren. Stockholm: AB Svea, 1958. By permission of *Fil. dr.* Gustaf Lindgren, Stockholm.

———. *Brev från nybyggarhemmet i Kansas 1870–1881.* Ed. Gustaf Lindgren. Gothenburg: Riksföreningen för svenskhetens bevarande i utlandet, 1960. By permission of *Fil. dr.* Gustaf Lindgren, Stockholm.

Mattson, Hans. *Reminiscences: The Story of an Emigrant.* [Trans. Axel Lundeberg.] St. Paul, 1891.

*Norra Kinda-Boken.* Linköping: Kommittén för Norra Kinda-Boken, 1973. "Befolkning och bebyggelse" by Paul Aineström. By permission of Paul Aineström, Brokind, Sweden.

Nyman, Anders Petter. Unpublished letter to his mother, Duluth, 1 January 1869. Provided by *Lektor* K. G. Gilstring, Linköping, Sweden.

Nyvall, Carl Johan. *Travel Memories from America, Among Swedish Pietists in America . . . 1875–76.* Trans. E. Gustaf Johnson. Chicago: Covenant Press, 1959. By permission of Covenant Publications, Chicago.

Olson, S. W., trans. and ed. "Early Letters to Erland Carlsson." Augustana Historical Society *Publications,* vol. 5 (Rock Island, Ill., 1935), pp. 107–33. By permission of the Augustana Historical Society, Rock Island, Illinois.

Olsson, J. S. Unpublished letters, 1883–1900. Provided by Fru Lisa Cederroth, Uppsala, Sweden.

Peterson, Conrad, trans. and ed. "Letters from Pioneer Days." *Yearbook of the Swedish Historical Society of America, 1923–24.* Pp. 45–117.

Peterson, D. A. "From Östergötland to Iowa." *Swedish Pioneer Historical Quarterly,* 22(1971):136–52. By permission of *Swedish Pioneer Historical Quarterly.*

Roos, Rosalie. *Resa till Amerika 1851–1855.* Ed. Sigrid Laurell. Stockholm: Almqvist och Wiksell, 1969. By permission of Sigrid Laurell, Stockholm.

Skarstedt, Ernst. "Vid hennes sida." Unpublished but privately duplicated, Portland, Oregon, 1889. Microfilm provided by Professor Franklin D. Scott, Claremont, California, from copy in Royal Library, Stockholm.

———. *Svensk-amerikanska folket i helg och söcken.* Stockholm, 1917.

———. *Vagabond och redaktör. Lefnadsöden och tidsbilder.* Seattle, 1914.

Stephenson, George M. trans. and ed., "Documents Relating to Peter Cassel and the Settlement at New Sweden." *Swedish American Historical Bulletin,* 2 (1929).

———. "Hemlandet Letters." *Yearbook of the Swedish Historical Society of America, 1922–23.* Pp. 56–152.

———. *Letters Relating to Gustaf Unonius and the Early Swedish Settlers in Wisconsin.* Augustana Historical Society *Publications,* vol. 7 (Rock Island, Ill., 1937). By permission of the Augustana Historical Society.

———. "Typical America Letters." *Yearbook of the Swedish Historical Society of America, 1921–22.* Pp. 52–98.

Stomberg, A. A., ed. "Letters of an Early Emigrant Agent in the Scandinavian Countries." *Swedish American Historical Bulletin,* 3 (1930):7–52.

Sweden. *Emigrationsutredningen.* 21 parts in 9 vols. Stockholm, 1908–13. *II: Utvan-*

*dringsväsendet i Sverige* (1909); *VII: Utvandrarnas egna uppgifter* (1908); *VIII: Bygdeundersökningar*, Del 2, G. Gerhard Magnusson, "Jösse härad i Värmland" (1908).

Swenson, Johannes. "A Journey from Sweden to Texas 90 Years Ago." Trans. C. T. Widén. *Swedish Pioneer Historical Quarterly*, 8(1957):128–35. By permission of *Swedish Pioneer Historical Quarterly*.

[Warberg, A. C.] *Skizzer från Nord-Amerikanska kriget 1861–1865*. Stockholm, 1867.

[Wermelin, Atterdag.] "Ett svenskt emigrantöde." Ed. John Persson. *Notiser från arbetarnas kulturhistoriska sällskap*, 34(1960):69–78. By permission of John Persson, Sigtuna, Sweden.

Westin, Gunnar, ed. *Emigranterna och kyrkan. Brev från och till svenskar i Amerika 1849–1892*. Stockholm: Verbum, 1932. By permission of Fru Ester Westin, Gothenburg, Sweden.

Widén, Albin. *Amandus Johnson, svenskamerikan. En levnadsteckning*. Stockholm: Norstedts, 1970.

―――――. *Amerikaemigrationen i dokument*. Stockholm: Prisma, 1966.

―――――. *Carl Oscar Borg. Ett konstnärsöde*. Stockholm: Nordisk rotogravyr, 1953.

―――――. *När Svensk-Amerika grundades*. Borås: Vasaorden av Amerika, 1961.

―――――. *Vår sista folkvandring*. Stockholm: Gebers förlag, 1962.

All used by permission of *Fil. dr*. Albin Widén, Bromma, Sweden.

# Index

# Index

The Swedish letters *å*, *ä*, and *ö* are alpha-
betized as though they were *a* and *o*
respectively. Place names are indexed
as they appear in the text, with modern or correct spellings indicated where
necessary. Every known locality from
or about which a document was written has been indexed, with the community and state given. Occasionally, it
was not possible to determine the state
and these few instances are indicated
by a question mark in parentheses (?).
Where the same note number occurs
more than once on a page, references to
such notes are as follows: 317n3(1),
321n3(2). The terms "America" and
"American" are used here in a North
American sense; where entries refer
exclusively to the United States or to
Canada, these latter designations are
used.

Adelswärd, Baron Axel, Swedish visitor
   to America, 6; document by, 79–81
Advertising, in America, 20, 76–77
Agriculture, conditions of: in America,
   30–31, 39–40, 58, 71, 81, 99, 100, 136,
   137–38, 154, 156, 182–83, 185, 186, 188,
   190, 199, 222, 227, 238–41, 245–47. 260–
   61, 264, 323n10; in Sweden, 9–11,

86, 90, 107, 139, 225, 256–57, 284–85,
   317n2(2), 318n7(1), 320n50
Ague, 14, 278
Ahlberg, A. P., Swedish religious educa-
   tor, 157; document by, 157–58
Ahlsborg, Småland, document from,
   157–58
Ahnfelt, P. G., Swedish pastor and
   author, 47
Åkarp, Skåne, 71
Alaska, 205, 206, 250–51, 323n12
Albany, N.Y., 14
Alberta, 205, 206, 264
Aldrin, Edwin, American astronaut, 309
Alfta, Hälsingland, document from, 44
Almquist, C. J. L., Swedish author, 6, 15,
   73; document by, 73–77
*Aln*, defined, 318n1
America: information and ideas about, in
   Sweden, 15–18, 33, 34, 88–92, 101–2,
   110, 134, 210, 241, 286–87, 319n15;
   physical environment, 19–20, 23, 30,
   35–36, 39–40, 58, 59, 84, 87–88, 114, 126,
   131, 141, 143, 167, 180, 184, 186–87, 190,
   220, 227–28, 236, 238–39, 257, 259, 260–
   63, 264, 267, 282; climate, 20, 32–33, 84,
   85, 120, 127, 130–31, 147, 153, 154, 174,
   179, 181, 182, 183–85, 187, 190, 199,
   245, 248, 282, 284, 299, 319n14, 322n22;